AN INCONVENIENT MINORITY

The HARVARD ADMISSIONS CASE and the ATTACK on ASIAN AMERICAN EXCELLENCE

KENNY XU

DIVERSION
BOOKS

For more information, email info@diversionbooks.com

Diversion Books
A division of Diversion Publishing Corp.
www.diversionbooks.com

First Diversion Books edition, July 2021
Hardcover ISBN: 9781635767568
Paperback ISBN: 9781635767810
eBook ISBN: 9781635767537

Printed in The United States of America

10 9 8 7 6 5 4 3 2

Library of Congress cataloging-in-publication data is available on file

Cover photo courtesy of Jorge Salcedo / Shutterstock.com
Author photo by Willis Bretz / Heritage Foundation
Jacket design by David Riedy

Table of Contents

Foreword
Within Our Many, an Inconvenient One

E Pluribus Unum. From many, one. This is the motto of the greatest and most successful diversity project in human history—the United States of America—successful, at least, until very recently.

There are, of course, reasons to regard this characterization of the nation with skepticism, even criticism. When the foundational documents of this nation were calling to an ideal of "all men are created equal and are endowed by their Creator with certain inalienable rights," the hand that wielded that pen also held dominion over people he, himself, enslaved. From that fateful date in 1776 until 1865, slavery and the racism and white supremacy that maintained it were institutional and systemic in this nation, despite its lofty ideals. Even then, for another 99 unjust years, legal equality for Black Americans would remain elusive, and racism would persist beyond even then, baked deeply in some ways into American life and still bearing material and psychic consequences to this very day. Few deny this.

Simultaneously, other forms of racism and discrimination applied to other groups, mostly of immigrant origin, even as they came in as "poor, huddled masses, yearning to be free," whether on Ellis Island in sight of the statue bearing that famous verse or elsewhere in the country. One of these forms of racism was anti-"Asian," that catch-all term for many immigrants from the various diverse nations of South and particularly East Asia and other regions of the Pacific. Though lesser known, this discrimination was in many ways severe, including overt exclusion and disenfranchisement via the Chinese Exclusion Act and internment of Japanese Americans during World War II. All of this was backed by racism and white supremacy as well.

These are dark stains on the history of this nation. They are terrible errors we should be proud to have made so much progress in mostly, though not completely, overcoming—to the great credit of the courageous individuals who stood up against the brutal effects of having their racial and ethnic identities imbued with unjust social significance and used as a basis for discrimination against them. E Pluribus Unum was, for far too long, a work in progress that stayed short on the progress. Progress came, though, and the idealistic American Experiment slowly proved itself to be the greatest diversity program in the history of the world.

Nevertheless, there is, even as you read this illuminating volume, already underway a concerted movement to re-introduce and re-institutionalize racism and discrimination throughout the West and in the United States in particular—in the name of greater or perfected progress. In academic circles, it goes by the name Critical Race Theory, and it holds that racism is the ordinary state of affairs in American life and thus relevant to all interactions, institutions, and phenomena. As a result, Critical Race Theory pushes the idea that one's racial and ethnic background should be made more materially relevant, not less, and it openly doubts, in its own words, "the very foundations of the liberal order, including equality theory, legal reasoning, Enlightenment rationalism, and the neutral principles of constitutional law."[1]

As if re-making one of the worst mistakes of our past wasn't bad enough, Critical Race Theory also openly denigrates a key American virtue—merit, that combination of talent and hard work that makes for genuine, well-earned success. This denigration of merit (as well as individualism) leads it not only to repudiate the foundational premises of America but also that has a disproportionate impact on one racial minority group in the United States more than any other: Asian Americans.

■   ■   ■

Why? Because, as Kenny Xu lays out in this sparkling volume (with no shortage of personality, I might wryly add), Asian Americans have disproportionately come to this country with little more than their talents, willingness to work hard to achieve, and a burning desire for a fair shake in a country that values fairness, equality, and more meritocracy than almost any other place on Earth. More importantly, they have succeeded in this regard, to their own credit and to that of our nation.

Asian American success—arising through little more than merit—positions them as an inconvenient minority for the narrative of Critical Race Theory. The Theory contends the opposite: that systemic racism, thus one's racial or ethnic origin, not merit is the most determinant factor upon one's life and that there's little or nothing an individual can do to make up for it. This presents a paradox for Critical Race Theory because merit cannot be the reason for the success of members of a "minoritized" group, but in the case of Asian Americans, it undeniably is that reason.

Critical Race Theorists attempt to resolve the Asian inconvenient minority paradox the only way the Theory will allow: by accusing Asian Americans of being "model minorities," "white-adjacent," or just "white," and arguing that they push to succeed because they possess and want to keep white (or "yellow") privilege and engage—as a group—in "anti-Blackness." Through their one lens of zero-sum racial conflict theory, Critical Race Theorists have only one explanation for Asian American success where it exists: participation in racism. Not hard work. Not sacrifice to succeed. Collusion in evil and oppression. And this must be their resolution to the paradox they write for themselves. In Critical Race Theory, merit is considered a feature of "white supremacy culture," so those who believe in it and succeed by it must be upholding white supremacy—even if they are Asian.

Critical Race Theory is, then, as anti-merit as it is anti-equality, and this causes it to be anti-Asian American—except when it can make use of other types of anti-Asian racism to co-opt "Asian solidarity" to their cause. In *An Inconvenient Minority*, Kenny Xu lays bare the many ways that Critical Race Theory and its activists cannot comprehend or tolerate the basic fabric of the American cloth—E Pluribus Unum—or see Asian American success as well-earned, well-deserved, and a valuable and crucial contribution to the course of American history and twenty-first century life for All of Us Many, as One.

James Lindsay
Author of the best-selling book *Cynical Theories:
How Activist Scholarship Made Everything about Race,
Gender, and Identity—and Why This Harms Everybody.*
February 20, 2021

Preface to the New Edition

At the time of this paperback publication, my book has been available for a little over a year. In that brief window of time, the issues addressed in these pages have only grown in their relevance to the current cultural and political climate of America. We will soon discover, through the outcomes of a series of broad national debates, whether we as a country will re-found itself upon colorblind meritocracy or cement in stone a belief in the fundamental immutability of race.

On one hand, our whole concept of race is quickly eroding in the face of demographic change and increasing colorblindness. According to a 2015 poll, 96 percent of Americans have no qualms living next to a neighbor of a different race, and 91 percent of Americans are comfortable having their daughter marry a spouse of a different race.[1] One out of five new couples are interracial, including one out of five couples involving a Black person.[2] We don't live in the 1960s anymore, when the primary races in our national consciousness were pitch-Black and pasty-white. Our entire paradigm of race is quickly eroding under the force of the successful American diversity experiment. We are truly on the path to becoming one race.

On the other hand, powerful new forces are soiling our colorblind experiment. Those forces, as you will see, prefer our divisions to be hardened and obnoxiously propagated in our discourse. They prefer the concept of white and Black embedded into the mainstream, even requiring different treatment based on skin color.

One of these forces is Harvard University. The institution proudly proclaims that it uses race in admissions decisions for the sake of "diversity" and a "well-rounded student body." Yet such "diversity" requires Harvard to go easy on some races and harder on others. For example, Black Americans were 9–12 percent of Harvard University admittees in the past twenty years despite making up 0.7 percent of all applicants scoring in the top academic decile. And Asian Americans were 16–20 percent of admittees despite making up 51.5 percent of all applicants scoring the top academic decile.[3] Effectively, Harvard cuts down the number of higher-qualified Asians to make room for lower-qualified Black Americans (as well as Latino and white Americans). That is the sad but harsh truth.

I will make the case in the pages that follow that this vast disparity in admissions rates is a result of Harvard's discriminatory policies that attempt to suppress or denigrate Asian American success. A version of my charge—though not as comprehensive—is being litigated in the highest court of the land. Asian Americans have sued Harvard University for discrimination. And on January 24, 2022, The US Supreme Court took up the Asian American plaintiffs' grievances.

This lawsuit, known as *Students for Fair Admission v. President and Fellows of Harvard College* is one of the core topics of this book, and the stakes could not be higher. (There is a similar lawsuit against the University of North Carolina-Chapel Hill that The Supreme Court merged with the Harvard lawsuit.) The Supreme Court's ruling has the potential to completely change the way our institutions approach race preferences and affirmative action.

At present, universities like Harvard are allowed under federal law to factor race into their admissions decisions. In the wake of the civil rights movement of the 1960s, various laws and court decisions allowed for racial preferences to be used to correct for the subjugation of Black Americans for generations past. However, there was always an assumption within those concessions that the race preferences would last only a short while, perhaps two or three decades; any longer and the attempt to restore racial justice would turn decidedly unjust. Supreme Court Justice Sandra Day O'Connor ruled in the 2003 case that the "Court expects that twenty-five years from now, the use of racial preferences will no longer be necessary to further the interest approved today."

This is the bill of goods that America was sold: give the universities a few years to play catch-up by preferentially admitting Black students, and in a few years all racial animus will be behind us. We will enter a new golden age where Americans live in a truly colorblind society.

Of course, this is not what happened. Twenty years has now passed, and we still have racial preferences that are arguably worse than they were in 2003. Affirmative action is more discriminatory than ever, and yet the gap between white and Black students at the secondary school level is sadly not closing. Furthermore, the gap between Black students and white students is increasing. There is no clear program by which our national educational leaders propose to close the gap, and so race preferences are set to continue unabated in perpetuity.

However, *Students for Fair Admissions v. Harvard* has the potential to completely shift this paradigm. If SFFA is victorious, Harvard (and by extension all American universities) will no longer have the right to privilege certain racial groups in their admissions process. No longer will well-qualified white and Asian students be denied admittance in favor of another student with worse credentials but a racial makeup that helps achieve a diversity goal. Beyond simply improving the lives of individual students and families, our institutions will once again be forced to confront stark realities in the racial achievement gaps in our nation. Instead of masking our realities with affirmative action, we as a nation actually may have to develop proactive action plans rooted in truth.

Of course, one Supreme Court ruling cannot fix the entirety of race relations throughout a nation of more than 300 million people. Many questions will remain: to what extent can we still attribute life outcomes to historical oppression? What is the place of personal accountability within generational success and failure? How does race factor into identity in a society desperately attempting to overcome racial animus?

Asian Americans lie directly in the crossfire of this conundrum. Asians are a diverse people with few longstanding ties to the United States, many of them immigrants or the children of immigrants. There are no "systemic" factors that act to prop Asians up, and many of them come from backgrounds that cannot be called anything but underprivileged. And yet, Asian Americans dominate our society across multiple metrics: income, educational attainment, family stability. Asian Americans provide an excellent counterexample to the whole notion of "systemic racism" in our country. After all, if America really is a white supremacist nation, why did they do such a poor job of limiting the success of Asians?

Herein lies the origin of *An Inconvenient Minority*: Asians simply don't fit into the box that the regime-approved narrative attempts to put them in. They inconvenience them. And with that inconvenience comes serious fear and resentment from the ruling elite. 36 percent of Harvard's 2022 class are legacy students; every single studious, first generation Asian American student threatens to take one of their spots. Asians are inconvenient both in the sense of collapsing the mainstream narrative surrounding race in America, and practically in terms of taking opportunities from lesser-qualified but better-connected students and young professionals.

Some narrow-minded academics, in a desperate attempt to save the systemic racism narrative from being debunked, call Asian Americans "white-adjacent." In other words, Asians have the benefits of white privilege even though they aren't white. The implication is that their success is undeserved. This is the most insulting thing you can say to Asian immigrant groups. The vast majority of Vietnamese immigrants come to America with little to no English-language experience, and yet through sheer hard work and cultural values, their children graduate from college at a higher rate than any other ethnicity. Their success is attributed to stern discipline and a belief in the power of education, not to "privilege."

Asian Americans are also starting to compete in more than just academics. From the mainstream adoption of anime, to the success of the film *Crazy Rich Asians*, to the athletic dominance of sports stars like figure skater Nathan Chen and gymnast Sunisa Lee, to the worldwide success of K-pop bands like BTS, Asian forms of art and entertainment are already well on their way to entering the Western zeitgeist. There is no indication this trend will slow anytime soon, and in an increasingly globalized world, American culture will likely continue to adopt Asian art forms.

On the political front, Asian Americans finally had a mainstream political voice in the person of Andrew Yang. Regardless of his politics, his national platform is a large step for a demographic group that has had little to no political presence in past decades. We will see more and more figures like Yang appear as the decade continues—Asian American, civically engaged, and ready to serve on both sides of the political aisle. In a political environment where individuals are increasingly encouraged or forced to consider their demographic characteristics, Asian Americans will come to be a stronger force in shaping the direction of this country.

As Asian Americans continue to push through in American culture, they will continue to stir up new questions surrounding race and diversity in our country. In particular: through the Asian American example, will we truly be able to adopt a colorblind system that judges individuals alone, based upon their merit? Will we be a country where we can learn good practices and habits from other cultures instead of resenting their success? Or will Asian Americans continue to simply be *An Inconvenient Minority*?

Kenny Xu
February 8, 2022

Preface to the First Edition

If you run in highly educated, professional circles in big cities, you have probably come across your fair share of Asian Americans. Your family doctor is disproportionately likely to be Asian American. The cellist at your local orchestra is likely to have straight jet-black hair and brown eyes. Your "quant," i.e., your math guy—perhaps the classmate you stole homework from when you were a kid—is disproportionately likely to have some connection to China. In some sense, many Asian Americans have developed professionally and ensconced themselves in lives of middle-class "stability," despite looking and acting different from the average white guy.

But how could this be? To be a minority is to be outcasted, to be subordinated. Black Americans are the most deeply ingrained example of the bearers of burdens that come with being a minority, of being enslaved, forced to work in a colorized world, and judged solely according to the color of their skin. But they are not the only ones. Asian Americans, too, were historically oppressed. One need only look at the 1940s internment of Japanese Americans or the 1882 Chinese Exclusion Act to understand Asian American alienation. If not in America, then certainly oppression pervaded in their former homes: millions of Vietnamese refugees escaping the fist of Communism, Filipinos escaping government corruption and malfeasance.

Indeed, the social advancement of Asian Americans despite historic marginalization is remarkable and, in fact, *inconveniences* the racial narrative advocated by today's culturally dominant intellectual Left. The intellectual Left likes to divide the world into privileged and oppressed classes based on racial status. If you are white, you are privileged. But if you are a "minority" or a "person of color," you are oppressed. The purpose of such categorization is to grant benefits to groups based on their oppressed status, in restitution for the oppression against them. Disparaging the privileged earns you preferential treatment, equity funding, and social currency.

Yet Asian Americans do not often receive preferential treatment due to their minority status. They are often victimized by preferential treatment designed for other minority races. In the starkest example, Harvard University's admissions office discriminates against Asian American minorities in order to preferentially admit less qualified minorities of other races (and even white people). There are many more shocking examples, and I will explore those examples and the reasoning behind them in great detail. But there is no question that Asian Americans are not given access to many of the benefits of being a "minority," even as they face some of its traditional disadvantages. Because they inconvenience the narrative, so too will they be inconvenienced. They are the inconvenient minority.

What's more, the attack on Asian American excellence represents the decline of a larger concept in American society that has allowed its culture of excellence to prosper: meritocracy. Asian Americans, largely without historical wealth or social connections and absent from the Left's preferred minority list, disproportionately rely on merit, their skills and talent, to move along in society. When identity politics undergird merit-based principles and replace them with Leftist divides along the lines of race and proximity to power, Asian Americans are squeezed out of positions for which they are well qualified, and the totality of our culture of excellence suffers.

When I first thought to write about the lasting consequences of Harvard University's diversity ideology and the impact of modern equity and social justice rhetoric on Asian Americans, a political science professor to whom I came for advice turned up her nose at the idea: "Good luck getting sympathy for rejected Asian American college applicants." A most casual dismissal.

But why would our culture be less than sympathetic to *anyone*, particularly a minority facing discrimination based on race? Especially when that discrimination continues to be abetted and validated by a culture that deems it morally unproblematic to trample on one group's individual rights in favor of another group? Asian Americans are afterthoughts in the racial discourse in America today.

An Inconvenient Minority tracks how the diversity-and-equity-obsessed movement has suppressed Asian American excellence, how it has consequently damaged our American culture of excellence, and how ordinary Asian Americans from unsung walks of life are fighting back.

Their political voices will not be ignored anymore.

A BROKEN MERITOCRACY

THE TENSION AND THE STAKES

There were just too many Asians.

Thomas Jefferson High School for Mathematics and Science in Arlington, Virginia, is widely considered the best high school for math and science in the region. It is the number one ranked high school by the U.S. News and World Report in the entire nation. "That place is so difficult and so rigorous, that you're just beaten," said Asra Nomani, the Indian American mother of a Thomas Jefferson student. "You don't even know if you're going to make it, like as a family, because your child is slogging so much. And I have issues with that because they almost crush the passion of math and science out of you because they are just so rigorous, so hard. But every Thomas Jefferson parent . . . remembers the day where you go to bed before your kid."

Before 2020, admissions to Thomas Jefferson involved a standardized test, along with grades, teachers' recommendations, and course rigor.[1] It is all standard fare that anyone would know. For a long time, admissions to TJ were mostly white. As late as 2002, Thomas Jefferson was 70 percent white, 25 percent Asian, and 5 percent Black or Latino.[2]

But starting in the 2000s, the composition of the class of Thomas Jefferson changed. It got more Asian. Way more Asian. The reasoning for this change was pretty simple: Asian immigrants started pouring into Northern Virginia in the '90s. They got married and had kids. In the new millennium, those kids were reaching high school age. And they were studying to go to TJ.

In 2020, Thomas Jefferson accepted 486 students from a pool of 2,539 applicants. Seventy-three percent of those admitted were Asians.

It's not as if Fairfax County Public Schools was failing its students in terms of classroom rigor. In 2013, FCPS required all eighth-grade students to take Algebra I, the culmination of teacher and individual school-led efforts to boost the region's proficiency in math. Surging ahead of this requirement, more schools and parents moved to have their kids take Algebra I in seventh grade—and some even in sixth. The standards at FCPS, at least in math, have increased for all students over the past twenty years.

But even with the increased standards, Asian kids still were doing better at math. There was no real secret to it: The Asian American parents moving into the area were simply investing more in their kids' math education from an early age. "Parents want their kids to be moving along at the pace that they can handle," Asra said about her own community. "[My son] ended up ready to take Algebra I in seventh grade." Asra had enrolled her son in gifted math in elementary school. And she made sure to keep him on track—she even homeschooled him for a year so he could get the enrichment he needed. You can call Asra what you want—overly ambitious, authoritarian, not a "well-rounded" parent. But the bottom line was that her son was excellent at math, and so were many other Asian American sons and daughters in Fairfax County. As Asian Americans continued to move into the district, they increased their advantage for spots at the math-and-science focused Thomas Jefferson High School admissions.[3]

Fairfax County had long yearned for more minorities to fill TJ's spots— just not these minorities. For thirty years, Fairfax County's entrenched school board had been hankering for more Black and Hispanic kids in

TJ's programs. They tried everything to get them in: Enrollment outreach programs. No effect. "Holistic admissions." No effect. Fairfax County even tried admitting more low-income students into the "TJ pipeline" of middle-school gifted and talented programs, drastically increasing the number of Black and Hispanic students in these middle-school gifted programs from 3 percent to 15 percent of all students in those demographics. That had the opposite effect—watering down the rigor of the nongifted middle school Honors courses caused the number of schools who sent fewer than ten students to TJ to increase from ten to eighteen. And all the while, Asian American students continued to dominate admissions to TJ. The school board was livid. How could they accomplish their diversity goals if these Asian immigrants and their children kept taking all the good spots?

Then, George Floyd was killed.

Across the nation, "wokeness" became a household concept, and a national conversation erupted over the role of systemic racism in every part of American life. And you can bet education was not left undiscussed.

In the wake of the country's racial reckoning and shortly before the school year began, the Democratic Party blog BlueVirginia wrote, "ZERO African-Americans were accepted into TJ" in 2020. *Washington Post* reporter Hannah Natanson wrote an article highlighting the issue, and it became a local sensation. (The claim itself is untrue—attributable to a publishing error in the original statistics. Although the number of Black students accepted was low, it was not zero —it was six.)

The newly woke Fairfax County School Board galvanized over the article. In August of 2020, they invited author Ibram X. Kendi to speak to the entire staff. Ibram X. Kendi is mostly known for his bestselling book *How to Be an Antiracist*, where he famously argues: "The only remedy to racist discrimination is antiracist discrimination. The only remedy to past discrimination is present discrimination. The only remedy to present discrimination is future discrimination."[4] They paid Kendi $20,000 to speak and bought $24,000 worth of his books.[5] The only requirements for Kendi's speech were that it be "confidential" and "exclusive," so no one else could see what was discussed.

Kendi spoke in vague generalities, decrying "systemic racism" and stating that "we need to create a system where no one's money will give them more opportunities."[6] But he didn't need to be coy; with one look at his book, thousands of which were bought by Fairfax County Schools, anyone can parse how he feels about the education system and how he would characterize the TJ admissions process that leaned heavily on the standardized test:

> "The use of standardized tests to measure aptitude and intelligence is one of the most effective racist policies ever devised to degrade Black minds and legally exclude Black bodies."[7]

With Kendi functioning as their woke cheerleader, Fairfax County decided to overhaul their entire admissions process, to force more Black and Hispanic kids to come to TJ. "I believe our country—in the middle of the pandemic and after the murder of George Floyd—has reached a moment where we have to with a fresh perspective to relook at equity in everything we do. We've had an over 25-year conversation about [improving] TJ admissions," FCPS Superintendent Scott Brabrand said in a town hall about TJ's admissions process. "I do believe it's time to do something other than the status quo."[8]

So the school board put forth the most drastic admissions policy they had ever done in the history of Thomas Jefferson High School: They created an admissions lottery. Yes. A lottery. For admittance to the number one high school in the nation.

Under the new lottery, "merit" admissions would be reduced to 100 of the 480 spots. The rest would go to any students scoring above a 3.5 GPA and with the required courses, by the luck of the draw. The proposal was drawn up to "increase diversity" and to allow TJ to "reflect the diversity, equity, and inclusiveness that is core to the mission and values of Fairfax County Public Schools," said Superintendent Brabrand.[9]

At least, that's one way of seeing it.

■ ■ ■

The issue of opportunity in Fairfax County is not that the admissions process for Thomas Jefferson, a single public school, is racist against Black and Hispanic students. In fact, one analysis by a George Mason University law professor showed that admissions officers accepted 90 percent of Black students who made it to the second round of the application process, while accepting less than 50 percent of white students who made it to the second round, suggesting evidence that the bias might in fact be in their *favor*. The issue is that the number of Black students who made it to the semifinalist round of the application process in the first place was so low. Remember, the semifinalist round is the *minimum* standard for admissions—it signals you have the requisite merit to even play the game. In 2008, 507 white students made it to this semifinalist round. The number of Black students? Thirty-seven.[10]

The problems of too few Black and Hispanic students in even the semifinalist rounds of admissions are problems of the entire condition of low-income Black and Hispanic education, problems that cannot be fixed or solved with racial quotas at one school—that can only be masked, not solved, with the artificial propping or boosting of certain races' admittance into the school at the expense of people who are more qualified. Rather, solving these problems requires addressing them at every level of education—not putting promising but underqualified Black and Hispanic students through the meat grinder that is Thomas Jefferson High School for Mathematics and Science.

But the chattering class governing the county did not want to hear this logic. They would rather believe that everyone would be equally meritorious and pretend that one can artificially increase racial diversity with no negative consequences.

The counterproposal—the antiracist proposal—to TJ's test and grade-based admissions was implemented in October 2020, calling for a "merit" lottery of admissions where anyone who crossed a minimum threshold would get an equal chance for admissions to the most excellent high school in America.

The issue is that the board of education gets to decide the "minimum threshold." They decided initially that the lottery was going to be open to anyone with a minimum 3.5 GPA. The school board's own analysis for this merit lottery predicted an upsurge in Black, Latino, and white admitted candidates. The Asian population, on the other hand, would drop by a projected 27 percent. A parents' coalition analyzed the data and found a steeper drop: 55 percent for Asian students.[11] In contrast, the white population would shoot up to 45 percent of the total student body. And the Black and Hispanic representation would both remain in the single digits.

■ ■ ■

What if restructuring TJ admissions wasn't just about increasing Black and Hispanic admissions? What if something more sinister was going on?

A 2013 study of white Californians found that when white people were told about Asian American success on standardized tests, their support for standardized tests fell significantly.[12] An ominous possibility emerges: The school board's radical transformation of the admissions process, publicly justified in the name of racial representation and antiracism, was latently a sort of envious clapback from wealthy, elite parents against the Asian American takeover of *their* schools.

Consider, for example, a favorite term of today's liberal elites: diversity.

"When it comes to ethnicity statistics, it becomes blatant that there is no such concept of diversity at Jefferson," wrote high schooler Sonja Kachan about TJ admissions. "As stated before, Asians make up close to 68 percent of the student body, followed by Caucasians making it 21 percent."[13] To these students at TJ, fed diversity ideology from their diaper-wearing days, Asian identity is *not diverse.* Why? Because there are just too many of them.

In the messaging of woke students and the woke school boards propping up their ideas, the writing on the wall is clear: Asian students can be sacrificed—but that's okay, in the name of diversity. Mind you, it did not matter that these Asian students put hundreds of hours of work into their academic careers, sacrificing a social life to give themselves the best shot to enter a school known for its brutal work hours. That depth and breadth of dedicated effort was to be lapped up and framed as "test prep," or "privilege." Virginia education secretary Atif Qarni called preparation for the TJ admissions exam the equivalent of "performance-enhancing drugs."[14] *Studying for the test* was comparable to sticking steroids into your body the day of a wrestling meet. Never mind *actually* cheating, a real epidemic across the nation's high achieving public schools. Extra-curricular work and simply studying for tests was labeled in those same denigrating terms.

How did we get to the point where it's morally okay, even encouraged, to justify halving the Asian American population at a popular gifted school, labelling them cheaters and test-preppers? Would this at all fly if "Asian American" were replaced with "African American"?

Such a question gets at the heart of this battle over Thomas Jefferson High School in Fairfax County, Virginia. Who are the people considered "minorities" in the Left's America? Who will get privileges doled out to them in a woke world? What does "diversity" really mean if Asian Americans are not included?

Or does anyone question the most fundamental consequence of it all—the fact that a "merit lottery" will inevitably result in a drastic decline in overall school performance? The simple mathematical facts beget this utterly logical conclusion: If before you selected the most meritorious in rank order and now will select from a lottery of students above a lower cutoff point, you sacrifice one immediate, clear principle that powerfully distorts the overall excellence and reputation of your school, your community, and your world.

That principle is meritocracy.

A CULTURE OF EXCELLENCE LAID TO WASTE

What is meritocracy? Thomas Mulligan, Georgetown professor and theorist of meritocracy, puts it this way:

> "First, we establish equal opportunity, and then we judge people strictly on their merits. When this is done—when we live in a *meritocracy*—citizens will have their just desserts."[15]

Asian Americans are the minority most ensconced in meritocratic thinking for several reasons. Firstly, Asian Americans by and large do not come from privilege and lack social connections to move up in society. Secondly, Asian Americans nevertheless achieve at a level commensurate with white Americans, and even higher in some cases. If you accept both premises, the logical conclusion is that Asian Americans have gotten to where they are in American society because of their own merit—their sheer hard work and cultural traits.

But where are they, exactly? We must start, of course, at the crux of Asian American success in this country to the extent it can be claimed. Then, we must look at the reaction to Asian American success and how it affects that population and our American meritocracy at large—to the extent that it can be called a meritocracy. We must look at the fundamental vehicle of Asian American prosperity in this country: Education.

Talk about an upper-middle class white mother's nightmare: An article came out in the 2013 *American Sociological Review* entitled "When White is Just Alright: How Immigrants Redefine Achievement and Reconfigure the Ethnoracial Hierarchy."[16] This foreboding title hearkened to an even grimmer picture for the nation's white mothers in densely Asian cities like New York City and San Francisco. The article's authors, Tomas E. Jimenez and Adam L. Horowitz, went even so far as to say, "In Cupertino [a suburb of San Francisco], Asianness is intimately associated with high achievement, hard work, and academic success. Whiteness, in contrast, stands for lower-achievement, laziness, and academic mediocrity."

According to Jimenez and Horowitz, white residents in these high-powered cities no longer set the norms for academic success. Increasingly, "fellow immigrant-origin Asians set the norms for success, and the evaluative frame through which they judge achievement therefore confers an advantage over whites." That is, Asians have become the superordinate populations in these cities—at least in education—and ambitious young academic achievers of all races, but especially white students, look and react to the Asian population for cues towards how to position oneself for success.

But from the Asian American's perspective, it's not the greatest thing to be looked upon as the top of the academic hierarchy—for two reasons.

The first is that academic success doesn't translate neatly to overall business and wage success. Life is more than a grade or an SAT score, and the winds of Asian success, strong out of the port, start to flag as they progress through life, not necessarily because of their own merit or lack thereof.

But the second reason is caught up in winds that could potentially upend not only the Asian-led academic order but the entire expanse of American political life. When then-presidential candidate Donald Trump focused his first campaign speech on undocumented immigrants characterized as being from Mexico, the variety of reactions focused on his alleged racism against and disdain for Mexicans. What most of the mainstream media missed, of course, was the underlying issue Trump pointed out: There was a deepening sense of competition between the native-born working class and the immigrant working class. Both have come to somewhat resent each other, and native-born working-class Americans saw the continuous influx of undocumented immigrants as a threat to their opportunities for social mobility, decreasing their leverage in business and local politics.

Now take those sentiments by the white working class against Mexicans and wrap them in a new casing: that of the upwardly mobile professional classes. Would it be so much of a stretch to consider that, just maybe, the sweepingly ubiquitous perception of academic success by first and second-generation Asian Americans—many of whom also retain artifacts and the seemingly weird practices of their home countries—also arouses resentment from other groups? We're not talking about the working class anymore. No, we're talking about those most likely to directly compete with Asian success: the highly educated professionals working in tech, finance, law, or medicine.

But it couldn't be, could it? These elite professionals talk nonstop about diversity and inclusion. They put signs on their front lawns decrying that "hate has no home here." They even glow about how much they love Chinese food and how well they can use chopsticks!

You have to look at how elites act to discover their state of mind. Consider the trends among the elite class—a nonstop work culture, a hypercompetitive race to the top, the calcified hierarchies for increasingly few winner-take-all spots—to see how elite professionals are being boxed into a culture of scarcity and Darwinian rules of survival. In today's cutthroat professional cultures, "you were always made to feel like you were just a little bit expendable," said Heberto Alexander Limas-Villas, a former Goldman Sachs associate.

> "There's only so many people you can promote . . . It's maintaining a cap to ensure quality over quantity. A year ago, we believed the partner culture was so large that it became diluted and opportunities for the partners were not as great. So [Goldman Sachs] encouraged the partners who weren't as great to leave the firm and pursue other opportunities . . . Want to keep it very simple and stable."

Thanks, Heberto! A moving illustration of the warm and forgiving nature of today's business elite.

Can you feel the stress levels rising? Elite professionals can. Perhaps many of them are parents and don't want their children to go through these meat-grinding work cultures. You can't necessarily blame them for wanting to relieve their progeny from the screaming anxiety of today's competitive atmosphere, which seems to treat scarcity as a kind of sadistic pleasure. Indeed, Harvard University faces allegations that it manipulates many Black and Hispanic students into applying for their college just so they can reject their applications, and so maintain their selectivity rate for the rankings![17] The more you reject, the more prestigious you look.

Let's say you are in this position. As an elite professional, you value maintaining your advantages, and you see this increasingly meager system threaten your child's ability to maintain his future leverage over the elite game. There are two ways you can attack. You can aim at the system of artificial scarcity—the Harvards, the elite jobs, the ruthless competition culture. But the system is entrenched, it is well-funded, and worse, it's probably populated by your friends. That makes going after the system an unattractive option.

The alternative, then, is to attack your competition. And who's your competition if you are an elite professional? Likely, Asian Americans.

Because Asian American students compete hard for their educational opportunities, they can be seen as contributing to "competition culture." Poor and rich Asians alike study an average of thirteen hours per week, more than twice as much as the typical non-Hispanic white student who studies a mere 5.5 hours per week at home.[18]

But this is unavoidable for Asian American students and their parents. If you are an immigrant parent, all you have are your skills. You don't have social connections or a network to buffer you or to absorb your mediocrity. If you aren't excellent, or have something to offer, you're done. So you bring that sort of attitude to your parenting. You seek to prepare your kids as best you can to walk the most well-trodden paths to stability in America today. You invest a far greater share of time and energy into your child's education than others. You develop a child who can get a good job—and have options that you didn't have when you came to America.

Royce Chen, a Bay Area student, describes the culture surrounding the Taiwanese American household as follows:

> "Family culture was defined by each person having a certain task to do. Be distinguished by each member of the family having certain tasks. Family seems to operate most effectively when everybody doing their own job. Whereas some families, everything was collaborative, in my family it was a productivity focus. Divide and conquer mindset. The tasks were built to complement one another. Mom would do the dishes and I would do the homework."

Say what you want about not learning household skills, but this style of "divide-and-conquer" parenting, heavily prioritizing what many Asian Americans perceive as one of the most worthwhile investments in a person's life—their education—does get results. This is not to say the Asian American strategy is best in the entire context of the American experience. But one conclusion is probably true: narrowing the focus of a child's life towards education tends to produce . . . a better-educated child.

And I don't just mean the effective test-taking child. Contrary to the stereotype of Asians being test-taking robots, Asian parents' cultural practices tend to emphasize creating a dedicated space for their children to do homework and become independent learners and thinkers.[19] Even poor Asian parents build practices conducive for their kids' future academic success like stressing the value of peer role models and getting extended family involved—as well as staying involved themselves—in the day-to-day academic routines of their kids. Sometimes, it gets excessive. Indeed, the extreme of this involvement, perhaps made most famous by Amy Chua's *Battle Hymn of the Tiger Mother*, carries with it some baggage. Chua described Chinese parenting as follows:

> "The Chinese mother believes that (1) school work always comes first, (2) an A-minus is a bad grade; (3) your children must be two years ahead of their classmates in math; (4) you must never compliment your children in public; (5) if your child ever disagrees with a teacher or coach, you must always take the side of the teacher of coach; (6) the only activities your child should be permitted to do are those in which they can eventually win a medal; and (7) that medal must be gold."[20]

Predictably, the book's more controversial statements—such as the fact that Chua once threatened to burn her daughter's stuffed animals if she didn't master a piano piece—inflamed outrage, but white "my little Johnny" liberals were not the only ones to criticize Chua's bestselling book. Many "Chinese mothers" also took Chua to task, arguing her book misrepresented Asian households as ruthless, repressive regimes. "I don't think what she said about Asian mothers or tiger mothers is true. In my whole life, I never saw one parent do that," said Ye Pogue, an immigrant of Chinese descent who married a white man. At the same time, Ye laments how the media used Chua's book to craft an image of Asian parents as exceedingly ruthless and despicable. "We need to show we are truly not monolithic. Somehow society thinks we're all tiger moms, tiger dads. I never saw tiger moms," she said.

Chua herself has even made it clear her book was about the *lessons* she learned trying to implement this mischaracterized Chinese system of parenting on her children.

Perhaps I am one of few authors out there who believes that Chua should not apologize for the spirit, if not the excesses, of her book. At the very least, it is undeniable that if one's goal is to nobly facilitate the educational fruits of their children, the cultural parenting styles of many Asian American groups tend to outclass the majority of other Americans in producing smart, competent, excellent students. And they should not be maligned for that.

■ ■ ■

Particularly, they should not be blamed in an age where American excellence, once indisputably boastful of the best talent in the world, is running into harm's way.

The millennial generation is the least likely generation to start their own business since before the Great Depression. John Letteri, an economic policy firm cofounder who testified in front of the Senate Committee on Small Business and Entrepreneurship, finds that less than 4 percent of American millennials report being self-employed/entrepreneurial—a stark decrease from 5.7 percent of Gen Xers and 6.9 percent of baby boomers.[21] Millennials are more likely to be employed than either generation—but less likely to start their own business. How could this be the case?

Or, if you prefer international testing metrics, why is it that American proficiency on international reading or math exams has fallen behind Canada and New Zealand—to say nothing of the rising East Asian powers whose students are dominating PISA (Program for International Student Assessment) scores? In 2015 America had to settle for fortieth in math.[22] Maybe overall test scores don't matter so much in terms of which country has the best workforce—the US still attracts the world's best talent—but consider that an increasing proportion of that talent is coming from elsewhere, particularly Asia. Consider this sobering statistic: 29 percent of US students did not meet the PISA test's baseline proficiency for math. However skeptical you are of international tests, it is hard to look at these scores and not walk away a little concerned about America's future competitive edge.

But the single most pressing—and probably discomforting—example of the decline in America's culture of excellence lies in sordid examples of our centers of excellence themselves.

Buried within the black-hole vortex of news that early to mid 2020 was a story not about Trump or China. It was about the Center of Disease Control in Atlanta, Georgia.[23]

The CDC, with an annual payroll budget of $1.1 billion, pays its 10,600 employees an average of $106,000.[24] (This, by the way, represents a 51 percent increase in taxpayer funding since 2003.) It has 168 executives who make over $200,000 a year. And it is entirely responsible for doling nearly $5.5 billion in research grants to scientists and administrators across the world. This makes the CDC America's biggest—and biggest budgeted—expert on infectious diseases, the leading light in the country's response to pandemics. It is the organization taxpayers trust with one responsibility: to protect their lives against the natural menaces of the world.

That is why the CDC's gross negligence at the cost of thousands of American lives should shut the mouths of anybody who believes that America's elite is as fundamentally sound and excellent as could be.[25]

In March of 2020, news headlines were trained on the Trump administration for failing to supply enough test kits to test for coronavirus in the American populace. It appeared to be a disaster of epic proportions. As the World Health Organization (WHO) supplied test kit information globally, and countries like South Korea were aggressively testing their population to the tune of tens of thousands per day, the United States couldn't seem to get its act together. Tests were widely unavailable, mere thousands administered a day until almost two weeks after social distancing measures were put into place. To many foreign observers, the US was a laughingstock. The richest, most advanced country in the world couldn't properly distribute a widely available COVID-19 test? It is just as ridiculous as it sounds.

The *Washington Post* reported that the Trump administration rejected the WHO test kit model in favor of a proposal by the CDC early in the coronavirus outbreak. In late January 2020, only days after the Chinese government released the full genomic sequence of COVID-19, the CDC got working on the test . . . only to discover with horror midway through the process that their COVID-19 test kits—which are built to detect trace amounts of the coronavirus—were being contaminated with the virus. This meant that as early as the twenty-fifth test, the kit would begin to register a positive trace of coronavirus even though there was none, such as in a sample of purified water. The CDC had only discovered this effect after they had already shipped out the first round of test kits to hospitals across the nation. The feedback that they received from hospitals revealed something they failed to catch in their own facilities.

The *Post* investigation deemed the CDC's failure to produce an adequate test kit for COVID-19 an "an unparalleled low in its often-proud, 74-year history." And it was. The result of the CDC's botched test kit was that widespread testing in America was delayed for nearly a month; in late February, while the rest of the world had tested 420,000 civilians for COVID-19, America had tested 1,000.

The CDC, America's highest center of research and public health excellence, is not a machine but run by people, people with warts and faults. It is essential that a program like the CDC, which carries the national welfare in its balance, is staffed by the best talent with the country's most disciplined minds. A slip-up here, a mental lapse there, and the country's health is jeopardized. This is the margin of error we have in our culture of excellence.

I don't speak of this story to throw shade on America. I speak of it to illustrate just how dire the circumstances of meritocracy are for the welfare of our civilized society. The marginal abilities and mental discipline of a few elite scientists at the CDC, the top of America's talent, meant the difference between coronavirus testing kits getting out in February versus March—and therefore the difference between public awareness of the coronavirus a month earlier, which would have resulted in containment of the virus a month earlier. One study projects that if the US closed even three weeks earlier, 95 percent of the initial upsurge in cases would have been prevented, resulting in thousands fewer coronavirus-related deaths.

One easily preventable quality-control snafu, if handled by even a few slightly better trained scientists and leaders, could have saved perhaps tens of thousands of lives. The United States might not have needed to resort to a costly economic lockdown to stop the spread of the virus. Lives, America's security, competition with China in the future tech war—all are at stake in the maintenance of a culture of excellence in which truly the very best need to be put in positions of the most responsibility.

No, this is not a Trump-era problem, or a problem that a Biden-Harris administration alone will be able to fix (although it will certainly be able to make it worse). We can no longer assume even the most general competency of our institutions, especially those that are paid most handsomely and considered most "elite." For a long time America thrived on "democracy and meritocracy"—the idea that American prosperity would be sustained on the hypothesis that the best leaders, the ones we elect, would naturally bubble over to the top because of the robustness of our institutions to both produce and identify top talent that would best serve our country. But what institutions do we actually trust to incorporate these ideals? The government, trusted by a mere 17 percent of the public?[26] Higher education, at 48 percent? Big business at 25?[27]

We must fix the accelerating decline of public trust in America's long-vaunted institutions of democracy. And in order to do so, we must fix our culture's ability to project, and then perform, one thing that they are sorely lacking: competency.

THE RISE OF CHINA

Americans have to look at another country, its history, and its future to understand the full scale of why a culture of excellence matters. That country is China.

How did the world's second-leading power rise to its current cultural status from its economic and social nadir, fifty years ago, during the time of agrarian Communism? To answer that question, we must understand the mind of the visionary who, more than most other leaders in world history, left his mark on his country. We must understand the mind of Mao Zedong.

Before Mao Zedong became the first dictator to kill one hundred million of his own people (a marker not even reached by the likes of Stalin and Hitler), he was a Chinese academic, a philosopher. In 1939, while hiding out in the caves of middle China and surrounded by enemies on all sides, he wrote that all on Earth was a sea of contradiction. Existence itself is a contradiction, and everything presumes its opposite. There could be no light without dark, not above without below—no oppressor without the oppressed.

> "Without landlords, there would be no tenant-peasants; without tenant-peasants, there would be no landlords. Without the bourgeoisie, there would be no proletariat; without the proletariat, there would be no bourgeoisie."

All these things, Mao wrote in his seminal piece *On Practice and Contradiction*, necessarily exist as opposites to each other, reflecting the ancient Daoist line of thinking. They are more than conveniently opposite, however. They are *metaphysically* opposite: The proletariat is destined to always struggle against the bourgeoise, the colonized against the colonizers.

Mao tapped into a deep hurt that Chinese people experienced at the time: the Century of Humiliation, when Western Powers and Japan took down the most ancient power in the world with a combination of opiates, political treachery, and gunboat diplomacy. Between 1830 and 1930, China was "carved up" into spheres of influence—each beholden to the hands of foreigners. Mao's way of thinking could be read as comforting: that imperialists rise and fall, and the conditions of the colonized also rise and fall, and change.

Mao's treatise came with a particular promise: Through the process of socialist revolution and the Communist Party command of industry, the landlords who own the land will lose it, and the peasants who work the land will own it. The bourgeoise will be subjected to the "dictatorship of the proletariat." Even the war and violence waged by the Chinese Communist Party would become peace, he argued. Mao justified his violence as necessary preparation for the eventuality of "permanent elimination of war."

It was embedded in Mao's philosophical being to oppose the successful. Whether that be the landowner, the industrialist, or the intellectual,

Mao saw all of them as enemies of the people. It was only the people *versus* the capitalists, the people *versus* the Westerners, the people *versus* industry and wealth and expertise.

Once he established the Chinese Communist Party as the guide star of all Chinese affairs, Mao implemented his personal vision for Chinese society with dizzying speed and force. In his Great Leap Forward (1955–1959), Mao targeted the industrialists and landlords—the successful men in commerce—by collectivizing agriculture and nationalizing industry. The resulting Chinese Famine (which wasn't a famine at all, but a government-arranged disaster) of 1959–1962 is widely regarded as the deadliest man-made disaster in the history of mankind. Over forty-five million died. One death is a tragedy; a million is a statistic. Nowhere is this sentiment more real, and realized, than in the mind of an elderly Chinese person today.

The consequences of the Great Leap Forward were so embarrassing to Mao and the Communist Party that he voluntarily retreated from public duties for five years. But Mao grew restless, and in 1966 he used the strength of his contacts to reassert pole position in Communist Party affairs. Emboldened, and reinvigorated, he sought a new target to rip on after utterly and thoroughly wiping out an entire generation of industrialists and landlords from 1959–1962.

This time, he went for the intellectuals.

There were pragmatic reasons for this—the usual getting-rid-of-political-enemies type thing—but it is important to note that Mao sincerely believed, with wholehearted conviction and incredible tenacity, that the socialist revolution could only occur if China was of one class and one mind, in lockstep with socialist ideals. In the Down to the Countryside Movement, he ordered promising young Chinese high schoolers to rural exile, denying them college in favor of hard labor in the farmlands. He encouraged the Red Guards, militia-like groups of young people who subscribed zealously to Mao's ideology, to attack and threaten anyone too intellectual for his own good, especially those studying Western thought. Those that failed to conform were beaten, tortured, and killed. Nearly two million died, and five years' worth of China's most creative top talent was washed down the drain because of Mao's suspicion of intellect and desire for class purity.

He called it the Proletarian Cultural Revolution: informally, the Cultural Revolution.

It was a profoundly anti-intellectual and anti-meritocratic revolution of thought. Yes, *anti*-meritocratic. There are policies and institutions all over the world that are *un*-meritocratic; that is, absent of principles of equal opportunity and merit-based hiring and elevation. However, the list of institutions that are expressly *against* meritocracy—in the sense that competence is hated and despised, and excellence is ridiculed and often tortured out of the person—is smaller. And make no question of it: The Cultural Revolution of mid-1960s China was *anti*-meritocratic.

It is not clear if, had the Cultural Revolution carried on for another fifty years, the minds of Chinese folk would have become molded into sincere camaraderie for the forthcoming peasant paradise, but early returns were not splendid.

Needless to say, after Mao died and the leadership of the Communist Party transferred to the pragmatic, French-educated Deng Xiaoping, Mao's "reforms" became hard-taught lessons to a tired and desperate party leadership sick of Maoism and ideological struggle. After grasping full power in 1978, Deng, with the support of the Chinese Communist Party, began to pave the way towards a new system of thought that repudiated Maoist ideology—even as he paid lip service to his predecessor. He called it "Socialism with Chinese Characteristics."

"Socialism with Chinese Characteristics" opened the Chinese economy to trade and business ownership while retaining state control of the biggest levers of the economy—most infamously its currency, the *yuan*, as well as its giant, state-invested energy and technology companies. Hardly a true "free" market, but it was a big step from agrarian Communism.

What must be understood about this phase of Chinese economic development is that China's primary motivation post-Mao was to gain international credibility for investment and establish a reputation for competence after the Maoist regime wasted so much talent and potential. "There was a terrible experiment with populism during the Cultural

Revolution, so there's a strong case to reestablish this kind of political meritocracy," said Daniel A. Bell, political theorist at Tsinghua University and author of *The China Model*.[28]

So the Deng Xiaoping regime did not simply "open up," as naïve Western scholars too often assume, but in a carefully calculated and conservative way—one that showed competence and contemplation.

One of Deng's first major decisions was to reinstitute *gao kao*, the annual National College Entrance Exam, the sole criterion by which a high school student will be admitted to a college. Although the *gao kao* sounds like a fixture of modern scientific thought, it is actually modelled off the Tang dynasty (618 to 907 AD) Imperial Exam for civil service workers. As the Tang dynasty is widely considered China's apogee in world dominance and historical respect, the exam's restoration served not only scientific or economic purposes but strongly *nationalistic* purposes—to show that China was returning to times of world leadership and competence.

Indeed, the Deng regime sought to make its people believe in the Communist Party again. *Gao kao* was a vehicle for public affirmation. Shelley Rigger, China scholar at Davidson College, states succinctly: "There's no trust, so the only thing that seems fair is a test." Because as much as people hate tests, they trust them to identify the most competent people in high positions; just take a look at the existence and formidability, despite criticism, of America's preprofessional exams (the LSAT, the GRE, and the MCAT).

The reinstitution of the test represented a nationwide effort to restore a perception of advancement by *merit*, instead of ideology and family, that would push the nation beyond the depressed and politically corrupt Mao years. And this was especially true within the Chinese Communist Party—even of its most repressive and authoritarian acts of governance! After the Tiananmen Square Protests of 1989, where hundreds to thousands of Chinese people were massacred protesting the Chinese Communist Party, Deng faced a crisis of leadership. He needed a "professional face-saver": someone who could deal with protesters effectively without repeating the disreputable mistakes leading to the international embarrassment of Tiananmen Square. After a nationwide search, Deng promoted Shanghai Minister Jiang Zemin, who was able to quell the protests in his city without having to, well, shoot anyone. There was a clear signal to the rest of the Communist Party: Want to get promoted? Do difficult jobs in your communities . . . and succeed.

That's what drove the promotional efforts of a regime trying to establish what Daniel Bell, China scholar and professor at China's renowned Tsinghua University, calls "vertical democratic meritocracy"—a form of meritocracy that relies on local governments to identify and cultivate the next generation of competent, able leaders—as a gateway to public trust. He writes:

> "For much of Chinese imperial history, public officials were selected first by examination and then by performance evaluations at lower levels of government. The fascinating thing is that this system has been reestablished in form over the past 30 years in China."[29]

Shelley Rigger describes the case of the Chinese hall monitor, a unique example of this schematic foreign to Western eyes. As early as first grade, local teachers would identify a strong student to whom they give the "hall monitor" title. The hall monitor carries immediate responsibility at the age of six or seven. (Consider what, if any, responsibilities Western parents give to their children at six or seven.) This child learns how to organize the books, assist the instruction, and even lead the classroom when the teacher was not available. A kid! Leading the classroom! How unthinkable would that be in America? But the hall monitor concept flourished across its provinces, as the Chinese Communist Party sought to find and develop the best community talent early and quickly—so as to produce the culture of excellence that it had run aground during the Mao years.

Did this new investment in a "culture of excellence" work? I can only say this: while the Soviet Union and its satellite states collapsed and utterly shattered its economic fortunes after transitioning from socialism to capitalism, China did not break. Instead, during the '80s, '90s, and 2000s, it grew exponentially. Now China is the world's second-largest economy and gaining. And while the authoritarian regime still represses and violates the rights of its own people, the Chinese Communist Party still rules—but the same cannot be said for the Soviet Politburo and its associated states.

■ ■ ■

Dr. Jun Ma was one of the winners in China's newfound reversal of fortune after Mao. But that didn't mean he experienced no hardships.

Before Jun became the director of the Center for Finance and Development at China's top-ranked Tsinghua University, he was an elementary school student outside Shanghai in the late 1960s and early 1970s. He was a vessel for education—or propagandization, in the eyes of Communist leaders under Mao. "We used chalk to write propaganda," he recounted bemusedly. "The Cultural Revolution wasted time in my elementary schools [with] propaganda."

Fortunately for him, Dr. Jun Ma's coming-of-age happened just as China came back to its senses in the realm of education. After Deng reinstalled the National Entrance Exam, a trickle-down effect followed; high schools and middle schools around the country got the message. Jun lived in Shanghai, at the time one of the country's most well-connected and globalized cities, and the public school system worked quickly to refine their education programs to fit the culture of competence Deng was trying to implement.

Jun's academic talent was identified by local leadership at a young age (another example of "vertical democratic meritocracy"), which allowed him to get into one of the most competitive middle schools in China's new academic system. Realizing he had to work exceptionally hard to leverage his middle school education into admittance to one of the city's most selective high schools, Jun studied hard and won first place in his middle school class rank. His position as first allowed him to attend a high school that fed into one of China's best universities, Fudan.

At the time China was just dipping its toes into world waters, Jun discovered computer science at Fudan. In this historical moment of opportunity, this was an opportunity to the third degree. "We considered computer science the future of the world," Jun said. Imagine if bright kids like Jun had got a hold of this technology—and the principles of modern businesses—*en masse* ten or even just five years prior.

Imagine if China had been able to harness the computer revolution instead of the US, creating and designing the first computers, pioneering the Internet, and getting the jump on smartphones before America did. Indisputably, we would be talking about China as today's next super-power, China whose dominance we'd be predicting over the world's tech infrastructure.

But China didn't, and Jun Ma didn't care much for computer science. He preferred business. "At that time there was no real economic research in China and you needed to study Marxism," he said. No one serious about becoming a businessman could take Marx seriously, and so Jun did what he thought would leverage better opportunity—he went to the US.

Jun became one of many bright, business-minded Chinese people who emigrated to the US when China was just getting its legs, further depriving China of its best talent and holding it back, despite its massive population and newfound commitment to productivity. America was too strong, and China, still too weak . . . at least, in the '90s.

But that isn't the end of the story. After working ten years in the States, Jun was approached with another opportunity. A branch of Deutsche Bank offered him a slot as its senior economist—in Hong Kong. So Jun packed his bags and left America. After making his bank a ton of money in exploding-growth Hong Kong, Jun settled into his current job as the founder of an economics-based think tank within Tsinghua University—arguably the top university in China.

For a long time, the best and brightest fled Communist China, with its outdated Marxist doctrines and intellectual barrenness, to come to America for freedom and opportunity. But as China has grown and developed into an economic superpower, some of its expats are finding reasons to go back. Although the country's illiberalism and repression remain, it is no longer a backwater swamp of intellectual decay. It has achieved a culture of excellence that now competes with America in a startling number of arenas. One only has to look at the Chinese video-making app TikTok, downloaded more than 165 million times in the US alone (at the time of this writing), to observe how China increasingly threatens American dominance in technology and business.[30]

This is not the time for America to rest on its laurels. If America does not improve its culture of excellence, the next century may indeed belong to China.

KEYING IN ON ASIAN AMERICANS

Why are Asians so significant to this culture of excellence? Why the focus on Asian Americans as the main case study in this discussion of the changing landscape of American ideals, and America's oncoming tech, science, and military competition with China?

One quote from a 2016 National Bureau of Economic Research paper by economist and data scientist Nathaniel Hilger says it all: "Asian Americans are the only nonwhite US racial group to experience long-term, institutional discrimination and subsequently exhibit high income."[31,32]

Here's the trick: Asian Americans were able to disproportionately build wealth because of their acquired skills that are considered valuable in today's economy; in short, by their merit. The bargain America cosmically struck with Asian Americans was for Asian Americans to do disciplined jobs like engineering, scientific enterprise, medicine, and mathematics, and for America to reward them with middle and upper-middle class status.

And this is exactly what happened. Asian Americans did not historically have success building wealth in the United States until about 1960, when most forms of legal discrimination were banned in America. They had barely any land from which to extract rent. They had no family inheritances. But they did have skills and educational discipline.

Hilger's study and data tracking Asian skillsets during the time of institutionalized discrimination from 1900–1940 reveal that Asian Americans had acquired skills and cognitive capabilities that, when finally allowed to trickle upward, gave Asian Americans considerable mobility in American society. The standardized Army General Classification Test (AGCT), for example, routinely rated Asians comparable with white

Americans during World War I and World War II, while educational data on Japanese Americans revealed greater educational success in the classroom than other comparably matched races.

Depressed wealth-building opportunities and the struggle to own land and acclimate to American life made Asian Americans one of the poorer ethnic groups in American life between 1880 and 1940, with low comparative social mobility from father to son. Asian Americans congregated in Chinatown ghettos isolated from the rest of American society.

But at the end of World War II, particularly after public outcry against the internment of Japanese Americans, institutional discrimination against Asian Americans was significantly lessened. In the midst of a postwar economic boom and without broad institutional barriers to entry in the workforce, there was a strong market incentive to hire based on the skills delivered, lest a competitor hire a better worker and gain a competitive edge.

Asian Americans thrived because market forces were finally allowing them adequate compensation for their skills.

Take California in 1940, where the majority of Asian Americans resided in the US at the time, for example. Asian Americans earned an average income comparable to that of the average Black American in California, which was to say much lower than that of the average white American. By 1960, however, Black wages in California and nationwide remained depressed compared to the average white American, while Asian American wages shot up—reaching parity with white Americans in barely twenty years. By 1980, Asian Americans had greater incomes than white Americans and exceeded Black incomes in California by a factor of an entire educational degree. A typical Asian American was achieving wage levels on par with a Black American with four more years of schooling.

Institutionalized bias kept Asian skillsets suppressed for a long time, and when finally released through the end of legal discrimination, unleashed a whirlwind of talent into the marketplace. They started businesses. They went into every industry. They built the American Dream for themselves.

■ ■ ■

The story of Asian Americans' social mobility is encapsulated in the life and travels of Binh Vo. Binh is studying to become an Air Force pilot. At the age of twenty-eight, he has already started his own real-estate business and built sizable wealth through home equity. He took every opportunity America gave him.

Binh Vo came to America from Vietnam when he was eighteen years old. His parents were "businessmen," he says—but with a caveat. "The title sounds cool, but they barely make enough." His parents eked out a living selling peppers. Not exactly CEO glitterati-types.

The majority of foreign-born Vietnamese Americans currently living in the United States immigrated in the aftermath of the Vietnam War, in the late 1970s and especially the 1980s, when President Ronald Reagan allowed for hundreds of thousands to flock American shores after Vietnam descended into Communist control. Before the war, there was Communist-controlled, USSR-sympathizing North Vietnam and capitalist, US-backed South Vietnam. When the US sent troops to ally with South Vietnam against the North's aggression, it was received with deep unpopularity and controversy in the United States. But to the South Vietnamese, America was a godsend. Binh, who is South Vietnamese, praises America like it is truly a heavenly land: "The United States represents freedom regarding the war between freedom and communism," he gushed.

Indeed, gratitude to America is a fundamental value of South Vietnamese Americans, says Binh. Of all Asian Americans, Vietnamese Americans are most likely to answer that they are "satisfied" with the direction of this country.[33] They are the ethnic group most likely to get naturalized. In 2015, 86 percent of Vietnamese Americans who were eligible for naturalization were already naturalized.[34] South Vietnamese immigrants jump for joy at the thought of getting naturalized. They line up. To them, it is a beautiful ceremony.

The thought of America being a racist country is repugnant to Binh. "This country is so generous and they are so welcoming," Binh said. "I do not see the racism in White people." He gives an example: "When I first got here in 2009, I was waiting for the bus. A police officer stopped by and asked if I needed a ride home. Today I realized I should have said yes. When I first came to America I stayed with a lady who was in her sixties. She was really patient with everything even though I couldn't speak good English."

Vietnamese Americans, in many ways, are the clearest-eyed example yet of what kind of land America is because most of them came as *refugees* from Communism-stricken Vietnam—between 1975 and 1990. Most arrived with nothing, not even English skills.

And yet, *and yet*, this immigrant group is blossoming merely thirty-some years after they first stepped into refugee resettlement camps in America. Today, the proportion of all Vietnamese in poverty is lower than the median. The proportion of impoverished *foreign-born* Vietnamese, who barely know English, is lower than that of the median American.[35]

How did this happen? "Popular professions among the Vietnamese are restaurants and nail shops," Binh remarks. "We took over the nail industry from Koreans in the 1990s," he adds. Asians are always competing with one another, aren't they?

But Binh's point illustrates a near-universal truth about these tough-minded immigrants, who came to America from a war-torn, destitute, Communism-racked country with no English skills and built a life to provide their children with the opportunities to succeed. "At a nail salon, you don't have to speak much English. You can work ten to eleven hours a day and get paid," Binh said. As Vietnamese immigrants integrated in the fabric of American society, small businesses sustained their community. Nail shops and restaurants.

But that doesn't mean Vietnamese immigrants want the same for their kids. According to Binh, there were four types of professions for an American-born Vietnamese: "Engineer, lawyer, doctor, or homeless because they get kicked out of the house." And the data reflects this. In a single generation, Vietnamese immigrants have produced sons and daughters with master's degrees. In the United States today, 52 percent of foreign-born Vietnamese have a high school or less education; among American-born Vietnamese—one or two generations younger, at most!— that number shrinks to 21 percent. Today, 51 percent of American-born

Vietnamese have bachelor's or higher degrees—compared to 30 percent of all Americans.

What is in the water for Vietnamese Americans? It is more than good values. It is a belief in America—a total devotion for freedom. These immigrants come in and start their own businesses with zero education, settle all across the country, and build their lives in states like California, Texas, Florida, Louisiana, and Oregon.

Vietnamese Americans, I believe, are a classic case of what we know to be the American Dream: that your background doesn't matter, but your attitude—your work ethic, your belief in the goodness and opportunity of this country—is what matters. To the extent that the American Dream is still a viable philosophy of living, it is encapsulated in the lives of Vietnamese immigrants.

■ ■ ■

What narratives do Asian Americans break? Perhaps all of them, from the Left and the Right. Take the narrative that artificial "eliteness" and social networks cultivated by privileged parents are what make a successful person in America. Daniel Markovits articulates this idea in his book *The Meritocracy Trap*—which is somewhat misleadingly named, as his book doesn't actually critique meritocracy so much as America's diversion from meritocracy over the last fifty years:

> "Middle-class stagnation, elite prosperity, and rising economic and social divisions all fit together, as meritocracy transfers wealth and privilege dynastically down through the generations."[36]

We see this narrative increasingly reinforced by elite firms' intensive cultivation of schools to reinforce the narrowing hierarchy of the elite class. But Asian American immigrants don't come from those backgrounds. They have been the victims of historical exclusion and discrimination in America for centuries. Yet whenever they are allowed to compete, they often outcompete the privileged students of the socially inbred elite. Asians break the narrative of privilege in vogue with today's socialists.

Asian Americans also don't fit neatly into the traditional definition of a "minority" as someone in need of help, a victim of society and the world. Oftentimes the term applied to Asian Americans is "model minority," a racial group that has been able to tap into the potential of the American engine rather than languish in the shadow of the white economic machine.

But we cannot extend this too far. A common conservative talking point is that "Asians are the new Jews," a persecuted but successful minority—and yet Asian Americans, unlike Jewish Americans, are so underrepresented in politics, media, and the upper ranks of business. Perhaps the character of Eduardo Saverin, a Jewish man portrayed by Andrew Garfield in *The Social Network*, said it most presciently when he pointed to a gaggle of Asian women at his fraternity and encouraged a stunned Mark Zuckerberg: "They like us!"—implying, perhaps, that they are who the Asians want to be . . . or be with. Why does it seem as if Asian Americans are a tier below Jewish Americans and other "model minorities" in cultural representation, and even by conventional standards of beauty (for Asian men, especially—this will be elaborated on further later in the book)?

There is no question that the status of Asian Americans has risen to a level of public interest unprecedented in the history of the United States, save for possibly World War II. Intellectuals look across the Pacific Ocean at China's rise towards world supremacy and fantasize about authoritarian China's efficiency and meritocracy, traits that they wonder, inevitably, whether they translate to the members of the ethnicity themselves.

But the truth is, Asian Americans do not fit cleanly into any of these predominant narratives about American life. In fact, the truth about Asian Americans in this country exposes these common narratives' flaws and failures across the map of all races and collectives. As the country begins to wake up to the contradictions that Asian Americans stab in the heart of sociopolitical narratives across the spectrum, resentment against Asian Americans will grow and fester. Until Asian Americans get a grip on themselves and organize into a coherent political identity, they will increasingly face the wrath of a country increasingly turning against their values.

Because they don't fit into your narrative. And by the way, they won't fit into your narrative.

They are an inconvenient minority.

ANSWERING OBJECTIONS TO ASIAN AMERICAN UNIQUENESS

There are a few obvious ways the Left usually responds to these inconvenient facts about Asian Americans. The first is by denying that Asian Americans are, in fact, more successful "in measures of citizenry" than white Americans. They point out how Asian Americans experience higher rates of poverty than white Americans, at about 12.3 percent compared to 9.3 percent, respectively.[37] They use this to show that Asian Americans are not "monolithic" and also fall into categories of privilege and oppression.

One popular statistic the Left employs to demonstrate that Asian Americans are not participating in the American Dream is a Pew Research claim that "income inequality in the U.S. is rising most rapidly among Asians." According to the report, Asians have surpassed Black Americans as the race with the highest income inequality. In 1970, the top 10 percent of Asians made about six times as much as the bottom 10 percent. Now, the rate is 10.1 times, which makes Asians the "most unequal" group among the races.[38] One of the most walloping claims is mentioned as a subheadline of the report: The standard of living of lower-income Asians stagnated from 1970 to 2016.

But this claim is extremely misleading. Low-income Asians' standards of living have not "stagnated," as the Pew Research report goads us to think. Rather, the previous generation of low-income Asians has advanced to higher levels. But concurrently, massively increased Asian immigration has brought in even more low-income Asians, who—despite starting out in this society with low wages—will turn out just fine, if American society functions as it had for the last crop of low-income Asians.

This chart provided by the Urban Institute proves the above point. It breaks down Asian Americans by country of origin and percentage on

SNAP (a federal food stamp program that proxies for poverty status) in 2015.[39]

Share of Population Receiving SNAP

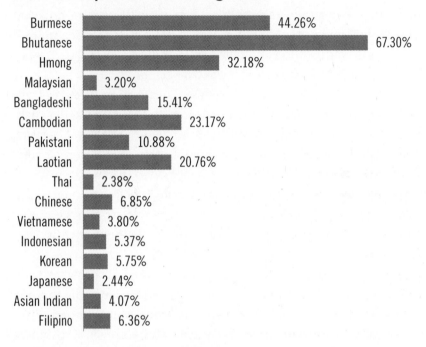

Burmese	44.26%
Bhutanese	67.30%
Hmong	32.18%
Malaysian	3.20%
Bangladeshi	15.41%
Cambodian	23.17%
Pakistani	10.88%
Laotian	20.76%
Thai	2.38%
Chinese	6.85%
Vietnamese	3.80%
Indonesian	5.37%
Korean	5.75%
Japanese	2.44%
Asian Indian	4.07%
Filipino	6.36%

Source: American Community Survey, 2015 data.
Note: SNAP = Supplemental Nutrition Assistance Program.

What is the highest percentage of Asian Americans on SNAP, by far? That would be Bhutanese-born immigrants. What is unique about these immigrants? Most of them came to the US in the late 2000s, prompted by a refugee crisis. And what is unique about both the Hmong and Burmese? Well, most of them recently faced similar levels of oppression. They didn't come to the United States to be oppressed; they came to *flee* oppression. And naturally—given that these people are victims of ethnic and identity violence when they emigrate—they would often come to America poor. These refugees form a highly disproportionate number of the so-called "bottom 10 percent" of Asian Americans—*not* Asians who have lived in this country for generations and participated in the so-called "anti-minority oppression" going on in the United States.

And while Asian Americans experience poverty at the same rate as white Americans (7.3 percent for both groups, according to 2020 Census data), they experience its crippling behavioral effects at a significantly lower rate than even white Americans.[40] Take crime for example. The white arrest rate in 2018 was 3.6 percent. For Black Americans, it was 6.7 percent. For Asian Americans, it was 0.8 percent.[41]

Or take single parenthood, one of the statistics most linked to exacerbating the cycle of poverty. Asian American children are less than half as likely to be living in a household that is not two-parent than the average American.[42] Remember, the government definition of poverty is simply an income threshold. But there are people who live in "poverty" who experience significantly fewer deleterious effects of living under that line than others. And it is clear from the accompanying statistics that Asian Americans in poverty are less prone to its culturally destructive effects than others.

So, when it comes to Asian immigrants, we can only say what is absolutely true based on the evidence: The American Dream seems to work—at least for this group of Americans—and Asian Americans who live in this country for a little while are likely to parallel, and even surpass, white Americans on many measures of social status or lifestyle in the United States.

The second attempt from the Left to discredit Asian success is their assertion that Asian immigrants, especially newer ones, benefit from certain advantages gained from their home country that allow them to thrive in this one.

I've heard this argument framed in even more conspiratorial terms: that the US government *actively tried* to recruit high-skilled Asians to shame Black people into denying racism. Per a viral College Humor video featuring Asian American studies professor Ellen Wu:

> "In 1965 . . . Congress approved a landmark immigration law that ditched racist restrictions. But it gave preference to immigrants who had skills that would benefit the US economy . . . and the

most sinister part of this myth is, it was used to put other minorities down.

"In the 1960s, government officials looked at socioeconomic data from African American communities and contrasted it to the so-called family values and stability of Asian Americans. Now this fueled racist claims that Black people had no one to blame but themselves if they experienced poverty and social disadvantages."

This claim falls apart on further analysis. If it was the US government's federal policy to only select for the "most educated" Asian immigrants, why did they accept 150,000 Vietnamese refugees, mostly peasantry, during the Vietnam War? Today, those same Vietnamese immigrants are among the lowest percentage of Asians on SNAP—below those "skilled" Chinese. And the claim unravels further upon examination of the skills and education of Chinese people who America "imported." In fact, over 70 percent of Chinese US residents obtained their green cards through family ties or through asylum—commensurate with the average percentage of all immigrant groups who came to this country via family ties or asylum rather than through skill.[43] And guess what—America also has a number of undocumented Chinese immigrants too, especially from the Fujian province.[44]

We absolutely must note that although Asian immigrants may perhaps score better on skillsets like math and science, they also come to this country with one extremely critical disadvantage, which only recently has softened—lack of English skills.

Lack of English skills is a huge blow to one's ability to progress in this country. UC-San Diego and University of Houston economists found in their controlled study that immigrants who came from countries with an overall worse English literacy have a 25 percent lower average income than those with better English literacy (when controlled for average GDP of country of origin and other relevant factors).[45] This is equivalent, in today's dollars, to a nearly $15,000 annual penalty per household per year. So it's not as if Asian immigrants come to America like Wonder Woman, bronzed-god Amazonian princesses with genius IQs. They're stunted in many senses too.

But let's say, just for the sake of it, the argument that Asian Americans disproportionately come with greater skills than the average American is, on balance, true—and I'm not denying it might be. It might be true that, on balance, Asian immigrants—particularly those from tech-savvy countries like China, Japan, India, and South Korea—arrive in America with higher skills in certain fields than other immigrant groups.

Doesn't this just prove our initial point? That culture matters; that building wealth in America depends upon the cultivation of particular marketable skills with value in society today. Whether you gain those skills in this country or in another one hardly matters. What matters is that you have those skills, and that you can pass on those skills—or at least the character and personal habits that would enable one to learn those skills —to the next generation.

THE REACTION AGAINST ASIAN SUCCESS: NATIVISM

Asian culture significantly bolsters Asian Americans' ability to transcend poor circumstances and achieve middle-class stability in American society, despite limited factors like language barriers and lack of social connections. But Asian Americans are still underrepresented in most sections of the American intelligentsia—including in politics, business, and media.

That's because the elite sphere of American life is not a meritocracy. It's not something you can simply drill or study for, a place wherein you can get by on your pure grit. There are gatekeepers to this elite—and these gatekeepers carefully scan for race.

When you are part of a race that has hit educational institutions so hard and so fast, it's not actually so great to be seen as the top of the academic and economic mobility hierarchy. Two reasons why come to mind.

The first is that Asian American academic success inspires resentment from the elite liberal establishment, which still controls the political and educational power centers in the United States. This establishment sees the creation of more meritocratic competition, especially in the form of an outside race like Americans of Asian descent, as a threat to their own welfare.

As the racial group of Americans closest in socioeconomic status to upper-middle class white people, Asians are the likeliest visible racial minority to live next to liberal, similarly-classed whites. Asian Americans also tend to congregate in the most liberal cities in America—particularly, New York, Los Angeles, San Francisco, and Seattle. That's basically murder's row of liberal cities. This doesn't mean, however, that Asian Americans are uniformly liberal. Their relationship with American *liberalism* in general is complicated and could in fact be interpreted as subversive. Nevertheless, Asian Americans are a fairly strong Democratic stronghold—63 percent of them voted for Joe Biden in the 2020 elections.[46]

Yet Asian Americans have become a suspicious entity to the nation's liberals. They have come too fast and too strong. They take up all the good magnet schools—a fact not lost upon the nation's disgruntled liberal school administrators. And when they graduate, they take up all the stable software engineer jobs at the big tech firms. I can hear the so-called Lefties mutter under their breaths: "The high-wage labor formerly done by my prep-school child is increasingly being done by a Chinese guy with an accent!"

Although liberals would likely not be keen to admit it, nowhere is the resentment more calcified and organized than in the nation's public school system. Because it has become so obviously stratified, there are scarce spots within the best schools, a fact not lost on *anyone* raising a child in America today. When these schools choose students for their spots based on merit, Asian Americans tend to fill them in disproportionate numbers. So little Johnny, son of the Prius-driving, Whole Foods-buying leafy liberal couple down the block, finds himself constantly competing—and often losing—to guys named Wong and Xu.

And this drives some elite liberals batty.

"I know they have the tests," said Byron Johns, head of the Montgomery County, Maryland, NAACP chapter (a liberal organization in one of America's wealthiest counties)—alleging that the Asian community retains copies of the local gifted and talented exams to memorize. "You have a suspiciously high number of Asians, who are 13 percent of the population, but they make up 35–40 percent of the magnet schools."

Johns is perhaps justified in his concern about the racial inequality he perceives in his district. He has reasons. The cultural and socioeconomic artifacts of discrimination perhaps persist in the comparatively lower socioeconomic statuses of Montgomery County's Black households. "Montgomery County never did desegregate," Johns asserted. "[Still today] there is statutory discrimination."

But the Montgomery NAACP chapter head goes further than accusing the county of discrimination. He goes so far as to say that Asian Americans are gaming the system to put their kids in the gifted and talented programs, while Black and Hispanic kids are left out in the cold.

Although Byron Johns is perhaps one of the more unfiltered examples of weaponizing Asian dominance in the education field to raise concerns over unfair treatment of "other" racial minorities, liberal brainpower eggs on this general line of thought at the school administrative level. Former school board member Chris Barclay probably spoke a little too candidly when he remarked to the local *Bethesda Beat* newspaper about the gifted and talented programs of Montgomery County:

> "In this region, that unfortunately is very addicted to power and ranking, there is a reality of folks wanting to be on top or have more than others . . . How are we going to have this conversation so it's not just again *the usual suspects* that end up knowing everything and then end up being able to leverage their knowledge to being able to get what they want for their children."

Or ponder the comments that Brooklyn Councilwoman Laurie Cumbo made about an Asian "wave" of migration into her diverse, well-educated Brooklyn district, inflaming nativist fear of Asians streaming into "their" schools and "their neighborhoods":

> "[My constituents] are having challenges in terms of understanding how one particular ethnic group, that speaks the same language across the board—I know that there are many different

languages and many different dialects—but how is it that one specific ethnic group [Asian Americans], has had the opportunity to move into a development in large numbers?"[47]

She calls Asian Americans a "bloc" and worries about what a wave of Asians would do to her diverse community—one that historically struggled with tensions between the Black and Asian communities in the 1980s and 1990s.[48] Yet instead of healing and repairing, Ms. Cumbo chose to dichotomize her residents.

Outside of the education realm, consider how lawmakers in California who supported Proposition 16, a 2020 ballot measure that would introduce racial preferences in public employment and contracting, described Asians in their communities. California assemblywoman Cristina Garcia, one of the most fervent supporters of the measure, said of the opposition to a similar race preferences bill in 2014:

"This makes me feel like I want to punch the next Asian person I see in the face."[49]

And sometimes, such exclusion is more than just subtle asides. Sometimes, it is completely out in the open.

Yangzi Jiang came to America as a student from China. Many international students come to America to learn about the culture, desirous of getting into an American university. But for Yangzi, the stakes were much higher.

When Yangzi was in middle school, he was diagnosed with bone cancer. Chinese doctors were underqualified to handle it, so his parents sent him to America to have his leg amputated and replaced with a metal affixation. (Yangzi's stride is perfectly normal, and only when he wears shorts do you ever notice that his left leg is made of metal.)

Even though the bone surgery and travel to America had already sapped the Jiang family of most of their savings, they decided to spend nearly everything they had to allow Yangzi to stay and receive an American high school education. "We had already lived in America for a year, so we might as well," Yangzi said. His parents wanted Yangzi to live in America for the rest of his childhood. So they enrolled Yangzi in high school and took a plane back to China.

But the catch was clear—if unstated—in the Jiang family: In order for this risk to work out, Yangzi had to go to an American college, *with financial aid*. Why? Because Chinese universities typically did not accept American high school transcripts for entry into college, and since his parents had little money left after paying for Yangzi's high school tuition, their son not only had to get accepted to an American college to have any hope of attending a decent university—he had to receive financial aid. "For high school my parents could barely support me, but for college there was no chance," Yangzi said.

Technically classified as an international student, Yangzi faced an even steeper hurdle: In American universities today, international students and *especially* Chinese international students are considered college administrators' personal piggy banks. Chinese international students often fixate on American universities, and university administrators utilize that fixation to an exploitative degree by charging full tuition for the "privilege" of studying at their university.

Yangzi called the University of Rochester, inquiring about need-based financial aid due to his family's income status. "[They said] we offer limited scholarships for international students," he told me. "And they asked me, what country are you from? And I said China. And they said: Oh . . . so we don't offer scholarships to Chinese students."

Yangzi was taken aback. "It's kind of funny, they made it very explicit. They see the Chinese passport, and they see Chinese students as a sort of revenue. Or there are enough rich kids who come from China, they don't need to accept a poor kid from China."

Need-based financial aid was thrown out the window strictly due to Yangzi's Chinese international status. It became clear to Yangzi: No one was going to do him any affirmative action favors even though he came from a poor family. And it was expressly for the reason that he was Chinese.

The result of that denial? Yangzi had to compensate by becoming a slave to his studies to try for merit-based financial aid. "I was the nerd," Yangzi said. For four years he was "the nerd," burying himself in books, forgoing a social life, and learning English at a rapid clip. He was already good at math (a product of early Chinese education, he admitted) but really needed to catch up on English. He spent many lonely hours memorizing vocabulary. When others would socialize with their friends, he drilled day after day at routine grammar exercises.

Yangzi ended up with stellar grades and test scores. He ended up getting accepted to Davidson College with merit aid. But it came at a price. He missed out on the "high school experience." He was ignored in class. Odds are, he was classified by the other students as one of those Asian test-taking nerds with no personality.

Of the education system, we always talk about how "humorless" and "socially unaware" Asians affect their treatment in the admissions process. But we never talk about how Asians' treatment before and during the admissions process can affect and shape Asians' ability to socially integrate—when they know that they have to work harder to get the same result as someone else.

The racial and nation-based stereotypes and judgments that these college administrators apply to Asian students don't just evaporate into the ether. They have real effects. They stick.

THE REACTION AGAINST ASIAN SUCCESS: ASIAN PRIVILEGE

Yet another maneuver elite progressives make to not only discriminate against Asians but morally legitimize that discrimination so they can feel good about it, too, is their accusation of "Asian privilege." That is, complicity in white supremacy—just because as a race they achieve on a level commensurate with white people.

In her 2018 article "The Whitening of Asian Americans," *Atlantic* writer Iris Kuo claims that Asian Americans "are making a case that, in the elite echelons of society, Asians are, like white people, a privileged class that is being brought down as other racial groups rise."[50] She believes that Asians are simply the next group to, like the "people of Irish, Italian, and Jewish heritage before them," participate in the great American "whitening"—the process by which "the white race has expanded over time to swallow up those previously considered non-whites."

Kuo goes on: "In the next wave of whitening, some sociologists have theorized, Asians and Latinos could begin to vanish into whiteness, as some assimilate culturally into white norms and culture, and become treated and seen by whites as fellow whites," she said. "Being in the good graces of white people helped me win plum housing deals. It helped bring me pay raises and perhaps even jobs themselves." She concluded with the ultimate put-down of Asian Americans: that their success is predicated on groveling to the tastes of white people. "Perhaps it shouldn't be surprising that some Asian-Americans are aligning themselves with white people when it comes to university admissions," she said. "Appealing to white taste, after all, is a baseline requirement for advancement."

The idea follows the liberal ideology categorizing groups as either "privileged" or "oppressed"; that is, Asian Americans are "privileged" because of their proximity to whiteness, especially in comparison to the lack of proximity by Black people. The term used by the Left is "White-adjacency." That is, whites are the dominant population, and Asians are their abettors.

Asian American progressive author Viet Thanh Nguyen states his perception of Asian privilege via proximity to whiteness more bluntly:

> "Situated in the middle of America's fraught racial relations, we [Asian Americans] receive, on the whole, more benefits from American capitalism than Black, brown or Indigenous peoples, even if many of us also experience poverty and marginalization. While some of us do die from police abuse, it does not happen on the same scale as that directed against Black, brown or Indigenous peoples. While we do experience segregation and racism and hostility, we are also more likely to live in integrated neighborhoods than Black or Indigenous people. To the extent that we experience advantage because of our race, we are also complicit in holding up a system that disadvantages Black, brown and Indigenous people because of their race."[51]

You can see the narrative Iris Kuo and Viet Thanh Nguyen are trying to build. They call out Asians for either trying to be like white people or benefitting from systems that prop up white dominance. Iris Kuo's use of the word "privileged class" is intentional. The application of the word "privilege" to Asians is a dog whistle— but not for the Right. In Left-speak, when a class is considered "privileged," taking things from them is morally legitimate.

■ ■ ■

To understand the true meaning of the word "privilege" and its implications on public policy, we must go back in history. In 1971, John Rawls— Harvard political philosopher and supposedly one of the most important philosophers of the twentieth century—published his magnum opus, *A Theory of Justice*, which became the iconic work for the contemporary liberal movement.

According to Rawls, *all* aspects of merit are arbitrary and due to luck. Rawls maintained that "the idea of rewarding desert is impracticable."[52] Yes, if you won a 100-meter competition, you did it because of luck. Yes, even innate talent for running was a function of luck. Your "effort?" Your "hard work?" Merely the result of top-tier coaching and top-tier parenting, a Rawlsian would say. Even if you didn't receive that, your "inner drive" was also a function of luck. Get the picture? You didn't deserve that running medal. The fact that you earned that running medal and someone else didn't is just pure luck, in this cosmic game of life.

From his total elimination of the idea of merit, Rawls created a justice system wherein he believed that the most just outcome in a society is the outcome that most benefits the lowest class of people. Calling it *the difference principle*, Rawls believed that if two complete strangers got together and created a society, it would minimize the poverty of the person who turned out to be on the lower end of their two-person society—even if that poverty minimization came at the expense of the wealth of the other. This is where you get ideas like making a lottery system for Thomas Jefferson High School. Their school board had such little faith in merit as a matter of justice, that they thought the only way to soothe their consciences was using random chance to determine the opportunities of the county's high-aptitude kids.

Now racialize it. In our current mainstream discourse, "white" is considered the highest class and "Black" the lowest. "Hispanic" is roughly above Black and "Asian" is higher than both Black and Hispanic. Yet, "Asian" is also perceived as more foreign than either "white" or "Black." The result is this influential graph of Asian Americans' racial triangulation, according to political theorist Claire Kim:[53]

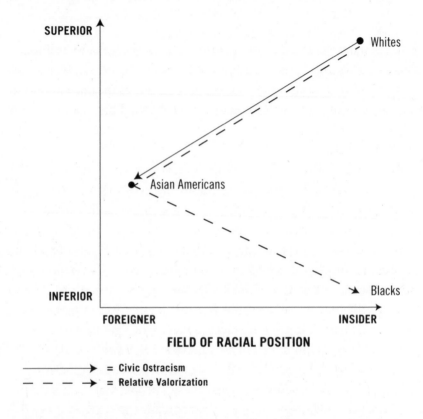

Based on this graph and Rawlsian reasoning, Asians are in a higher class than Black people, and so there is moral justification to strip Asians of societal benefits if those benefits would instead flow to Blacks, the "lower class" under the difference principle. And, because Asians are considered outsiders, it would be easy to do so—because they don't have the social capital to fight back.

■ ■ ■

Daniel Tan does not think he is all that privileged. His experience is not one of Asian privilege but actually of seeing another group claim "oppression points" and favors that he himself could not because he is not of an "oppressed" status.

Born to a family of Chinese-Filipino minority businessmen living in the Philippines, Daniel's original plan was to take over the family business. Then the Great Recession of 2008 hit, and Daniel's family businesses collapsed amidst Filipino government corruption. "My dad told me and my brother we had to move because our tax system was very corrupt. My dad was tired of living this way. Better to find greener pastures." They chose to come to America.

Interestingly enough, Daniel's mom—as opposed to his businessman father—secured the family visa to come stay in the United States. "Mom was a nurse during 2008 and there was a nursing shortage, so the US let her in on a work visa because trade was in demand." When they finally got to the US, Daniel's family relied upon local churches that were able to supply them with decent living conditions. Daniel's dad was lent a foreclosed home for the family to stay in, and so Daniel came to America in the middle of a recession with a degree from a foreign high school, mediocre grades, and not much of a plan to fit into this new society.

Daniel's mom was the one to first suggest the medical profession to him. "Your father and I expected you to take over the business one day, but that's moot," she said. A medical career would provide stability and leave room for his business interests.

Daniel decided his mom's advice was sound and enrolled at San Joaquin Delta Community College to pursue an associate degree in respiratory therapy. But he was handed a rude awakening before even his first day. "I had to pay out-of-state tuition because I wasn't a resident of California for long enough," he said. Even though he had to pick up extra shifts at diners and his second job at a clinic where he worked to make ends meet, Daniel accepted this as the cost of achieving a college education in America. "As I was washing those dishes at Red Lobster, I remember reflecting, 'I don't want to be a dishwasher for the rest of my life.'" He grew more determined to get a college education, although he would initially have to pay extra for it. He would get out of dishwashing, even if it meant paying extra for college and grinding to make ends meet.

But one incident on campus shattered his conception of the value of hard work and doing things the right way in America.

"Early on I was applying for community college and I saw a little booth for DACA students." (DACA, or "Deferred Action for Childhood Arrivals," is an Obama-era program that offers residency status to children of undocumented immigrants.) "I went up to the booth and they were asking 'are you DACA,' and I said no, and then I asked them what this was about, and they said 'oh, if you're DACA, you get to . . . I think California was somehow paying for DACA students for their tuition or they were getting funding.'" Daniel winced at the strong sense of unfairness he felt right then and there. "I'm doing everything the right way and I have to pay twice as much."

The 2011 California Dream Act gave in-state tuition to all DACA students, waiving non-resident tuition for *them* that *Daniel* would have had to pay his first year. The average in-state tuition at San Joaquin Delta College is $1,288 per year. For an out-of-stater like Daniel, it was $9,072 a year.[54]

How was this fair, Daniel asked himself, when his mom was the one who fought for a visa to legally enter this country—and then the children of undocumented immigrants, those who didn't go through the legal entry process, not only cut him and his mother in line for immigration but get a fat tuition cut on top of it?

Plainly: "It was a very nascent feeling of 'this is not fair.'"

What Daniel's story shows is that privilege is not a universal one-way street. While progressive elites would call him "privileged" for being an Asian American, Daniel—an immigrant who obeyed all the laws and worked for months at a Red Lobster to pay for college—remained unaided while the children of undocumented immigrants received the benefits for college that he had been left to scrounge up through dishwashing from the government.

ASIAN AMERICANS AND THE CULTURE OF EXCELLENCE

America has a choice to make. There are legitimate concerns regarding equity and inclusion in this country. The fact that the average Black American has one-tenth the acquired wealth of the average white American ($17,000 to $171,000) is a national travesty.[55]

But at the centers of intellect, equity-increasing initiatives to bring racial representation onto elite campuses and businesses in the name of "diversity" uniformly deny more qualified Asian Americans—who have worked hard to achieve at the level they have achieved—to receive the opportunities for which they so diligently work.

And this conflict presents a crucial dilemma. In our institutions, designed to produce our most excellent students—those who will invent the next national security innovations, found our next great businesses, produce vaccines for whatever new pandemic strikes next—at what point must equity take a backseat to excellence, *bar none*?

In a knowledge-based market, Asian Americans are uniquely qualified for the battles America will wage, especially in the economic and technological sphere, with an increasingly aggressive and competent China.

But the creeping diversity ideology of today's intellectual epicenters discourages Asian Americans from putting their whole heart into advancing the society in which they live. By uniformly calling Asian Americans "privileged," today's progressive intellectuals foster Asian American guilt about their achievement. By not-so-subtly driving Asian Americans away from educational opportunities, intellectuals cause Asian Americans to question whether they should want to work in this country and engender in them resentment to create in a society that needs their talent. We see these developments in college admissions, in media representation, in business, and in politics, wherein the lasting imprint of the Left's diversity ideology might not actually wreak any significant increase in Black and Hispanic success, but will likely rather wreak damage to Asian American consciousness.

That is, unless Asian Americans fight back.

And they fight back. But they're fighting for more than themselves. They're striving for a principle, meritocracy, that has elevated not only millions but has established a framework in which America's many diverse people may fairly interact with each other in an integrated way—instead of resorting to the fires of identity politics.

This is the story of Asian Americans battling a thorny, anti-excellence diversity ideology that has spread across the elite power centers pulsing across this country. America's culture of excellence hangs in the balance.

HARVARD IS ROTTING

JUST WHAT DOES IT TAKE TO DEFEAT HARVARD?

There were two protests that day, each one conjoined to the other.

On October 14th, 2018, a stream of Asian Americans gathered at Boston's Copley Square. Signs abounded. "I HAVE A DREAM TOO," some read. "SUPPORT RACE NEUTRAL ADMISSIONS." They were protesting Harvard's longstanding policy of including race in their admissions context, which they perceived to be weaponized against Asian Americans.

That week, the 1st District Court of Massachusetts would hear the *Students for Fair Admissions v. Harvard* case. At that time, several revelations about Harvard's admissions process had already been unveiled. Harvard had:

1. Rated applicants on scales of 1 through 5 on academics, extracurriculars, athletics (if applicable), and a "personality" score;
2. Used the "personality score" as the determinant factor for most admittances to the college;

3. Rated Asian Americans significantly lower than all other races on the "personality score," despite them having received the highest academic and extracurricular scores of all races.[1]

The court was tasked with finding evidence of discrimination against Asian Americans in the highly anticipated, nationally covered *Students for Fair Admissions v. Harvard* case. But the stakes at Copley Square presented a greater issue at hand.

Several miles away, a group of Harvard students, faculty, and others raised counter-protest signs in support of Harvard's admissions policies. "SUPPORT DIVERSITY," one read. There was a tailgate atmosphere at sections of this rally, complete with chants: "We are more! Than our scores!"[2] It was a little bit of an odd sight: not one but two competing protests, each with hundreds of attendees, over a few admissions spots to Harvard University.

But these protests weren't over a few admissions spots to a single college. Everybody there knew the stakes were far greater. The future of affirmative action—in particular, the Ivy League diversity protocols that gave points for being of certain preferred races—was at hand. If Students for Fair Admissions, a group comprising rejected Asian American applicants to elite colleges, could prove that Harvard discriminated against Asian American applicants in order to make room for other races (Black and Hispanic applicants), then they could argue against those who were for affirmative action: "Now, you're not just discriminating against white people, but a minority." The affirmative action side would be dumbfounded! How could they justify the exclusion of a nonwhite racial minority in order to make room for their preferred races? Game over.

To some Asian American kids, the court's decision on the SFFA vs. Harvard case was a bellwether for how elite society looked at them: short, nerdy kids raised by Asian parents with no social connections. Of another Ivy League college implicated in these cases, physics researcher Sam Dai said: "The reality is just that Princeton and other colleges are trying to build a student body that 'looks kind of like society.' You want your academic people, your sports people, your wide array." The implication: not too many people like him.

Harvard knew the stakes. Fortunately for them, Harvard practically invented race preferences.[3] With a $40 billion endowment and the nation's top lawyers at its disposal, Harvard has the resources to buffet the college from any challenge to its prized "race-conscious" admissions system. Edward Blum, leader of Students for Fair Admissions, revealed to me that a lesser-known university, UNC-Chapel Hill, spent $17 million defending its own version of race preferences against a similar lawsuit, and so "it's not unreasonable . . . [that Harvard] spent close to $40 million or more" to save race preferences (Harvard will not release its total expenditures on the case). The confirmed public bill for what Harvard spent on its defense is staggering on its own. A cadre of lawyers, its own public experts, marketing campaigns . . . Harvard raised an army to rescue race preferences. The college was preparing for war.

Students for Fair Admissions, led by Blum and representing rejected Asian American applicants in the Harvard case, hired Peter Arcidiacono, a Duke economist, to prosecute the case against Harvard. Arcidiacono delved into Harvard admissions data from the past decade and found that even relative to white applicants, Asian Americans faced a particularly stiff penalty for admissions in the personality score section, a penalty that would increase Asian admissions to Harvard by 19 percent—to the midforties, as a percentage of the Harvard student body—if removed.[4]

Furthermore, when Arcidiacono separated applicants by academic decile (with the best academic applicants in the tenth decile), he found that Asian applicants suffered a beleaguered rate of admission in every decile compared to white and especially to Black applicants. The prosecutor most notably found that Asian American applicants to Harvard scored significantly higher than every other race in both academics and extracurricular ratings, and comparably on all observable metrics (alumni interviews, teacher recommendations), demonstrating that Asian Americans maintained a lead among races in "personality"-related factors—yet were still starkly penalized in the personality score, to the point where they were the lowest of all races.

Either Harvard admissions officers were biased, then, against Asian American applicants, or the personality score was simply a pretext to include race as a defining category of admission, Arcidiacono argued.

It wasn't as if people hadn't noticed the Asian penalty before Arcidiacono found it within the admissions data. Ron Unz, a conservative writer, authored a 2012 front page article in the *American Conservative* entitled "The Myth of American Meritocracy" where he observed that Asian Americans at Harvard in 2009 had an SAT score on average 140 points higher than white students, who in turn had an SAT score on average 310 points higher than Black students.[5] This meant that an Asian student had to score an astounding 450 points higher on a 1600 point SAT test than a Black student to have the same chance of admission. That is a steep merit penalty. And conservatives weren't the only ones documenting it: Harvard's own Office of Institutional Research admitted that if academics were exclusively considered with no regards to race, Asian Americans would be estimated at around 43 percent of Harvard's admitted class, instead of flattening around the 20 percent range.[6]

And it's not just at Harvard either. Many lawsuits allege that racial discrimination has spread across the entire cabal of elite colleges. In October 2020, the US Department of Justice brought a lawsuit against Yale University for discriminating against Asian Americans (and white applicants). A thirty-two-page filing revealed to the public that racial preferences were a cancerous tumor in Yale's admissions department. Every applicant is screened by two readers, an Area Committee, and then a Final Review Committee. *At every turn*, evaluators were instructed to increase their applicant ratings if the individuals were a preferred race, Black or Hispanic as defined by Yale. The first reader would give a plus factor to a Black applicant and penalize an Asian applicant; the second reader would give a plus factor to a Black applicant and penalize an Asian applicant; the Area Committee would then give a plus factor to a Black applicant and penalize an Asian applicant. The Final Review Committee would neatly tie on its own plus factor, too—with the corresponding penalty for being Asian. The end result? A compounding effect of racial preference that was—get this—multiplied *four* times over.[7]

A graph on Asian American admissions at Ivy League universities and Caltech (one of the few elite schools in the nation that explicitly do not practice racial preferences) is reproduced below:[8]

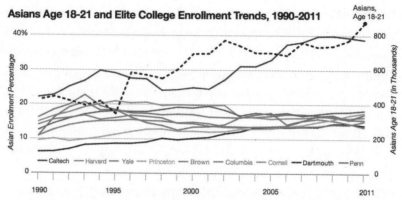

Asians Age 18-21 and Elite College Enrollment Trends, 1990-2011

Trends of Asian enrollment at Caltech and the Ivy League universities, compared with growth of Asian college-age population; Asian age cohort population figures are based on Census CPS, and given the small sample size, are subject to considerable yearly statistical fluctuations.

If there's not a ceiling in Asian American admissions at MIT and Harvard reaching thirty years back, I don't know what that is.

So what did Harvard do about this lawsuit? Lie down and beg? Admit defeat? *No*, these are not dogs. We're talking about the world's richest, elitist, most prestigious, most narcissistic institution of higher education. When Harvard got hit, they hit back harder.

Every action taken by Edward Blum and the Asians students suing them, Harvard had to do one better.

Blum's partner organization, the Asian American Coalition for Education, had sixty-seven Asian American organizations file complaints against Harvard. Harvard, retaliating, finds "hundreds of experts, scholars" to back their position—and then brags about it in the August 2018 issue of the *Harvard Gazette*: "More than 500 social scientists, 16 statisticians and economists, numerous Asian American organizations, Harvard student and alumni groups and coalitions, the American Civil Liberties Union, and the Asian American Legal Defense and Education Fund filed briefs on Thursday in support of Harvard University's admissions policies."

Blum commissioned a buzzy Duke Economics study of Harvard's obvious racial preferences against Asian Americans. Harvard recruits their own economist, David Card, to defend them against the damning accusations made by Duke economist Arcidiacono.

Until Harvard hired him, Card, a labor economist at the University of California, Berkeley, was perhaps best known for an early 1990s study where he found that minimum wage increases in New Jersey did not lower the number of fast-food jobs available, contradicting most economists' positions at the time. Card's methodology in that study came under fire, however, and in 1996 a response paper by two other economists found that payroll data in New Jersey contradicted Card's view. His study became notorious not just in the Economics community but in political circles, as well. Liberals stepped up to defend him. Conservatives reviled him.

Across America, economists of all kinds flocked to the issue of Harvard's alleged discrimination. "[It] divided our faculty," said Jonathan Arnold, a PhD student of economics at the University of Pennsylvania. Arnold's professors, Hangmin Feng and Michael Keane, signed an *amicus* brief supporting Students for Fair Admissions. Other professors, including past and future Federal Reserve Board Chair Janet Yellen, signed an *amicus* defending Harvard.

What did Arcidiacono have to say about Card? "[He] has always been good to me," he said on the *Glenn Show*. "I understand why Card did what he did, I mean, he was a paid expert for Harvard." He smiled. Only this mildest of put-downs to underscore one of the biggest recent economic and *econometric* controversies in the entire discipline.

It was a true duel between economists at the top of their games going toe-to-toe with each other. Let's break it down.

David Card produced his own dataset on the Harvard admissions cohort, which drew the conclusion that the Asian American penalty was statistically insignificant. The study became the basis for the legal argument from Harvard: that race was an eensy-weensy factor out of "many other factors" that determine admissions, per Harvard President Lawrence S. Bacow.[9]

The first thing Card did was methodologically seek more controlling variables—that is, variables Harvard uses to determine admissions in addition to race, factors like neighborhood schooling, parental occupation, intended career, and geographical diversity. Card maintained that Harvard did not have racial preferences so much as it had preferences for other aspects of one's background unrelated to race. He writes:

"Although Prof. Arcidiacono controls for an applicant's admissions docket (i.e., broad geographic region), he does not control for the much more detailed neighborhood attributes available in the College Board data, such as the median income of the neighborhood . . . In addition . . . Prof. Arcidiacono also fails to include in his model several available variables that reflect differences in applicants' family background and life goals."[10]

The issue with Card's reasoning is that these other "available variables" he alleges that Harvard uses actually target Asian Americans. A key example of this: Harvard's preference for people of different geographical stations is a proxy bias against Asian Americans, who tend to congregate in the same areas of the nation (big cities in California, New York, and Texas). In a similar example, when the School Board of Montgomery County, Maryland, reformed admissions to its gifted and talented programs, it justified its policies as race-neutral but also sought *geographical* diversity. In fact, the county preferred neighborhoods that targeted certain races over others. Because Asian Americans in Montgomery County (and America) tend to congregate in the same schools and areas, the county's zip codes preferences were used to exclude Asians. The immediate result of the Montgomery County School Board's supposedly race-neutral policies is that the percentage of Asian students in its gifted and talented programs went down by 20 percent.[11] By the same methodology, Harvard could easily use Asian Americans' congregation in cities like California and New York against them.

Or take "intended career." Card played off a stereotype: "Asian American applicants are much more likely to intend to pursue a career in medicine or health," suggesting that Harvard wouldn't want to bring in too many doctors or engineers. But "intended career" is flaky—and Card knew it. Over a six-year period, the number of people annually applying to Harvard for Law varied between 703 and 2,093 applicants, and Teaching from 17 to 660. And just how many applicants end up in the career they mark on a high school application? Arcidiacono blasted Card's oversight: "Like parental occupation, the applicant's intended career also varies in ways that are inconsistent over time, casting doubts upon the reliability of this metric and further undermining Professor Card's models."

What Card doesn't acknowledge about Harvard's use of so much applicant data is that these "proxies" to determine admission would be strictly illegal in most other major contexts in public life—*because* of the potential for race discrimination.

"We're not allowed to use data like zip codes, income for targeting purposes," said Daoshan Sun, a former banker at Wachovia (now Wells Fargo), about his industry. Bankers like Daoshan were disallowed from using even a fraction of the data Harvard was allowed to use.

"It was very stringent . . . We're not allowed to say, 'this guy lives in a bad zip code, we deny him a loan.' *Absolutely not.*" Daoshan's bank "and most other banks, I'd imagine," were only allowed to use income when directly addressing an individual's financial risk—but not for analytics, and were certainly barred from using most neighborhood factors to determine the basis for giving someone a loan. Why? "We could be sued for racial discrimination."

I explained to Daoshan what metrics Harvard uses to determine who they admit: race, household income, parental profession, high school, geographical area, percentage of high school students going to out of state college, et cetera. Daoshan scoffed at the court standard: "There's a double standard . . . Courts can say there are fewer Blacks on the team [at my bank], that's discrimination. But here at Harvard they don't even care if you use the information to approximate race."

Card seems to think it's no big deal that Harvard uses all of these background factors to determine admissions. Did it ever once cross his mind that the agglomeration of these factors could be combined to approximate race? Did he ever have that inkling when he decided the race penalty was eliminated by controlling for all these other factors that proxied for race?

Card wasn't out of tricks yet. To further show there was no Asian discrimination, he greatly expanded the dataset beyond its statistical capabilities. Claiming Arcidiacono used a dataset that excluded recruited athletes, legacies, children of professors, children of donors, and other specially admitted kids, Card argued that when those kids are included, Asian Americans suffer less of a penalty.

Arcidiacono did exclude those categories of applicants. And it was right to do so. Racial preferences aren't the only ones Harvard has: Their well-documented preferences for legacy applicants, children of elites and elite donors, and the 1 percent is part of what makes Harvard, well, Harvard. It would make no sense to compare students without those social connections or legacy statuses—which are, as we know, disproportionately Asian American—with students who have extensive social connections to the university.

Card's study, propped up with stilts and sophistry, relied too much on an assumption of Harvard's benevolence and gave the institution way too much benefit of the doubt. One error's consequences of inherently siding with Harvard's good intentions simply proved too extreme and harmful to the nation's Asian American community at large.

In order to deflect arguments about Asian suppression in admissions at every academic decile, Card argued that Harvard was right to admit Asian Americans at lower rates than their academic positions would dictate because it was *true* Asian Americans had lower personality skills than white Americans. "White applicants are in fact stronger, on average, on non-academic factors that Harvard values [than Asian applicants]," he wrote.

The idea of "non-academic" strength is an odd one. What does it mean to be strong in "non-academic" factors?

Card's continued chain of logic reveals the answer: "Asian-American applicants tend to have higher academic ratings and slightly higher extra-curricular ratings than white applicants," he argued, "while white applicants tend to have higher personal and athletic ratings and are more likely to be multi-dimensional." Ah, now we get it. "Non-academic" means to be an athlete, or to have a higher rating according to Harvard's personality score.

Yes, to prove Asian Americans really do have weaker "non-academic" traits than whites, Card uses Harvard's *personality score*—the very factor that Students for Fair Admissions alleges maintains the discriminatory animus against Asians. He bakes the racial discrimination right into the cake!

Arcidiacono blasted Card for his error in a public response:

"In similar fashion, Professor Card includes the personal rating in his measure of 'non-academic achievement.' But as I have shown . . . the personal rating incorporates preferences for African American and Hispanic applicants and penalties against Asian American applicants. Using the personal rating as a marker for non-academic achievement is thus highly misleading."

Imagine you hypothesized that your friend was exclusively attracted to members of his particular race. Every time he went on a date with a member of another race, he would report back, "Nah, man, she was just ugly." Would you then use your friend's comments to say, "Oh, all the girls my friend went out with who were of this race were just ugly. I guess that means he has no racial preferences?" It's the same as what is happening here.

Look. It is entirely possible that Asian Americans grade lower in some evaluations of character or interview performance. But there's just no evidence in Arcidiacono's dataset to suggest that. When accounting for all observed factors that could possibly measure one's personality rating, such as alumni interviews and teacher recommendations, Asian American applicants outscored or at least paced white applicants in every observable metric. Look at this graph pulled from the Arcidiacono dataset:

Academic Index Decile	Final Reader Overall Rating					Alumni Interviewer Overall Rating				
	Whites	African American	Hispanic	Asian American	Total	Whites	African American	Hispanic	Asian American	Total
1	0.00%	0.00%	0.00%	0.00%	0.00%	7.26%	7.31%	7.14%	7.35%	7.34%
2	0.18%	0.47%	0.08%	0.15%	0.22%	13.35%	14.89%	11.82%	12.22%	13.37%
3	0.26%	2.05%	0.68%	0.23%	0.63%	19.38%	23.88%	19.07%	17.51%	19.86%
4	0.69%	7.16%	2.15%	0.40%	1.54%	26.23%	33.46%	24.84%	23.11%	26.12%
5	1.57%	15.50%	4.54%	1.34%	2.71%	32.68%	43.48%	35.08%	29.71%	32.87%
6	2.95%	23.82%	8.82%	1.80%	4.05%	38.07%	51.38%	39.65%	36.08%	38.34%
7	4.15%	30.79%	12.01%	3.11%	5.22%	42.62%	56.18%	44.89%	42.37%	43.30%
8	7.63%	37.42%	15.61%	4.61%	7.39%	49.26%	59.20%	50.98%	46.95%	48.50%
9	10.97%	45.41%	19.67%	7.59%	10.12%	56.69%	61.22%	59.18%	54.16%	55.91%
10	15.64%	46.97%	23.37%	12.93%	14.70%	63.13%	66.67%	64.47%	63.10%	63.28%
Average	4.44%	5.29%	3.88%	4.85%	4.60%	36.50%	20.82%	23.64%	40.91%	34.59%

* Note that those who do not have an alumni interview are coded as not having received a 2 or higher on the alumni overall rating

On the alumni interview rating, Asian applicants in the top four academic deciles (7–10) scored a two or better at a nearly identical rate to white applicants. But on the overall rating, Asian applicants in the top four deciles faced a significant disadvantage. Perhaps there were unobserved factors in which Asian Americans did not score as well as white Americans, like the personal essay, which was not assigned ratings in court documents. But there is no evidence either way to support that Asian Americans had better or worse essays than white students, and the evidence that *would* link to a personal rating—namely teacher and alumni recommendations—showed comparable performance to white students.

So fluky is this personal rating discrepancy that John M. Gore, acting assistant attorney general of the Department of Justice, was unable to link these low scores to any observable factors in the applications: "The personal rating significantly harms Asian-American applicants' chances for admission despite their superiority in the academic rating, and Harvard has failed even to attempt to defend the personal rating as narrowly tailored to a compelling interest."[12]

The bottom line was that Card messed up.

We can talk about statistics all day. We can discuss personality scores and Card's tactics in this standoff, tactics that seem precisely designed to punish Asian Americans for every statistical coincidence about them—that they live in concentrated big cities, get good grades, and are not often legacy applicants. We've gone over the legal responses. Peter Arcidiacono's report, one that was emotionless and fact-driven, made a legal case for Harvard's discrimination. But that doesn't mean he didn't read the essays.

After the initial district court ruling, Arcidiacono was legally cleared to speak in public about the case, and he went on a podcast with economist Glenn Loury to talk about his findings. They talked about the case for a little. Then Loury asked him if he had anything left to say. This is the exchange.

L: Anything else you want to bring up before we conclude?

A: I like to try to approach research fairly detached from what the outcome is. I will say over the course of the Harvard case I've become more attached to the Asian discrimination case and it was reading the files that tipped me over the edge.

You see these negative results against Asian Americans. And then I read the file and about this one [Asian American] woman in particular whose dad suffered a severe mental illness. Her and her mom were hit by a drunk driver the summer before college, which she writes about. She spent time in foster care, which she writes about. And the reader gives her the usual score on the personal rating . . . and the only comment on the application was "SS," which means "standard strong," which means good but not good enough.

And it stands in contrast to the alumni interview who was like "this is one of the best interviews I've ever had."

David Card went to Queens in Canada and Princeton for his PhD; Peter Arcidiacono never attended an elite school. He completed his bachelor's at Willamette and his PhD at Wisconsin—elite for Wisconsinites, but not the world. Arcidiacono is also a devout Catholic. "My faith is important to me," he said on the *Glenn Show*. "I know I mess up all the time. We're all in the same boat. Every person has dignity, period, and I want that affirmed."

This case became, to him, not about gaining the spotlight or settling a feud with Card or being vindicated in the eyes of a judge. Point of fact, he didn't even believe the court would necessarily take his side. "I've come out of [this case] a bit cynical," he said. "The rulings are going to come out to fit whatever the desired policy outcome is, not based on the statistical evidence per se."

Listening to Arcidiacono tell that story about that young Asian American woman who was hit by a drunk driver—who spent time in foster care—it becomes clear that to him, this case was about *dignity*. It was about giving someone due respect despite the fact that he or she looks different from you. And it was that equal respect that Harvard was taking away.

■ ■ ■

On trial day, October 2nd, 2019, Judge Allison Burroughs of the Massachusetts District Court—a Barack Obama appointee assigned to hear
the case—addressed her rejection from Harvard as an undergraduate.
Burroughs joked about her rejection to "chuckles" from an anxious
staff, according to the *New York Times*.[13] And although she has done
well for herself as a US District Court Judge, she must have thought, as
many other ambitious kids do today, about what she could have done
had she gone to Harvard. What Judge Burroughs's opening comments
reveal is that Harvard does matter in our cultural discourse. By virtue of
being at the top of America's academic hierarchy, every policy or action
it implicates reverberates throughout the culture, directly impacting
high-achieving students all over the nation.

A year after the trial date, Burroughs found "no evidence of any discriminatory animus or conscious prejudice" on the part of Harvard's
admissions officers. She described Harvard's admissions programs as
"imperfect," but "the court will not dismantle a very fine admissions program that passes constitutional muster, solely because it could do better."[14]

In making this decision, Burroughs took Harvard admissions officers'
claims that they were not consciously discriminatory against Asians at
face value. And they probably weren't. College admissions officers are
not Confederacy glorifiers. Although the implicit bias debate rages on,
few people in this country consciously and explicitly discriminate against
Asians or any race. In 2014, back before the *Washington Post* went down
the rabbit hole of wokeness, the paper analyzed data obtained from the
World Values Survey and concluded that "Anglo and Latin countries," and
in particular the United States (95 percent+), are among the world's most
likely to not disapprove of having a different racial group as a neighbor,
compared with other countries like France (70–80 percent), Germany
(90–95 percent), and China (80–90 percent).[15] So no, I don't imagine
Harvard admissions officers are consciously anti-Asian.

But the issue was never that the Harvard admissions officers were
actively and explicitly racist. It was that Harvard's admissions process
evaluated people based on their race, and *judged it moral* to attack Asian

Americans for their character and low "personality" in order to prop up lesser-qualified applicants of other races. Harvard's commitment to "diversity" eliminated the potential of people born within certain constrictions due to the color of their skin to be able to break from that path. In pushing for diversity, Harvard eliminated a true hope of Americans of all races in this country—that people would be able to sculpt their own narratives for living rather than be trapped into archetypes of a group in which they did not choose to participate.

I would contest Judge Burroughs's ruling. But it almost doesn't matter. Ironically, Judge Burroughs's ruling of no discrimination found against Asian Americans, while helping Harvard win round one at the district court level, may actually help Students for Fair Admissions win a possible Supreme Court challenge to the wholesale use of race as a factor in college admissions.

If Burroughs sincerely believes the narrative spun by David Card—that Harvard's "Asian penalty" is practically nonexistent, and that racial considerations against Asians are sincerely as miniscule as Harvard asserts them to be—it then brings up the constitutional question: Why maintain race preferences in admissions in the first place?

It is logically contradictory to have meaningful race preferences without discriminating against one minority in favor of another. In the zero-sum game that is college admissions, if someone wins, someone else has to lose. Either Harvard gives a "plus" to Black and Hispanic applicants or it doesn't. Either Harvard discriminates against Asian Americans in the name of uplifting less qualified Black and Hispanic Americans or it doesn't. Judge Burroughs found no discrimination; therefore race-consciousness has no meaningful effect on admissions. So why keep it?

Edward Blum followed the ruling to its logical conclusion. "This lawsuit is now on track to go up to the US Supreme Court, where we will ask the justices to end these unfair and unconstitutional race-based admissions policies at Harvard and all colleges and universities," read his statement following the US Court of Appeals' ruling affirming Burroughs's position.[16]

Burroughs handed down her judgment. At the time of this writing, the Supreme Court has yet to make theirs.

"I CAN'T BELIEVE IT TOOK THIS LONG"

Harvard's admissions process has relevance far beyond its Cambridge quads. It is culturally imprinted on the American mind, re-instantiated on our consciousness because of the zeal of the Asian Americans who immigrated to this country evangelizing it. It has taken on symbolic life, a kind of cultural gatekeeper into high society that our nation's most ambitious young people are well aware of.

And so targeting it, seeking to dismantle it, was going to come with its own set of cultural reverberations. Harvard—an institution so embedded in the nation's elite fabric that to challenge the behemoth would be a rematch of David and Goliath—is *dialed in* on racial preferences. Even though everyone knew about Harvard's game for twenty years, no one had the guts or the resources to take them to task. Enter Edward Jay Blum.

The white, wavy-haired Jewish man with an earnest face concealing stormy thoughts may not at first seem like the ideal candidate to represent Asian Americans in the trial against Harvard College. But Harvard is hardly his first rodeo.

"I don't know Ed Blum's motives, and so I am in no position to comment on whether he is a good guy . . . or not," said Julie Park, one of Harvard's most prominent defenders, in front of a public audience of higher ed diversity types at a conference in Washington, DC. Oh, yes. Edward Blum has a reputation.

He may not be the perfect face (and his whiteness was certainly held against him in the court proceedings), but he had the fortitude—and legal resources, with deep-pocketed donors interested in his crusades—to take Harvard on. At his home in Tallahassee, Florida, he wakes up at 4:30 and by 5 in the morning, he is on his iPad in search of the next affirmative action or race-based issue to take action on. No wonder the higher ed diversity types hate him.

On a crisp January morning, Blum started scrolling through his iPad. "You arrived at the perfect time," he said to me, with just a hint of pleasant boastfulness in his voice. Then he showed me the screen. It is a Google news search with the keyword "diversity."

"Lots of this is from India, the African continent," Blum said, perusing the search engine. "But I am gonna run across something that every now and then . . . aha! . . . is called 'diversity scholarship.' I'm gonna look through this." He motioned for me to take a closer look. "I came across an article where [in] the state of Wisconsin, someone did a story about a new bill that had been passed called the Wisconsin minority teacher loan program. And what this is," he explained excitedly, "is a loan forgiveness program for any new student who wants to become an elementary or secondary school teacher and teach in a school that has a significant minority population . . . This program is a college loan forgiveness program.

"If you're a sophomore and you're studying mathematics at the University of Wisconsin-La Crosse, for example, and even though you're a mathematics major you're also going to [get] a teaching certificate, and your ultimate goal is to go and teach high school mathematics—and if you're Black or if you're Hispanic, or if you're American Indian, or if you're Cambodian, Laotian, or Vietnamese, *not* Chinese . . . then you could have all of these loans forgiven! But if you're Chinese, or you're white . . . no."

The legal strategist's voice rose. "Now, this is unconstitutional. This is completely unconstitutional! I knew this the minute I read these."

Blum is diversity advocates' worst enemy. It makes him very effective at generating a lot of publicity, and maybe a little cultural change, in this country. His first Supreme Court challenge to racial preferences—*Fisher vs. University of Texas* (2013–2016)—set him in the crosshairs of the diversity industry.

For that case, Blum recruited a young white redhead, Abigail Fisher, who was rejected from the University of Texas under its "Top ten percent" admissions policy, which used neighborhood as a proxy for racial preferences in admissions. (As Blum tells it: "I know a lot of people in Texas, and kind of network and talk about people, and Richard Fisher was a business associate . . . he introduced me to Abby and we talked and . . . we ended up suing the University of Texas!")

For a little while, the case went well. Blum and Abby "won" the first Supreme Court case in 2013 when the five-justice majority remanded the case—that is, sent it back for correction—to the lower courts, objecting that they had used an insufficiently strict standard to evaluate whether the University of Texas's diversity admissions program was racially discriminatory. When the case came back to the Supreme Court, it was under the revised, stricter standard, making it harder for a diversity program to pass. Blum and Abby Fisher exuded confidence. "We all thought we were going to win," Blum said.

Then Justice Anthony Kennedy, a Harvard Law School graduate, made a pact with the liberal justices and, in his 4–3 majority opinion, wrote to affirm the University of Texas's diversity program: "Considerable deference is owed to a university in defining those intangible characteristics, like student body diversity, that are central to its identity and educational mission." Kennedy's statement argued against his own 2003 dissent in *Grutter v. Bollinger*, where he stated, "[d]eference is antithetical to strict scrutiny, not consistent with it."[17] Kennedy, considered at the time the most libertarian justice on the court, had seemed the most passionate about eliminating racial considerations from admission programs. But just like Justice Powell fell under Harvard's extraordinary spell in *Bakke*, so did the Harvard alum eventually bend in deference to his alma mater.

After all, how deep is our tolerance for discrimination so long as that discrimination can be justified in the name of diversity? If we allow Harvard to discriminate, will we allow businesses to do the same? How about our public institutions? The Army? Will we allow our US Army to turn down a better-qualified Asian person so they can hire a soldier who is less qualified to protect our country?

Although he lost the case, Blum spurred a national conversation over race and individual merit that, for a moment, threatened the whole diversity establishment and even generated an anti-Fisher Twitter hashtag: #ByeByeAbby. That gave him hope for a rematch. After a long march to loss in *Fisher*, the Supreme Court regular was hungering for round two.

But Blum needed to find a still better plaintiff than Abby—an amiable and curious person, yes, but a white woman, not the most sympathetic of cases in today's identity politics discourse. He also needed a better target than the University of Texas's obliquely-motivated "Top Ten Percent Program" (the university frequently referred to its program as racially fair due to its acceptance of "everyone" who graduated in the top ten percent of their class).

Blum went hunting again. This time, to California. "[S]omeone who is very senior or well-known within the Asian advocacy groups knew somebody whose kid was just rejected from Harvard . . . we went to California and met with the family and explained what we wanted to do, and then the family flew out to Washington, DC, to meet with a legal team there and make sure this is what they understood and how this was going to take place." He called the group of students—more of which were added every year—Students for Fair Admissions.

Now here was a match that was even better than the last one. A university with a long, ill-kept history of exclusion—first of Jewish applicants, now Asian—and a series of motivated students embittered by their rejections from Harvard. This was a case that could go all the way.

Even Dr. Julie Park, one of Edward Blum's biggest critics, begrudgingly showed some respect for the man: "I can't believe it took this long for affirmative action critics to use an Asian American rather than a white person."

Blum's group filed a lawsuit against Harvard University in November 2014. "The thrust of the Harvard case is that we assert that Harvard purposefully discriminates against Asian American applicants in order to create an incoming student body that reflects the racial composition of the country," he said.

His initial evidence is as follows: First, Harvard's student body has been kept between 18 and 22 percent Asian for twenty-five years, despite there being the highest growth among the young Asian American population out of all racial brackets. Second, Asian Americans suffer from the lowest acceptance rate for each SAT test score bracket, having to score on average 140, 270, and 450 points higher on average than their white, Hispanic, and Black counterparts for equal chances of admission. And third, Asian Americans have the lowest admittance rate out of all the races despite having higher grades and test scores.

All this was old news to the Asian American community. Asian Americans first filed federal complaints against Harvard University in 1988. But no federal action was prompted until Edward Blum, fresh off the national publicity he gained with *Fisher*, turned up the heat with his millions in fundraising capital and organizational prowess. After Blum filed his lawsuit, sixty-four more Asian American organizations joined in filing complaints of Asian discrimination to the federal government.

Although Blum was himself perfectly capable of generating media attention, the Chinese American community, sensing the opportunity, made the lawsuit a national story. To this end, they used WeChat, a Chinese social-messaging platform. In the midst of this, Chinese American leader Yukong Zhao united the sixty-four Asian American organizations under the umbrella of his organization, the Asian American Coalition for Education (AACE). Yukong, an immigrant to America who escaped from Chinese Communism, believed that Harvard's repression of Asian admissions resembled the kind of tactics the Chinese government used to turn its university system into a political arm during the Cultural Revolution. "People were admitted based on their background, what kind of family they were from, and whether they positioned fealty to the Communist Party," he said. With greater conviction, he leaned in: "Merit was not involved."

And this is the crux of the philosophy behind Ed Blum's and Yukong Zhao's views: A college admissions process should be fundamentally *meritocratic*; that is, it should only consider students on the basis of their individual merit, of which race is not part. And if admissions wind up 40 percent Asian . . . "Well, that's a sign that the other races need to step up and do better," Blum argued. "I believe competition makes you stronger."

LEGAL DISCRIMINATION

Immigrant kids are dazzled by the false notion that the Ivy League is the meritocracy Edward Blum spoke of.

"When you're an Asian kid, you grow up and you think of . . . the best schools as a standard, as a bar," Sam Dai, a Princeton reject, lamented about the school that crushed his worldview. "It's not something you look at that you need to stretch for. If I don't get in, I'm a failure." That is, if you don't get in, it's on *you*.

But that's simply not the case. Furthermore, it never was. To borrow a phrase from the Harvard defense team, merit is just "one of many, many factors" Harvard uses to determine one's admission.

Let's not lean too far the other way and fall into the temptation of the Ivy League Kool-Aid: that elite college admissions are by chance. This is the position of some defenders of Harvard. "It's a crapshoot," said Fatima Shabbaz, a Harvard student who supports the college in their lawsuit. "No one deserves to get in. I was lucky."

Fatima *was* lucky. But that doesn't make Harvard's admissions a crapshoot. To attribute their process to mere *luck* is to willfully ignore Harvard's exacting, hyper-intentional sculpting that attempts to balance everything from legacies, to donor wants, to admitting the children of elites, to race. Asian Americans, who are disproportionately without legacy, donor status, elite desirability, and the correct skin color, are screwed four times over.

The truth is that Ivy League admissions is neither a meritocracy nor a crapshoot. It's closest to a *clique.*

What percentage of the Harvard student body do you think belongs to the top 1 percent? The top tenth? The top fifth? Even in today's enlightened era, *fifteen* percent of the Harvard student body comes from the top 1 percent of household income, while another 70 percent of Harvard students come from the top 20 percent.[18]

A shocking article from the National Bureau of Economic Research journal says it all: 43 percent of Harvard's white students are affiliated with Harvard's alumni, faculty, or donors. And since athletes, legacies, and children of faculty applicants are admitted at a rate 5.7 times higher than those that don't fit those categories, the end result is that *certain* privileged white (and legacy Black) applicants to Harvard get major, unmerited advantages in the admissions process, while Asian Americans, with negligible elite history in the United States, gain few.[19]

The interest of the entrenched elite at Harvard is most definitely to perpetuate their entrenchment. Harvard needs this top 1 percent strata. They need the clique mentality. It allows them to bankroll their $40 billion endowment, to maintain their aura of unattainable prestige. It allows the people fortunate enough to gain admittance to carry an eliteness that generates their unmerited social respect. It preserves the entitlement an Ivy League degree affords alumni in the world today.

And just like any elite clique, Harvard needs someone to pick on, that "tryhard" they laugh at while throwing a big fat rejection in their face.

Fifty years before Asian Americans were the target, Jewish Americans faced Harvard's wrath as the college sought a very different goal in its affirmative action program—to keep the character of the college white, Protestant, and non-immigrant. Once Jewish Americans arrived in America and started outcompeting non-Jews in many arenas, one being merit-based school admissions (making up 80 percent of New York City's Hunter and City Colleges' student bodies and 40 percent of Columbia's), Harvard President A. Lawrence Lowell sought to "remedy" the influx of Jewish students into his school by lowering their percentage at Harvard to 15 percent. His justification, ironically, was to quell hate at Harvard: "The anti-Semitic feeling among the students is increasing, and it grows in proportion to the increase in the number of Jews. If their number should become 40 percent of the student body, the race feeling would become intense."[20]

Or, more plainly: there were just too many Jews at Harvard.

Of course, Harvard has felt embarrassed by this incident ever since they rescinded their formal Jewish quotas, and so they rarely acknowledge it. But though the college's WASP demographic has faded, its exclusionary mentality and desire to balance races has not. Like any clique that thinks of itself as special and exclusive, Harvard liked coming up with arbitrary rules for "belonging" in this "community." Rules like, not too many Jews. Not too many Asians.

But with the sweep of civil rights in the 1950s and 1960s, public scrutiny grew of institutions discriminating on the basis of race, as Harvard had. The issue was that the antidotes to discriminations were different depending on which side of the political aisle you camped with. The Left wanted discrimination corrected by discrimination in the other direction (also known as affirmative action). The Right and various center groups ascribed to Martin Luther King Jr.'s proposition that "one day my children will not be treated on the color of their skin, but on the content of their character," pursuing a blanket ban on racial preferences of any kind.

Harvard College, by virtue of being the American intellectual center of liberalism, went immediately the affirmative action route, seeking to atone for their previous exclusionary sentiments by aggressively recruiting minorities (of Black, Hispanic, *and* Asian descent) and even setting goals for getting them on campus. The 1968 race riots informed their policies, as colleges were put under pressure to show that they were committed to relieving racial injustice.[21] However, many conservative alumni and donors were concerned that Harvard's obviously racially preferential programs would hurt the prestige of the college and constitute reverse discrimination.

Eventually, tensions boiled over into a Supreme Court case: *Regents of the University of California v. Bakke*, held in 1978. The defendant was UC-Davis, but the thinking was firmly Harvard.

Allan Bakke, a white male rejected applicant from the University of California, Davis Medical School, was described as "friendly, well-tempered, conscientious and delightful to speak with" by student interviewers.[22] His benchmark exam score was 468 out of 500, placing him among the best-qualified applicants to the school. He was twice rejected from the program, during a period when UC-Davis's special admissions programs had asked for applicants from particular racially or economically challenged backgrounds. Bakke, who had applied under the general admissions program, noticed that the special admissions program still had four vacant spots in the year he applied—but they were clearly not reserved for people like him. He sued for his admission, and the trial court where he made the case found that "the special program [of UC-Davis] operated as a racial quota because minority applicants in the special program were rated only against one another."

The case went all the way to the Supreme Court, where it faced a cadre of justices now tasked with determining the future of affirmative action. Among these justices was Harvard Law School alum Lewis Powell. He would cast the deciding vote on whether Bakke was to be admitted, as the decision split the court. Four judges (Burger, Stewart, Rehnquist, and Stevens) wanted UC-Davis's minority admissions program struck down with no further action taken on the question of race preferences. The other four (Brennan, White, Marshall, and Blackmun) wanted UC-Davis's racial quotas to be constitutionally allowed.

In the winning opinion eventually issued (there were six total opinions delivered in the court), Justice Powell split the baby, reversing UC-Davis's admissions process but passing constitutional muster on race preferences in general. He contended that affirmative action was acceptable not because it would reverse America's racist legacy but because a *diverse student body* was so beneficial to the health of a college campus that it was compellingly deemed a governmental interest to promote. The decision reads:

> "[O]ur tradition and experience lend support to the view that the contribution of diversity [to a school department] is substantial."[23]

The diversity rationale.

This is not the last time you will read about its use in this book. In fact, this line in *Bakke* is the functional progenitor of what is now the diversity industry. This rationale is used over and over . . . and over again. Mostly to exclude Asian Americans.

It was the next part of *Bakke*, however, that set the stage for what is going on in Harvard and the culture today. The most natural response to Powell's proposition that diversity was a *compelling governmental interest* would be to say: "Great! Let's get X percent Black students and Y percent Hispanic students next year." Diversity-oriented people would get busy setting quotas and admitting people on the basis of race.

But as usual, Justice Powell was thinking like a Harvard man—that is, worried about how the image of such racial quota programs would affect the reputations of the Ivy League, these representatives of elite America. Racial quota programs could not survive strict scrutiny, Powell wrote, appealing to a standard of race classification wherein such considerations could only be brought forward if they advanced a compelling governmental interest *and* were tailored narrowly to advance that governmental interest only.

Powell argued that racial quota programs could not survive strict scrutiny, leading him to reject UC-Davis's affirmative action program because of its use of them. But racial balancing programs *could* occur— they just had to be executed without setting explicit goals and without the use of quotas. Racial considerations could be a "plus" factor, but not a specific goal.

This kind of thinking feels especially tortured when comparing it to the very standard of "narrow tailoring" (to explicit governmental interest) that Justice Powell used to characterize his decision. After all, odious as they seem, racial quotas are at least explicit about their intentions; they make absolutely certain why people are being admitted, i.e., for this certain governmental purpose of diversity. But Justice Powell called quotas expansive, and instead argued for the *much more expansive* definition of racial preferences, which was to have no explicit racial goals but to allow race to be considered as a "plus factor" for admissions—as if vague and general "plus factors" were somehow more clear and transparent than an explicit quota.

And get this. The *piece de resistance*. The truly gobsmacking part of this entire decision.

As an example of an admissions process that he admires for its ability to toe exactly the line he wants, Powell cites Harvard College. Yes. Harvard. His *alma mater*.

> "In Harvard College admissions, the Committee has not set target quotas for the number of Blacks, or of musicians, football players, physicists or Californians to be admitted in a given year . . . In such an admissions program, race or ethnic background may be deemed a 'plus' in a particular applicant's file, yet it does not insulate the individual from comparison with all other candidates for the available seats."[24]

Powell wrote that the program "treats each applicant as an individual in the admissions process," and thus urges colleges and universities to model their admissions off . . . Harvard's.

But he did not anticipate—or perhaps he did—that Harvard would use the deference he gave it to shelter from accountability even as it imposed an unofficial ceiling on an entire race. What Powell legitimized, the use of race as a plus factor without quotas, actually provides *more* cover for a school like Harvard to do what it wants with regards to race while falling back on the old defense: "Oh, race was just *one* factor. We didn't have any quotas." His decision was nothing less than a kiss on the ring of Harvard administrators.

The result of Powell's decision was to uphold Harvard's implicit ability to discriminate without conceding the true intentions of their programs. This is the landscape in which Edward Blum and Students for Fair Admissions must work today. As long as Harvard keeps their program sufficiently vague, declaring that race is just "one factor" among many and obfuscating the investigation with weird controls and odd methodologies, Blum has less of a chance to win this case. Basically, the more mendaciously Harvard attempts to foil the face-value data—the common-sense proof that Asian Americans face a ceiling—the more Harvard gains an advantage in a post-*Bakke* landscape, one constructed by loyal Harvard alum Lewis Powell.

It is said that Harvard alumni pay back their alma mater in many ways. Many become rich and donate to the school's world leading $40 billion endowment. Some become president of the United States and hire Harvard graduates to work in their administrations.

Supreme Court Justice Lewis Powell, a class of 1932 Harvard Law School graduate, remembered his *alma mater* by handing it the biggest Supreme Court win of its history. When a 1978 case came before him challenging UC-Davis's rejection of a white man in part due to its reserved spots for minority applicants, Powell's rebuttal may have written of California, but his thinking was firmly of *Harvard*—as evidenced by his opinion. Protective of one's reputation by language and sophistry. Exclusionary by design.

So as long as the judicial system plays by Harvard's rules, as Burroughs and the first circuit of appeals did, Harvard can keep its clique, maintaining the system that once kept striving Jewish Americans out and that destroys the dreams of Asian Americans today.

ELITE GUILT

Harvard is so exclusive and its network so entrenched that it leads its students, faculty, and administrators to behave irrationally, promulgating narratives about themselves that are either sadistic or masochistic—but definitely not normal.

As a set of elite institutions serving the elite, the Ivy League obsesses constantly with the pursuit of prestige and status. Look at this *Washington Monthly* magazine profile:

> "Why are so many Harvard and Stanford students vulnerable to getting caught up in such competitions [of money and prestige]? Most are well aware that they are competing for a narrow band of jobs, and that however boring and purposeless those jobs may be, immediate prestige will go to the winners of this highly structured competition."

How do bigwig firms recruit from these elite schools? They tack glossy marketing posters all over campus advertising their programs and staff. You recognize them immediately: Goldman Sachs! McKinsey! Bain and Company! Where recruiting presence goes, highly attended information sessions follow. "[Consultancies had] some of the booths with the longest lines," Grant Guan, an associate consultant at the prestigious Boston Consulting Group, said. At dinners, brown-nosing students dress in their best. And the big firms bring their best too. No hiring managers or HR guys. They bring their actual financial and consulting staff—most from the alma mater that they are targeting—looking their sharpest to show how successful and great their careers are.

Now, students are hooked—totally dazzled by the prestige, the name, the alumni stories . . . all manufactured with the collaboration of the Ivy League's Career Service Departments. Then come the interviews. Recruiters cloud the process in mystique so as to enhance hype, flying the students out in prepaid jet flights to fancy dinners (pennies in the bucket for these megarich firms), and leaving students agape in the sheer power of their corporate world. The prospective Ivy League employees have *Wolf of Wall Street* visions of themselves drowning in money. They fall over themselves making it their goal to get into Goldman. The hires are known on campus, their names associated with their company as a mon-identifier. "That's Tyler. He's going to *Bain*."

You might say, "This only represents a subset of Harvard and Yale students." But do you want to know how large this subset is?

Seventy percent.

Nearly three-quarters of Harvard's senior class submits résumés to Wall Street and consulting firms. And 31 percent of them eventually take a Wall Street job.[25]

And worse yet—the very fact that these Ivy League colleges are such recruiting bogs for McKinsey and Goldman Sachs puts pressure on the students to conform with their high-strung, high-achieving peers rather than explore what they're truly interested in to confirm whether it actually *is* finance and consulting, or whether it's art, math, business, health care, or public service. As such, Ivy League colleges inbreed a pipeline of vapid achievement and prestige, a hotbox of anxiety over status, that diminishes the creative potential of these extraordinary kids.

Take the response from '22 Yale student Enrique on the question of why he, a bright-eyed freshman with many professional and social interests, eventually settled on McKinsey:

> "I liked that the job was low-risk and high-reward. Consulting allows me to dip my toes in various industries and markets without serious commitment. And boy, am I afraid of commitment."[26]

Or take the experience of the aforementioned Boston Consulting Group (BCG) associate, Grant Guan. "On a personal level, I don't think I took as much time to think about that role [with BCG] as I wish I did," he said. He describes consulting as a product of "inertia": "It takes a lot of effort to go and find the kind of role that can satisfy what you're looking for . . . Consulting markets [itself] as the safe option to try. A cool opportunity to try a bunch of new industries. If you don't like it, you can always go and do something else."

There is such a thing as *too* much exploration. Duke economist Michael Munger describes higher education as a kind of "finishing school," where a person learns about his interests and passions. But even finishing schools must, in the end, offer some direction and path to prioritization. Yale seems content to let their elite students stay in the well-compensated wilderness. Per a *Yale Daily News* article:

> "When I was looking at colleges, Yale's marketing slogan was '*and* rather than *or*.' At Yale, I could be a singer and a student. I could take classes with Nobel Prize winners and Pulitzer Prize winners. At 18, I couldn't handle the thought of choosing one life over another, so I chose Yale. And that was probably the last big decision I've had to make. In college, I've filled my schedule to an outrageous degree, simply because I'm afraid of prioritization. I need six extracurricular activities, so I don't close any doors to the future!"[27]

The author, Yale graduate Nancy Walecki, later goes on to talk about how McKinsey consulting has topped Yale's fig tree by being "the lucrative career decision for the indecisive."

Just how indecisive are the bright young'uns that enter these Ivy League doors? "I would say 50 percent of the kids I know get their first job through Harvard's career services," said Harvard '20 grad Dody Eid. "We're naïve and uncertain about our own futures, so we go for the school-validated options," Harvard graduate Saffron Huang told *Palladium Magazine*.[28] The schools, it seems, are not only the gatekeepers but the validators and rubber-stampers of their students' early futures too.

Knowing that you have benefitted drastically in the elite rat race by an admissions officer's simple decision to admit you carries a great burden of guilt. There is an existential anguish among Ivy League elites to "do something" besides climb the elite ladder—while they climb the elite ladder. All that climbing makes young people weary. They need a moral salve.

That salve is *bourgeois* social justice.

The grounds of Princeton University are an awesome display of absolute financial and intellectual dominance, the most unabashedly glorious island of privilege on the East Coast. The lawns are perfectly manicured. The streets are fabulously walkable. A Brooks Brothers graces the main road, Nassau Street. The Institute of Advanced Study, which has singlehandedly produced more Fields Medalists (recipients of the highest honor in mathematics) than any other institution in the world (forty-one out of sixty-four recipients), is nestled in this little island paradise. The idea was to provide a place where the nation's top researchers could conduct their research *unbridled* by the specter of daily life. Princeton's campus is one multimillion-funded building after another.

The university and corresponding town could be described as one of the most privileged places on Earth. And yet, in a 2020 letter issued to all members of the Princeton Class, Princeton President Christopher Eisgruber proclaimed:

> "Racism and the damage it does to people of color nevertheless **persist at Princeton** [emphasis added] as in our society, sometimes by conscious intention but more often through unexamined assumptions and stereotypes, ignorance or insensitivity, and the systemic legacy of past decisions and policies."[29]

Eisgruber goes on to say, "racist assumptions from the past also remain embedded in structures of the University itself."

As evidence, the president points to a single concrete example illustrating his contention: "Princeton inherits from earlier generations at least nine departments and programs organized around European languages and culture, but only a single, relatively small program in African studies."

To the extent that this can be considered a problem (if Princeton had nine African studies departments, would anyone enroll within them? Would the university be doing a service to their students by forcing enrollment within them?), the idea that this "problem" could be born of racism is unfathomably absurd—especially from a college president who fashions himself as an intellectual. Princeton is a university founded by Europeans in the intellectual tradition of the Greco-Romans and Judeo-Christians; it has an obvious, vested interest in the study of its own heritage. It is not racist to prioritize study of one's own heritage. I don't think China's Xi Jinping loses sleep over mandating Chinese history classes over the travels of Christopher Columbus and George Washington.

If racial disparities in department studies are the best example of Princeton's modern systemic racism, then maybe the university is not exactly justified in pronouncing itself an epicenter of racist thinking.

Princeton does not actually believe that systemic racism is entrenched within its own institutions. We know this because when former Secretary of State Betsy DeVos's Department of Education filed a civil rights complaint for potential racism and discrimination at Princeton, Eisgruber immediately walked back his letter: Princeton "disagrees with the premise of the Department's argument."[30] But the premise of the DOJ complaint—that systemic racism was embedded within Princeton—came directly from the president's letter. An elite college foundationally infected with racism? That would be scandal-of-the-twenty-first-century material.

No, Princeton didn't mean it, of course not. But why did they say it? To paint Princeton as a righteous crusader marching in the name of justice for all oppressed. So desperate is the Ivy League elite to find some commonality with societal members it has excluded, it must resort to rising in defense of self-flagellating letters, injecting its campus with virtuous morale before students go off to their McKinsey and Goldman jobs, and the pipeline gets refreshed with the next crop of little elites.

RACIAL PREFERENCES PRESERVE THE EXCLUSIVE SYSTEM

Oh, right. There's one more way in which Ivy League colleges signal their virtue and morality while keeping their exclusionary mentalities safe.

You guessed it. Racial preferences.

It makes me suspicious—with ample reason—that part of the reason Harvard and Yale spend tens of millions of dollars and so much effort standing guard against racial balancing is that to students and staff, racial balancing remains the last pillar of morality allowing students to believe these elite schools are fundamentally worthy places. As racial wokeness becomes emotionally tied to a new fervor among liberals, hard and fast demonstrations of enthusiastic support of racial preferences would galvanize Leftist students and motivate privileged future bankers to champion Yale as a moral body. Think about all the students picketing *in support* of Harvard's racial balancing policies during the district court trial. Wow, discriminating on the basis of race—what bravery!

We've seen this play out. Students and administrators are not just approving of Yale's admissions policy. They are *passionate*.

How passionate are they? Yale student Eileen Huang wrote an entire viral essay about Asian anti-Blackness partly in response to affirmative action complaints from her Chinese American community. (The Chinese American website that published it chose, hilariously, to title it, "A Letter from a Yale Student to the Chinese American community," milking the Yale name to get the interest of Chinese immigrant parents.) "We Asian Americans have long perpetuated anti-Black statements and stereotypes," Huang wrote in her letter, which scored thousands of shares on WeChat just a few days after the George Floyd killing. "I grew up hearing relatives, family friends, and even my parents make subtle, even explicitly racist comments about the Black community: *They grow up in bad neighborhoods. They cause so much crime. I would rather you not be friends with Black people. I would rather you not be involved in Black activism.*"[31]

It's a searing letter, one that gained immediate viral traction on the Chinese American platform WeChat. In base fact, her allegations are certainly true: Of course there are some racist Chinese grandmas who dislike Black people. But there are racist Black grandmas who dislike Chinese people, who call Chinese Americans superspreaders of the novel coronavirus. And there are racist white grandmas who don't like either Black or Chinese people. It's that old adage: "Christians killing Jews, Jews killing Muslims, Muslims killing Christians."

But where Huang goes with her point borders on shocking: "Though we cannot compare the challenges faced by Asian Americans to the far more violent atrocities suffered by Black Americans, we owe everything to them." Embedded in her essay is the intentional privileging of the Black narrative over the Asian American narrative, which provides moral justification for race preferences. If one could prove that the Black victim narrative deserves more attention than the Asian American victim narrative, then one has justification for privileging Black people in everything from admissions to hiring to political identity politics—say, for example, when compared to a similarly qualified Asian.

"Instead of pointing out those larger structures of oppression, I think conservatives on WeChat and conservative Chinese Americans often scapegoat Black and brown people or Indigenous people for all of the racist trauma that Chinese Americans have experienced, which is just very harmful and absolutely false," she said in a Yale interview, taking a not-so-subtle jab at the Chinese immigrants on WeChat who opposed affirmative action.[32]

Eileen Huang became the darling of the Yale progressive community for a long while. Featured on the *Yale Daily News* and the *New York Times*, she even made her way to Chinese shores in publications like the *South China Morning Post*. Any guesses as to why? Because she unequivocally labelled her entire race as a privileged class, the end step to any comprehensive theory that would put Asians back in that white-adjacent box, and that would then back race preferences for Black and Hispanic Americans over Asian Americans.

As the logical answer to a worldview that divides society into a network of "privileged" and "oppressed," affirmative action provides an easy moral answer: Just give them preference. It allows an elite community to feel good about what it's providing for a world in which it doesn't functionally exist, while controlling the keys to the gates. *We decide who gets in. And you're going to feel grateful about our generosity.*

Eric Price II, a Georgetown University master's student, sees the elite game for what it is. "Diversity and inclusion are often paired together, but they're not often the same thing," he said. "Diversity is a quantitative topic: Yes, you're addressing diversity in a numerical standpoint, always focused on racial diversity . . . yet, the increasing of diversity officers does not automatically make for an inclusive experience on campus."

Price added: "You can speak to the actual minority students on campuses and they are negatively affected in these Predominantly White Institutions [such as Yale and Harvard] . . . it's easy and doesn't require any heavy lifting to say a school is doing great things, but schools will really improve if they do qualitative research on inclusive environments."

To Eric, higher education has a rotting core, what he calls the endless cycle of the "Three R's"—Resources, Reputation, and Respect. The more resources an elite institution cultivates, the more resources it spends to cultivate a reputation. When a PWI cracks that reputation threshold, it gains public respect, which enables the institution to gain more resources to do the same thing over again, *until their resources become greatly disproportionate to the actual quality of services they provide.*

And the result of that great disproportion is an embedded awareness that these students are in fact coasting on leverage they don't deserve. So they feel guilty. Like Eileen Huang.

This absurd, unserious narrative of endemic racism at these rich liberal universities—married to their policies of racial preference—is the opiate for their guilt.

THE SICKENING PART

Just because race preferences preserve the exclusionary system doesn't mean that they don't have serious consequences. They do.

The following story may seem a little extreme. Perhaps even a little too on the nose in how it articulates the harm of desperately wanting admittance to a university that doesn't want more people like you. Not every Asian American applying to elite colleges thinks this way.

But some do.

Sam Dai grew up as one of the only Asian American kids in a farm town, Cranbury, New Jersey. His mom and dad were both immigrants from China. His middle school barely had any Asian students. Probably in some part due to that latter fact, he was able to coast through middle school without exerting himself. "I stopped working hard after seventh grade," he said. "I could go on autopilot and get As in all of my classes." Coursework was easy to him. It seemed apparent that Sam Dai was going places—academically, at the very least.

Sam grew up in a culture many Asian Americans can recognize. His parents instilled the value of hard work as the family's primary tenet. "It was always about applying yourself . . . are you working enough? Enough, what does that mean? We don't know." Sam said.

From a young age, elite schools were at least implied as worthy of reverence in his world. "My parents would tell stories of, like, how they didn't go to the best name school, and they regretted it, and I think it was implicit . . . They were like, 'Where do you want to go to school,' and they would say, 'Well, there's *Princeton* down the street.'"

His family's mentality of adherence to hard work, rather than talent, drives success. "I remember my mom telling me that 'You shouldn't be proud, don't be proud, because this is just the result of hard work.'" It's not that Sam was smarter than anybody else. It was just that his parents worked him hard.

In middle school, Sam was the best math student in his school. But he wasn't the best math student in his state. It didn't really irk his parents, but it irked him. "I got third in the region," he said. "And my parents were more or less like, 'He's doing fine.'" Sam actually didn't have to work very hard past age thirteen. But that was also when he felt he started to lose his edge. Not his edge against the average student—Sam excelled gloriously at math compared to the average student. But it was against his fellow *Asian Americans* that Sam began to make comparisons.

"After seventh grade I started doing AMC [American Math Competition] tests every day. This may seem like a lot of hard work, but to other Asians, it was nothing. If you asked me, I did not say I was working hard. I could hear stories about competitive programming. I heard this guy who said, 'I used to code for 3 hours a day.' [Another said,] 'I used to practice piano 3 hours a day.'"

The truth of these stories does not actually matter. Sam wasn't around many Asians of whom he could make direct observational comparisons. His school was mostly white farm boys. Instead, he relied on word-of-mouth, little pieces of gossip about the Asians "over in West Windsor" [a highly educated, predominantly Indian American township thirty miles away]. Those stories fueled a silent competitive drive in Sam, that he had to be the best; not merely in his school but among other Asians.

"You compare me to the *other* Asians, there's *other* Asians who are doing harder things. I have no idea how to compare myself to the average student. I really don't. But I would not say I was working hard."

One day, when Sam was in eighth grade, a lone Asian boy joined the school math team with Sam. Immediately, the sixth grader started scoring close to him. He was hitting forty-four or forty-five points, very close to Sam's near-perfect scores in the math competition. "I was *nervous* about that kid," Sam remembered. "I certainly didn't feel kinship towards him."

Then, in ninth grade, Sam moved up to the much more competitive Princeton High School, an institution with many more Asian students. There, his nervousness about Asian competition culture grew only more sickening. "Some people in ninth grade took AP Chemistry, but the really special person took AP Physics," Sam said. In ninth grade, "I was taking the AP Chem and AP Physics class at the same time." Sam remembered the pervading sense of competition between him and the fellow Asian students in his class. "In my Chem class, this kid . . . and I were very clearly the top scores and we sat next to each other. And I was not thinking to him, 'Good job, A!' whenever he got an A. I was thinking, 'I beat you!'"

Was it friendly, at least? "It was friendly . . . but we were competing with each other."

For Sam, there was a preternatural sense—if it wasn't already implied by his parents— that sometime in the not-too-distant future, he would be put in a single-file line with all the other Asian-looking people at his school and be judged exclusively against them. And that sense would, of course, turn out to be true.

It is perhaps understandable that elite liberal parents would try to enforce the suppression of Asian students from admissions in order to make it easier on their white kids. But by making it easier on the little Johnnys of America, these parents drive up the competition culture for Asian Americans to one hundred. Sam Dai was collateral.

■ ■ ■

"I was pretty confident getting into Princeton," Sam said. "I was taking two classes in Princeton. I was doing science and math. None of my scores were particularly bad. My AP test was ten 5s. Above 2300 SAT [out of a 2400 score]. National Merit Scholar."

But as application day approached, Sam grew more and more anxious. He second-guessed himself, starting with his essays. "I wrote about my faith, which was a very poor decision. A kid writing about his religion. Most people would say 'this guy's a sheep.' They want to see individual desire and insight."

Would Sam's sterling test scores and faith-based essay be enough to land him at exclusive, liberal Princeton?

Sam remembers Decision Day like it was yesterday. "We were all in my statistics teacher's classroom . . . in a row of six. Me and a group of friends, we all applied to Princeton. We all get into a line, and we open up our computers. First of all, it's bugged, everyone's trying to check it and it's slow . . . You definitely know everyone's kind of nervous . . . And I open up the email and it says 'deferred.' And I think somebody got in actually . . . I remember running out immediately and breaking down crying and calling Aditya, my best friend at the time."

I asked Sam why he thought he was crying, and what he told Aditya.

"It was like my world had exploded. You spend all of high school thinking you're *Asian*, you're good, which means among the Asians, you go to the best schools, right, you go to the Princeton, the MIT, the Harvard. If you're like the captain of all of the Science teams, and you took classes at high school, you're going to think [I'll] get into Princeton, you would just think it's the natural thing, right. You think you're good enough. And they tell you, no, you're not.

I asked Aditya [who got into Harvard], why are you even friends with me? It's like, I don't contribute anything. You're smarter than me. I can't even get into Princeton. He's at Harvard at this point. I basically told him I was useless.

This rejection from Princeton turned my world upside down. I could no longer think of myself in the same way. It's just not possible. This is what you build your identity on.

I think I got 25k to Rutgers, which in state is basically full. And I wasn't proud of that. I eventually went to CMU [Carnegie Mellon University], which is a pretty good school. But I remember, even when I graduated from CMU, I felt nothing. Nothing."

Getting rejected from Princeton crushed Sam's carefully cultivated worldview, one that was about striving to preeminent places, competing with top talent, and working the hardest to be the best he could be. But to Princeton, he was just another Asian kid good at math.

Was Sam obsessed with Princeton? It wouldn't be a stretch to say so. But Sam had dreams to study with the world's best mathematicians and scientists. He put in the work. He toiled every day of his middle and high school career to take the highest-level math courses, to take classes at Princeton while he was in high school, to prove he could compete with top level college students—classes he aced with flying colors. Sam had better grades, higher test scores, and more club achievements than nearly all of his peers. But because his competition was fellow overachieving Asian kids, he looked "standard" rather than "special" in the eyes of Princeton admissions officers.

■ ■ ■

Sergiu Klainerman could have used a student like Sam. The world-renowned professor of mathematics at Princeton often crossed the bridge into physics, with additions to the theory of general relativity and groundbreaking theories on hyperbolic differential equations.

Klainerman's study of math was in part driven by his upbringing in a communist country. "Mathematics was an island," he said. It is why, in the USSR, "a lot of people went to science. It was the least ideologically controlled." Mathematics was the one place in Romania where Sergiu could pursue what he loved. But he wanted more. He wanted freedom.

He applied to America. "I was accepted to the place of my dreams at NYU. Being paid, [getting] a fellowship to study." His voice rose with emotion. "It was the happiest time of my life."

Mathematics, to Sergiu, was the one place where things were *just true*. He had lived "in a country where everything is a lie." He knew what lies were. He wanted the truth, which math simply was. "This kind of postmodernist idea there is no truth is completely at odds" with the mathematical realities of the world, he said.

It was this distaste for the "your truths" and "my truths" language of the current milieu that led him to express his opposition to President Eisgruber's letter of Princeton's "systemic racism." Sergiu slammed Eisgruber in a public response, stating flatly that he distrusted the intentions of his letter. He writes of his experience in the United States, where he had the good fortune of being treated in accordance with nothing but his personal merit:

> "A larger part of the credit [of my success] is due to the sheer good fortune of being able to pursue my career in the US within an academic system which has been, at least until today, the freest, most competitive, and fairest in the world. By "fair" I mean the remarkable ability of this system to reward talent and hard work, with absolutely no regard for ethnicity, religion, race, sex, age, or any other considerations."[33]

If there is any systemic racism at Princeton, Klainerman told me, it is in the treatment of Asian Americans in his department. "The administration doesn't care about consequences, but wants good percentages." And those percentages systematically exclude qualified Asian Americans like Sam.

But there *are* consequences for substituting race and gender for merit. Consequences that reverberate across the ages, that can scandalize an entire department.

"There was [a] Black woman [at Princeton's PhD math program], very bright, fantastic recommendations from NYU, came to Princeton, but she was a musician and became interested in math late, of course you're not prepared," Sergiu told me. "She was brought to Princeton, and people fought for her[:] 'We have to make an exception because she is so bright.'"

She was bright. But she was unprepared. "Princeton is by far the most advanced PhD program in the world," he said. Then he talked about this woman. "You come in, you compete with kids from all over the world. She was just overwhelmed, and it was a disaster to her and to the department. Because she became extremely bitter."

The sad, sickening part of this whole situation is that it could have been avoided. This bright young Black woman could have been a paragon for Black women in math everywhere if she had gotten the appropriate training for her level of competence, and not been immediately discouraged from math through Princeton's absolute hellhole of a PhD program.

"There are kids who come, they want to do math, they are very excited, they are bright, but they don't have the level of preparation. They compete with kids who went to Olympiads from China or Romania," Sergiu said. What do you expect to happen? That these students will suddenly do well?

One more consideration here: Frederic Bastiat, a leading nineteenth century French economist, posited the idea of the "seen" and "unseen." We, as humans, are generally enamored by stories about things that we did to cause immediate help and satisfaction, even when the costs are greater but more invisible.

For every student unprepared for the rigor of a Princeton PhD program in math—who is "seen," who you brought in for diversity purposes—you reject a student who is prepared, who worked every hour he could to get in, who wanted to do elite math with the best of the best, and who, with that level of research excellence, could go on to discover world-changing things. But who, "unseen," fades into invisibility. A student approximating Sam Dai. And you embitter him too. Because he knew that he was rejected for reasons he couldn't control.

MISMATCHED

Dr. Richard Sander joined UCLA Law School as a mild-mannered professor who liked talking about housing policy, and left as a fiery lightning rod of political controversy over racial preferences.

"The fundamental problem is not that mismatch exists, but that higher education ignores it," Sander said. "Instead of racial effects or things correlated with race being used as a way of understanding what's going on, it's used as a way to shut down inquiry."

Mismatch: How Affirmative Action Hurts the People It Intends to Help, a 2012 book by Sander and his colleague Stuart Taylor, explicates his studies on how racial preferences at elite universities tend to harm Black and Hispanic students' graduation rates and performance on important graduate-level statistics, like bar and STEM exam passage rates.

Sander's findings can be summarized as follows: Black and Hispanic students who attend colleges that heavily weigh race into their consideration for admissions tend to perform worse in certain subjects, like STEM and law, than those who are accurately "matched" to their levels of aptitude.

Sander's passion for this issue comes from his own campus: The University of California, Los Angeles, one of the most competitive public colleges in the United States. In 1996, the state of California banned affirmative action in all public universities—UCLA included. Many in UCLA's liberal administration fiercely opposed the ban on affirmative action. Even in 2014, nearly twenty years after Prop 209 was passed, UCLA Chancellor Gene D. Block still harped on its ill effects for students on campus. "Nearly two decades have passed since Californians voted to end affirmative action in admission to public colleges and universities," she wrote. "Today it is clear that we have suffered for it." (The rest of the statement discusses a few isolated racial incidents on campus, but says nothing of actual admission and graduation effects for UCLA.)

How did California's Black and Hispanic population suffer for it? Dr. Sander studied data released by UCLA's Law School. "There were huge gains at some of the other UC campuses. The number of applications went up dramatically at UC campuses . . . [Media] never reported on the higher graduation rates before Prop 209 was passed. They never reported on the higher grades students were getting."

In Sander's analysis of law school admissions with and without racial preferences, he found that the median salary of graduates of "Tier 1" (highest prestige) law schools that practice affirmative action, in general, is about 21 percent higher than that of graduates of Tier 2 or 3 law schools without racial preferences. You might think that it would therefore benefit Black students to go to a Tier 1 law school, even one that admits them by affirmative action. However, this bump is immediately offset by the "grade penalty" in Tier 1 law schools that disproportionately affects Black students; Black beneficiaries of affirmative action also tend to do significantly worse (about two standard deviations worse) in median law school GPA at these Tier 1 schools. Per Sander, the difference of two standard deviations predicts about a 25 percent median salary *decrease*. What does this mean? A Black student who chooses to go to a Tier 1 school that practices racial preferences, and suffers the grade penalty for racial preferences, would end up making roughly the same salary as the average Black student who goes to a Tier 3 law school and receives grades comparable to the average white Tier 3 law school graduate. At lower tier schools, the grade penalty becomes an even bigger factor than the positive value of prestige, and the Black student who chooses the affirmative action school actually *suffers* compared to the student who chooses the overall nonprejudicial school.[34]

UCLA's affirmative action supporters point to one statistic supporting their viewpoint: the decreased number of Black enrollees after Prop 209. "This is true," Richard said. But if the Black students that failed to get into UCLA instead enroll in a program that is better suited for their skill levels, and they graduate at higher rates and get higher grades in them, then are they truly worse off for not having enrolled at UCLA?

Sander dealt with the criticism. But what he didn't expect was the ensuing extraordinarily intense campaign to discredit his reputation as a leading social scientist and tenured law professor. After his papers came out, the UC system shut down his ability to do more research. Previously, he could easily obtain public admissions records to UC schools; now, he found steep resistance. "I had 100 percent cooperation [before my study] . . . Five years after that, I had 25 percent cooperation," Sander laments. "[There was a] steady erosion of transparency." When Sander sued the University of California for access to the updated public admissions data, university administrators spent "close to a million dollars" just to defend the withholding of data that they had released to him just ten years before.

"If the original reception of my article had been, 'Oh, I guess we didn't consider that, let's get to the bottom of it,' then it would have been enormously productive, it would have led to a richer discussion about how education works," Sander reflects. Yet, "the dominant reaction to [my research] was, 'Oh, this is a threat to affirmative action, which must not be questioned, so let's figure out how to destroy the message.'"

And that's because the university system saw an existential threat to its worldview in the annals of Sander's research. Indeed, UCLA's concern is not that Prop 209 would individually harm Black individuals in their college-faring years—indeed, the evidence points to the fact that it did the opposite—but that Prop 209 would harm *the school's reputation* by lowering the number of diverse enrollees at the school. A far different thing to acknowledge.

Why would you care what your school's racial composition looks like, even though the members of that once-preferred race are doing better off without you? Should we be sad or happy that a couple broke up and found partners better suited to them? UCLA's affirmative action supporters seem to believe we should be sad.

One possible reason is because the real beneficiaries of affirmative action are not, after all, the minorities we are most sympathetic to. The real beneficiaries of affirmative action, if it benefits Black and Hispanic minorities, tend to be the children of the privileged Black elite.

Seventy-one percent of underrepresented minority kids (Black and Hispanic, largely) at Harvard come from well-off backgrounds, says Harvard's own analysis of its admissions data.[35] Turns out, Black Americans can be rich. And the rich benefit from the luxury of having their kids get preferential treatment into elite schools on the basis of their Blackness, even though their skin color does not speak to the full story of their life—and, in the minds of some, even contradicts prejudices they have about Black people being poor and need of help. But because this preference is allowed to exist and institutionalize itself in the practices of Harvard College, it continues to pay unmerited dividends for the country's Black elite.

Corey Alexander Walker, former Yale student and current graduate student at the University of Michigan for Business, is well aware that being Black helped him get into Yale for undergraduate college. He also went to Deerfield Academy High School, an elite private school in Massachusetts. He knows, then, that he had the inside track to Yale—doubly privileged. "If I had a kid I wouldn't try to get them into Stuyvesant [a top public school that is 70 percent Asian American], I would get them into Phillips Exeter [an elite private school], because it's a much less stressful environment, and they have the same rate of kids who get into Harvard anyway."

Corey is also familiar with how race preferences at his elite colleges don't help the Black people Americans might think they do. "At this point you have [affirmative action] not helping the generation that came from slaves, but Black immigrants," Corey said. And it is true. In a 2004 survey, 41 percent of the Black students at the twenty-eight most selective campuses in America were Black immigrants or the children of Black immigrants. But they are close enough on paper, so for the purposes of diversity, they are preferred.[36]

The Black elite does not mind the fact that they—rather than the ordinary Black person—are most helped by race preferences. Some Black elites actually view this kind of privilege as representative of racial justice, through a modern-day relative of what is widely known as the "Talented Tenth Theory." In the words of leading civil rights advocate W.E.B. DuBois:

> "The Negro race, like all races, is going to be saved by its exceptional men. The problem of education, then among Negroes must first of all deal with the Talented Tenth; it is the problem of developing the best of this race that they may guide the mass away from the contamination and death of the worst, in their own and other races."[37]

An interesting theory, notwithstanding its *Atlas Shrugged* vibes. But does it help the ordinary Black person?

Eric Price, education studies student at Georgetown, has the same thought.

"[There are] two important points . . . yes, there is the top ten percent of the race that will rise and become elite of the Black race, the leaders, etcetera, etcetera," said Eric. "And that's fine, but the second part of it is a responsibility of that top ten percent to reach back and pull up the ninety . . . However, when people are to believe the thought process of 'I got mine, you have to get yours,' then you will now think it is not your responsibility to reach back and to pull up the other ninety. So there is a level of disconnectedness between those who have reached the level of Black elitism and those who have not." He is hearkening back to what Malcolm X said at a 1963 speech at the University of California, Berkeley: "The wealthy, educated Black bourgeoisie, those uppity Negroes who do escape, never reach back and pull the rest of our people out with them. The Black masses remain trapped in the slums."

Raised in an economically diverse, middle-class Black neighborhood in Washington, DC, Eric grew up with this idea that people and institutions were usually well-intentioned, that white elites knew what they were talking about when they tried to coax Black students to their schools to join them in the elite. But when Eric attended Winston-Salem State University, a Historically Black College (HBCU), for his bachelor's, his idealistic worldview was shattered. It was not as if he didn't get a good education there; he got a *great* education there. "The impact of seeing professors who look like you, who experience similar plights as you, leads to a level of kinship," he said. Eric described the culture there as being one of real understanding, not having to "fake it," not always feeling like a fish out of water. He supports his story with facts: 55 percent of Black HBCU graduates say their college prepared them well for life after graduation, compared to 29 percent of non-HBCU college graduates.[38] HBCUs are diamonds in the rough, Eric argued. But the higher ed intelligentsia is obsessed with elite centers of gravity and getting Black students into the Ivy

League. As a result, HBCUs are underfunded and struggle to survive despite their quality education.

We talk about Asian American "proximity to whiteness." But Eric believes the Black elite may suffer from a similar fate. And by beholding the Black elite to white generosity, racial preferences only reinforce that proximity. The losers are the Black affirmative action students who don't play the white elite game, and so must attempt to succeed within a culture that is overwhelming and foreign to them—at an elite college that claims to respect and care for them, but more often than not appreciates them for the cosmetic additions they make to the university aesthetic.

THE SCANDAL OF THE IVY LEAGUE

This is what is happening at the Ivy League.

The world's most exclusive and prestigious colleges, with all the airs of an exclusive prep club, nevertheless feel guilty about their lack of inclusivity. Harvard wants to make amends to assuage the consciences of its administrative officers, but it doesn't want to lose the flavor of exclusivity that it has learned to be proud of, its brand of unattainability. So Harvard engages in an aggressive racial preference policy that excludes "no-personality" Asian applicants in favor of other preferred races, including white applicants. Black affirmative action admits do not threaten Harvard's exclusive system; they are equivalently token invitees to the exclusive country club, broadcasting the progressiveness of the country club to all its rich patrons. In contrast, Asian students—those test-taking nerds with no personality—threaten Harvard's air of prestige, and there are just *too many of them*. Harvard can indulge in the best of both worlds: praise from the progressive establishment for how virtuous their college is, and the continued flow of alumni dollars, so their kids attend a college that sits at the peak of unattainability and cultivated prestige. And to top it all off, Harvard receives the full blessing of the Supreme Court; now, they can tout their clearly discriminatory admissions program as an exemplar of virtue and cosmetic diversity. They have peak prestige, money, and legitimacy. You can't win this much and this thoroughly without something having to give.

But something has given. The Ivy League and the establishment that props it up are losing their edges—the same edges that make Harvard, Princeton, and Yale the envy of the world in the first place.

What happens when over a generation, you artificially suppress an entire coalition of excellent thinkers solely on the basis of race, to the point where they scatter to other universities?

This systematic discrimination already happened once before, to Jewish Americans; Jews rejected from Princeton attended other colleges and built up those colleges' research credibility. When Columbia University rejected iconic physicist Richard Feynman because of its quota on Jewish attendees, he instead matriculated to the Massachusetts Institute for Technology (then less lauded), where he promptly developed some of the leading physics theorems of his day and—for all intents and purposes—put the decidedly middle-class MIT on the map as a leading research university.

Today, we can point to an example of a school that has benefited greatly from other schools' distaste for Asian Americans. That school is the California Institute of Technology in Pasadena, California. Onetime home to Feynman, the science and engineering-focused California Institute of Technology's undergraduate campus is now 48 percent Asian American, by far the most predominant race or ethnicity on campus. Caltech remains one of few truly elite universities in the United States—because it does not practice racial preferences in admissions. According to education scholar Peter Wood, "Caltech remains a benchmark for American higher education in the sense that it is the closest thing we have to a major university that sticks by a merit principle in admissions."[39]

We must give merit its due part: Even though Caltech's name recognition is perhaps lower than MIT, and its endowment more than six times smaller, and its program smaller than that of any Ivy League, Caltech is fifth in the nation in scholarly citations per faculty member while MIT is second.[40] Caltech is fifth in the widely regarded QS world university rankings while MIT is first.[41] Caltech maintains its edge as one of the most highly respected universities globally. The so-called "lack of diversity" has not hurt it or produced a lackluster culture, so to speak. Maybe you would look at Caltech's nearly fifty percent Asian American percentage and conclude you wouldn't want to go there. (Never mind that a school that is seventy-plus percent white seems little out of the ordinary for most of the country.) Regardless of your personal predilections, that loss is purely your own—it's not Caltech's!

A student like Sam, highly competent but embittered by the rejection of the nation's elite colleges, will usually find a way out. But it is the university that loses. Princeton's donors fund each student that walks its artificially scarce halls to the tune of $273,191 per student per year.[42,43] The research done at these elite universities is the highest level of research done in the world. To waste a precious spot on a less qualified applicant because the other guy was the wrong race seems a precious waste.

The reality is: When a cabal of top universities, including the Ivy League, MIT, and Stanford, enact artificial racial preference policies against Asian applicants, it's the competing "second-tier" universities that win out from this arrangement—unless they practice the same preferences, of course. Well-qualified Asians storm those campuses and help those universities catch up to the elite, top-tier ones.

Therefore, top universities bet not only against Asians but *their own place in the college hierarchy* when they practice longstanding discrimination. Translation: They are so committed to not having a meritorious number of Asian students that they are willing to compromise their own welfare.

Yet the Ivy League maintains its brand of prestige that has not yet succumbed to the level of public scrutiny it should receive.

This doesn't mean its brand will last forever. Scandal and social justice have tarnished elite colleges over the past ten years. In 2018, two prominent actresses—Lori Loughlin and Felicity Huffman—were indicted for bribing their daughters' colleges for unmerited entry to what they considered elite universities, the University of Southern California, for one. Loughlin paid up to $500,000 to get her daughter designated as a coxswain for the USC crew team, although her daughter did not row. Huffman paid $15,000 to rig her daughter's test.[44]

The cheating scandal implicated more than thirty other rich and influential parents who saw college not for its educational value but for its brand capability. It also further soured Americans who saw the scandal as emblematic of both how the rich game our system, and how worthless colleges have become, save for their branding. This scandal is not a morality play. There are no saints. The rich offered bribes and colleges accepted. It was transactional, almost professional.

The public has noticed this. As such, trust in elite colleges has fractured—predictably, under partisan lines. According to Pew Research, Republicans have fallen from 53 percent positive of higher education to only 33 percent positive in the span of just eight years, from 2012 to 2019.[45] Democrats have remained positive (at 67 percent), but trust fractured by political party is never good for a healthy democracy. And overall negativity on higher ed has increased dramatically—from 26 to 38 percent of Americans over the same span.

How has the Ivy League responded to this? Not by outreach to the communities it has polarized. Not by pledging to adhere to its ultimate mission—and the missions of any reputable university in America: to identify and train the best and brightest *tout court*, pursue truth and excellence, and refocus on its core task of producing excellent students and citizens. Instead, the Ivy League defines a *new* set of behaviors that accords it unmerited prestige and go down that rabbit hole. These behaviors are in accordance with the moral superiority garnered from so-called diversity and inclusion, wherein by merely admitting people who *look* different, the Ivy League can attain greater—and yet ever more limited and fragile—social respect.

Of course, this form of moral superiority is unmerited. But it is worse than that. It is deeply inequitable.

As it turns out, the wealthiest of the wealthy have the money to spend—and the talent pool from which to choose—to craft elaborate diversity schemes, pledging to status-enhancing but functionally useless "equity" and "inclusion." Meanwhile, costs burdening the unwealthy who might embark on these same initiatives is far too prohibitive to justify.

Bottom line: The elite wealthy can spend money and resources on diversity and inclusion for its status benefits, without it significantly harming them; nonelites cannot. So Harvard, the elitist of the elite, is a natural fit to propagate diversity ideology as the religion of the upper-class woke. It is a tithe the Pharisee of diversity, Harvard, will gladly make to show its great virtue, as it does not harm them in the short run.

And as the liberal elite adopts Harvard's diversity premises, they cheerily display their proud virtue while leaving diversity ideology's true cost—that is, the disruption of meritocracy via identity politics—to be borne by the rest of America.

It is borne as follows: One, lesser-qualified grads who are hired for leadership in our country do not live up to their Harvard-name billing, and so damage the top level of our society.

Two, an applicant's focus on self-cultivation shifts from building skill and talent to building the correct victim story, hurting America's overall productivity.

Three, racial identity politics seep into the broad reaches of our discourse and infect our young with resentment against white and Asian people in our country, poisoning our talent pool for generations to come.

We have an elite diversity ideology that props up Harvard's brand but is parasitic against the rest of the country. And our legal system gives it rapt applause.

THE TRUTH ABOUT ASIAN STEREOTYPES

THE HOPE OF ASIAN AMERICANS

C hinese Americans were the only group to ever be subjected to a formal exclusion law in the United States. Japanese Americans were the only group to ever be interned in American camps. And now "Asian Americans"—the category of people with historical roots in Asia, a deep and diverse continent—are the only race in America openly subject to more stringent admissions standards by an elite American university than white people.

When people think of Asian Americans, they might think of model students. They might think of "nice guys" and "hard workers." Of noodles and rice. They might even think, as Army Officer Mark Kahanding says about the barren dating scene for Asian men, of "small you-know-whats." But I think of something different. To me, the word "Asian" in America is invariably resonant with the word *invisible*.

"Invisible" rings most salient perhaps because of how much Asian Americans have sacrificed to aspire to be part of the American fabric. By geography alone, no other group has moved so far from their origins in an effort to become American. Asian Americans intermarry—that is to say, marry white Americans—at the highest rate of all the races. According to a 2012 Pew Research poll, Asian Americans are also most likely to believe that hard work pays off (69 percent of Asians versus 58 percent of the general public), to respect traditional family values (54–34 percent), and to experience the effects of upward social mobility. This is despite coming to the US with almost no wealth.

Pew Research notes that "Asian Americans are the highest-income, best-educated and fastest-growing racial group in the United States."[1] Despite severe historical discrimination, Asian Americans have persevered and built a home in this country that many of them love.

Asians emigrate for a variety of reasons and motivations, but one thing unifies them: a desire to experience the American Dream.

"[I] feel the kindness of this country. I feel very appreciative of the opportunity I was given," said Chinese immigrant and former Google engineer Tian Yu. The polls don't lie: The American Dream is not some Rightist or nationalist myth. It is a genuine belief, a representation of America that immigrants hold onto when they risk the entire trajectory of their lives to come here. Oftentimes, they flee from war, poverty, or Communism. In the case of some Southeast Asian countries, like the Philippines or Indonesia, they also flee calcified racial resentment that threatens to upend or destroy their lives.

"My parents owned several businesses in the Philippines," said Daniel Tan. "We weren't in the highest tiers of society in the Chinese community [in the Philippines] so our businesses were very vulnerable. There were a lot of tax collectors who said you need to pay up because you're Chinese, you're a business owner, you have lots of money, or we'll make life difficult for you. My dad was tired of being treated this way. Our business was at a low point. Better to find greener pastures," he said. America was that greener pasture.

Asian immigrants who faced racial resentment in their home countries, like Daniel's family, did not expect preferential treatment when they came to America; so long as treatment was fair, that would be an upgrade for them from their home countries. It only takes a passing glance over immigration history to understand America's storied exclusion of Asian peoples. The first wave of Chinese immigrants, at the height of the gold rush and the railroad boom of the late 1800s, often forged papers, claimed false identities, and endured brutal interrogations to prove their worthiness of admittance to this country. But when America opened its doors to Asians through the 1965 Immigration and Nationality Act, a "second wave" of Asian Americans saw a future America—which would genuinely welcome any hardworking person to prove themselves on these shores. That would give Asian immigrants a chance to be defined by the "content of their character, not the color of their skin." Dr. King's words echoed far beyond America. They touched every hopeful spirit in Asia.

Remember that MLK's mentor was the great Mahatma Gandhi. He and Gandhi were worldwide figures who stood up for racial equality across all mankind. So powerful was their message that they inspired freedom fighters in notoriously unfree countries like China. When MLK's sculpture in the National Mall was commissioned, the arts council awarded the project to a Chinese sculptor living in his home country, Lei Yixin, who called the work "the most important work of [his] life."[2]

But little do they know, the new home that they have chosen—America! Land of the Free!—still has some issues that need to be tinkered out.

For one, immediately upon coming on these shores, these immigrants are slapped with the most undignified name: "Asian American."

"As a Christian I chose to convert from atheism. I chose to be naturalized. Chinese is sort of an identity because it is a country. I *choose* to honor that Chinese identity," Ye Pogue explained, a first-generation Chinese American who emigrated as an international student.

"But 'Asian?' What kind of identity is that? It's a label."

David Azerrad, Professor of Government at Hillsdale College, puts it more bluntly: "I think that term is bullshit. The implication that there is solidarity with all people because they have a yellowish hue? I mean, look at what the Japanese and the Chinese have done to each other in the twentieth century, how much they hate each other. And what, suddenly they come here and they—I mean—that's just—"

So exasperated is Azerrad by the ridiculous thought, he cannot complete his sentence.

We must recognize the fact that the term "Asian American" (just like its sister, "Latino American," or more recently, "Latinx American") is manufactured, an attempt to tie down an agglomeration of identities together into one—for political reasons. The cost? This mass identity is often imposed upon these disparate peoples without their consent. As identity politics scholar Michael Gonzalez says in his book *The Plot to Change America*:

> "The leaders of organizations such as the AAPA [Asian American Pacific Alliance] . . . wanted the Asian American category created, of that there is no doubt. But do the people so designated even accept the huge pan-ethnic collective, any more than 'Hispanics' accept that label? The indications are that the answer is a resounding no. According to a 2012 Pew Research study, 'the Asian American label itself doesn't hold much sway with Asian Americans': 62 percent describe themselves by their country of origin, just 19 percent describe themselves as Asian American, and 14 percent just call themselves American."[3,4]

The idea of the pan-Asian American is an imposed one, but it is also one in which the significance of its imposition is often lost on Asian American people, who are generally too focused on assimilating in their new country to worry about shedding labels. When they finally realize that they are "Asian American" solely because they don't look like white or Black people, the reaction is often confusion and frustration.

"Race always came up in a positive light until you applied for college," said Jonathan Kim, a Duke Medical School doctor-in-waiting and second-gen Korean American, born in the United States to Korean parents. Jonathan went to an upper-middle class high school in diverse Montgomery County, Maryland. His high-achieving academic strata was predominantly Asian American, but people "would make fun of their own racial stereotypes and make fun of nonconforming."

"I'm an Asian American, but I do this [nonconformist thing]," Jonathan said. The idea of Asianness was largely humorous for his Asian American peers—to be dissected and laughed at. That worldview shattered when he and his classmates began applying to college.

"I sensed a lot of resentment about what you considered a minority. Up until that point, the minority [of Asian Americans] was the majority. What we considered was a minority wasn't what the world considered a minority."

"There were a lot of conversations about the Ivy Leagues and MIT," Jonathan continued. "People would say, 'How did *five girls* get into MIT? There's nothing different about them, in fact we scored higher.' And we feel like we wrote a pretty good personal statement. 'It's because they were women, and they want women in STEM.' 'Why did this guy get into Duke?' He would say 'I'm half-Hispanic' . . . people [would say,] 'You're the whitest guy I know, how are you half-Hispanic? The numbers didn't add up. Is it [because] you marked yourself Hispanic versus white?'"

The understanding of his Asianness as negatively negotiated by an institution shocked Jonathan. It was a coming-of-age moment, a transition from racial innocence to awareness. Before entering the college admissions process, Jonathan was naïve, an immigrant child. After recognizing discrepancies in the admissions process that he could only trace back to the color of his skin, "Asian American" became a term that carried greater significance, and potentially greater harm.

When Asian Americans arrived in this country, at the least they expected a country willing to move past—instead of reimpose—the constructs of race and origin upon its own citizens. What they didn't realize was that people were still being negotiated on the basis of their race, and in polite society too. Asian Americans, having faced exclusion on one side of the Black-white divide in the 1800s, now face exclusion on the other.

THE ONE STEREOTYPE ASIANS HAVE ALWAYS FACED

There is a stereotype of immigrants filling jobs that American citizens do not want to do. In a 2020 Pew Research poll, 77 percent of Americans said that undocumented immigrants mostly did jobs Americans would not do (as compared with jobs that Americans want), and 61 percent said the same for legal immigrants.[5] But there is a flaw in this stereotype, and it relates specifically to Asian Americans. The first immigrants from Asia came to America and immediately sought jobs that many white Americans wanted as well.

In the early and mid-nineteenth century, Chinese Americans first arrived on California shores. There were various reasons why they came: to flee rebellion, search for gold, and trade with Americans. The first and second Opium Wars, fought between the Chinese and the British (and resulting in a devastating loss of Chinese sovereignty), caused many to seek their futures elsewhere. At first, most Chinese planned temporary stays to help their families back home; however, more economic opportunities in America prompted them to remain permanently.

Nearly all Chinese people who came to America during the first wave of immigration in the mid-nineteenth century were male. This is significant: The implication is that nearly all who emigrated came to work, compete, and make money. Most had families back home. The rare woman who came was truly from another world. Indeed, Afong Moy, the first Chinese woman to come to the United States, was paraded around by two fellows named Nathaniel and Fredrick Carne and exhibited as "The Chinese Lady." The few Chinese women who came to America were gawked at and fawned upon by white and Chinese American men alike.

As such, stereotypes of both Chinese men and women surfaced almost immediately. The women were exoticized, deemed rare objects. And the opposite occurred with Chinese men: They became associated with curs and mongrels. A deeply bitter resentment against Chinese men grew in white, male Californians. To the white miners and gold rushers out West, Chinese men, with their idiotic long braids and slanty eyes, were invading space that was rightfully theirs. In the eyes of these white miners, who had journeyed from the East Coast into the wilderness to scruff out a living in the unmarked West, the last thing they needed was foreign men from the opposite side of the Pacific Ocean coming in to take their jobs.

And yet they came. Hundreds of thousands of them. Nearly all of them men. By 1850, 25,000; by 1880, a whopping 300,000. They epitomized undesirability to these white miners. Competing with them for jobs, Chinese men worked hard on the railroads, mines, and shops to feed their families back home. They also had to pay off debts to the merchants who financed their cross-country travel. They had little choice but to put their heads down and work any job they could take. And that meant they *would* take whatever job they could.

They worked hard for what they earned. And they became known as *hardworking*.

HOW A STEREOTYPE BECOMES A WEAPON

You might think that being known as hardworking and reliable is a good stereotype. But it depends on the person you ask. James Ahn, a Korean American corporate relationship manager at a large financial services company, claims the Asian stereotype of being hardworking helped him in his career. "[My race] is only helpful. I don't think it's ever not helpful."

James's position as a corporate relationship manager for his investment firm required him to get his foot in the door with a number of different high-profile clients. His youth initially disadvantaged him; nobody wanted to see a young guy. But James had an ace in the hole.

"It was one of my greatest advantages to be Asian. It was, 'Oh, I'm Asian, I'm pretty smart,' and I played the role a little bit more." How did he play the role? "I wore fake glasses to work . . . If I can't sell you with my youth, then I could sell you with my Asian personality; I became very deep, almost robotic, in a sense. I knew that jargon that I needed to use."

James was able to leverage the stereotype of the nerdy Asian dude leveraged against him to *his* benefit. Now, isn't that something? Stereotypes *aren't* exclusively harmful for the ones who carry them.

The correct interpretation of any stereotype is that it is a *weapon*, an instrument of power. All weapons, depending on who carries them, can be used either for good or bad—or good for them and bad for the other. And the skilled carrier can use weapons much more effectively to their advantage, while the novice will likelier find the weapon blows up in his face.

James Ahn, a three-sport high school varsity athlete standing six-foot-five and nearly three-hundred pounds, was a skilled and intimidating weapons-carrier, both physically and intellectually, able to leverage the hardworking stereotype of Asian people to his advantage.

But this is not the norm. Historically speaking, Asian Americans' stereotypes are usually weaponized against their subjects, oftentimes because Asian Americans lack the knowledge to compete on the cultural front.

Think about the Chinese immigrants who came during the California gold rush. By all accounts, they were hardworking and kept their heads down. Indeed, they frequently gained a higher yield than white miners and departed the fields happier than their disgruntled Caucasian counterparts, who were growing increasingly wary of their work being taken away from them.

Hardworking Chinese immigrants were also a bit naïve in not interrupting this growing resentful perception in the white community. Forced into self-sufficiency, they developed enclaves across the West Coast that blossomed into Chinatowns, hives of male economic activity that came with hairdressers, grocers, and entertainment. But these cloistered communities came with only more isolation from white people and increased their bitterness. The Chinese only came together with whites when they were working the same land—both groups competing against one another in the struggle to find gold.

This landscape was not primed for racial acceptance, or even mere tolerance. White resentment, motivated by competition with Chinese miners, birthed the complementary negative stereotype that became Yang to the hardworking Yin: the idea of Asian *coldness* and *selfishness*.

Which leads me to this influential 2007 study done by sociological researchers at Princeton, Northwestern, and Lawrence universities: "The BIAS Map: Behaviors From Intergroup Affect and Stereotypes."[6] It quickly became one of the leading stereotype studies in the nation, influencing many others like it after publication.

Its groundbreaking finding was that people tend to stereotype groups based on two axes: *competence* and *warmth*. Researchers asked a broad range of Americans questions about twenty select groups that highlighted their perceptions of these two traits. As hypothesized, groups like the middle-class, Black professionals, Christians (their findings about which are likely to have shifted by now), and the Irish were perceived to have

both high competence and high warmth. The homeless, welfare recipients, and Arabs were perceived to have low competence and low warmth.
Here's an incredible map of its findings:

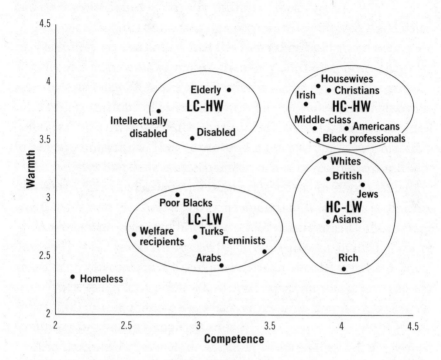

The groups were organized on axes of competence and warmth.
(LC means low competence on the graph, to clarify.)[7] And guess which
groups were perceived to have high competence but low warmth: the
rich, Jews . . . and Asians.

In line with the historical perceptions of Asians during the gold rush?
Absolutely.

The study went further than just this map of common attitudinal
perceptions by all races of Asians. It extended to how each of these
quartiles of competence and warmth correspond with four different
emotionalites, which lead to different actions performed towards members of these groups. This updated graph from 2021 showed the emo-
tionalities and actions associated with each stereotype. Those high in
warmth would be actively helped (facilitated), and those low in warmth

would be actively harmed. Those high in warmth and competence would be associated with admiration, but those high in competence and low in warmth would be associated with envy.

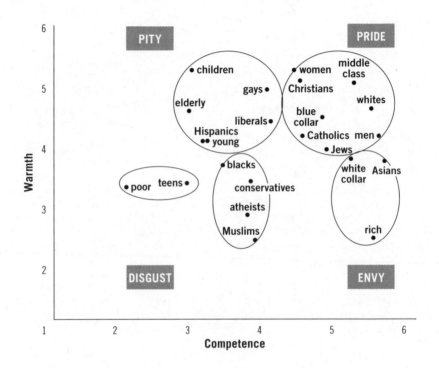

Asians, being in the high competence, low warmth category, were considered by Americans to be a "competitive group"—and, as evidenced by questions that researchers had preapproved to judge emotionality, hence stimulated measurable envy from the nationally and racially representative study sample of 571 adults.

White miners performed exactly by this book when they encountered "high competence, low sympathy" Asians. They envied them. And since envy had a .79 correlation to anger (a 95 percent significant correlation), it was not surprising that white miners sought to get rid of their competition. They vented their frustration to local and state governments, which of course had no representation sympathetic to Chinese Americans. With Chinese Americans unable to muster their own political support, California lawmakers passed a Foreign Miners' Tax that collected half of the typical Chinese worker's wages. And when that didn't scare the Asians miners away, anti-Chinese activists pushed through a Supreme Court decision that disallowed Chinese witnesses from testifying in court, *The People of the State of California vs. George Hall*. It allowed whites to lynch Chinese migrants with impunity and drive the Chinese out of gold mining entirely. The Snake River massacre, when white miners killed thirty-four Chinese Americans and faced little legal punishment, was a prime example of how the Chinese were eventually driven out of mining.

Still, Asians didn't give up on work entirely—they just took it out of California. Inland, backbreaking work remained to be done. The Central Pacific Railway corporation had dreams to build the first truly cross-nation railroad in North America. They needed reliable labor. White laborers were not attractive candidates, as they demanded high wages and the lodging, whereas Chinese laborers were willing to work on far less with no lodging. Capitalism won over racial misgivings. As libertarian economist Thomas Sowell wrote, "Capitalism knows only one color: that color is green; all else is necessarily subservient to it, hence, race, gender and ethnicity cannot be considered within it." The Central Pacific Railway brought the scraggly, lean Chinese men to do the dangerous work of exploding mountains, making room for revolutionary rail.

And boy, did they perform. Despite being underpaid and worked to exhaustion, Chinese laborers proved clean, reliable, and remarkably efficient. In no time at all, the Central Pacific sent messengers to import more and more Chinese labor until they formed a clear majority of the railroad workforce.

Now not only white miners but also white *railroad workers* were pissed. Chinese men walked in and just *worked*, day and night, without complaint and even appearing ever-grateful for their meager wages, while these white workers sat out in the cold without jobs. They couldn't outwork the Chinese laborers. They had to resort to different measures.

These measures, it turned out, were political. Specifically—ethnic identity politics.

Enter Denis Kearney.

■ ■ ■

Denis Kearney was like a lot of the Chinese immigrants in California: hardworking, industrious, entrepreneurial. An Irish immigrant to the American West, he gained quick success running a drayage business in San Francisco, owning five wagons and shipping goods across the city. He parlayed that success into becoming one of America's most notorious anti-Chinese campaigners.

What's surprising about Kearney's turn towards ethnic agitation was that he initially forayed into politics by criticizing the conditions of big business—a position many Chinese workers would probably have been sympathetic to. After all, these ideas were expressed in Kearney's infamous "Our Misery and Despair" speech:

> "Our moneyed men have ruled us for the past thirty years. Under the flag of the slaveholder they hoped to destroy our liberty. Failing in that, they have rallied under the banner of the millionaire, the banker and the land monopolist, the railroad king and the false politician, to effect their purpose . . . "

You can hear the Chinese railroad workers now: *Huzzah! Huzzah!* Kearney continues:

> "A bloated aristocracy has sent to China—the greatest and oldest despotism in the world—for a cheap working slave. It rakes the slums of Asia to find the meanest slave on earth—the Chinese coolie—and imports him here to meet the free American in the Labor market, and still further widen the breach between the rich and the poor, still further to degrade white Labor. These cheap slaves fill every place. Their dress is scant and cheap. Their food is rice from China. They hedge twenty in a room, ten by ten. They are whipped curs, abject in docility, mean, contemptible and obedient in all things. They have no wives, children or dependents."

Chinese railroad workers: *Uh oh*.

Yet even this anti-Chinese screed, a vile diatribe against the Chinese race, makes note that they, too, are being exploited by greedy capitalists and big businesses. Indeed, Kearney attacks those big businesses for soliciting "the slums of Asia to find the meanest slave on earth." He indicts them further, orating that these businesses treat Chinese laborers "as serfs [who] worked like slaves, and at last go back to China with all their earnings."

The nuance of Kearney's position must be acknowledged. It would be easy, in a more reductive environment, to simply debase Kearney as a racist lunatic. Perhaps he was; but one also must understand that Kearney's hatred of the Chinese intermingled with a more fundamental hatred: that of big business and their exploitation of American labor. In speeches, he generally referred to Chinese immigrants as passive creatures with no agency. They are "slaves," "docile," "obedient in all things." Obedient to what? The whims of big business, of course. Kearney believed Chinese laborers were so inimical to the American Way because he saw them as exploitable, weak, unwilling to fight for what he perceived to be the central American struggle against robber barons and their exploitation of "real Americans."

These Chinese are servile workers, he speechifies, but they will never gain our sympathy because they will never fight *with* us against the big corporations—only ever for themselves. They are *selfish*. Kearney played directly into envy inspired by "competent and cold" Asians, a stereotype still sowing discord today.

We must learn—yes, *learn*—from Kearney (and his legions of followers) how to present an effective attack on an ethnic group that convinces enough of the ruling elite to squash them. What Kearney did to destroy Chinese American hopes on these shores cannot be underestimated. Appealing to a sense of competition, a sentiment many whites already felt in the gold mines and railroads, he declared: "The Chinese are competing for your jobs! They're out to overwhelm you! 900,000 Strong!" as read one California news headline. Kearney degraded Chinese workers by *perverting* a supposedly positive stereotype of character into a broadside on their fitness for residence in this country. That is the power of rhetoric. That is the power of political will when demagogues wield it.

Kearney and his legion ultimately attempted to drive out Chinese by commanding the narrative and turning a label that should have helped the Chinese community—their reputation as hardworking—into a stereotype that completely wrecked it instead. This is meant when I define stereotypes as weapons advantaging the most skilled beholder. Denis Kearney knew how to utilize a stereotype. Chinese immigrants did not. And they paid dearly for their ignorance.

YOU MEAN ASIANS AREN'T GOOD AT EVERYTHING?

The many successes of the Asian American community are genuinely impressive and directly challenge the Leftist narrative of minority victimhood. But we also need to examine the Asian American community's failures. After more than 150 years on the American shores, they have not gained anywhere close to the kind of sociocultural capital that can fight stereotypes and political will; the kind of capital that stands up to Harvard University and says a resounding "f- you" to their race-based admissions policies and dangerous exploitation of damaging stereotypes against Asian people.

What is cultural capital, precisely? It's more than a bevy of A-list celebrities—although Asians have few of those either. Rather, cultural capital is knowledge and sympathy that other people have of your own culture and history.

As Americans are familiar, gaining cultural capital in our culture is not about working as hard as you can and keeping your head down. It's about presenting yourself in the best and most attractive light, and—when needed to—presenting your enemies in the most unattractive light.

The number of genuinely notable Asian celebrities known by nearly everyone in America—first-name people like Oprah, LeBron, Rihanna, and the Rock—is scant.

You can't just pin this one on racism. Many immigrant groups of smaller size have come and stayed in this country for shorter periods of time than some Asian American groups, and yet have accumulated more cultural capital. Cuban immigrants only started arriving in the US in the '50s and '60s, are maybe a third of the population of Chinese Americans, and yet have come to be one of the most culturally influential groups in the United States—boasting of several A-list politicians like Ted Cruz and Marco Rubio, celebrities like Cameron Diaz and Pitbull, and athletes like Tony Perez and Ryan Lochte.

Though celebrities are not necessarily indicative of cultural capital, it's doubtless that Cuban Americans, in part by dominating and influencing the culture of one of America's most vibrant and famous metropolises—Miami, Florida—have been able to achieve great heights and even influence in electoral politics due to their presence in the most powerful swing state in America: Florida. Cuban Americans, who make up 0.5 percent of the American population, have ten members in today's 117th Congress, or 1.8 percent of the congressional body.

In contrast, the names of "top-tier" culturally influential Chinese Americans, who make up six times the Cuban American population, are far scarcer as of this writing (Bruce Lee? Jackie Chan? Jeremy Lin? Priscilla Chan, Mark Zuckerberg's wife?). Andrew Yang, the former Democratic presidential candidate and a 2021 candidate in the New York City mayoral election, headlines Asian Americans well known in national politics (Kamala Harris is Indian American, but subordinated that part of her in favor of her Black identity during the 2020 Democratic primaries). Yang's breakout could portend greater cultural capital for Asian Americans; only recently have Asian Americans begun to establish more of a foothold in national politics. The 117th Congress has twenty-four Asian American members, 4.5 percent of the congressional body, many who were just added recently.

In terms of advancing the Asian American cultural image in society, there's no question there's work to be done.

Cultural capital is important to attain. It bolsters the positive case for your identity to be fully respected in society. Think about what the gay rights movement was able to do in the twenty-first century with the legalization of gay marriage. They used media both old and new to convey a normalized image of themselves—starting but not ending with nationally-beloved talk show host Ellen DeGeneres. And they leveraged stereotypes against their enemies: conservative Christians as hateful, prejudicial bigots, none bigger than the Westboro Baptist Church. And they won the cultural battle for their marriages to be recognized and respected in polite society.

Asian Americans' failure to obtain cultural capital—a result of the community's de-emphasis of American political matters—continues to allow both the Left and Radical Right to ignore them. As such, they are ignored in admissions and identity politics, even among the Left. No matter that the battle against white privilege results also in Asian discrimination. No matter that Harvard's discrimination against Asian Americans exploits the stereotype of Asians as head-down, test-taking nerds with no personality.

These negative stereotypes didn't just come about. They've festered in our society for centuries. And Asian Americans are due to recognize them and respond accordingly—though not in the way the Left wants them to.

THE RACIAL DATING GAME

Asian Americans' lack of cultural capital drives home some unfortunate realities. I'd like to begin with a relatively innocuous (well, depending on perspective) foreshadowing of the way that cultural stereotypes or ignorance affect ordinary Asian American lives.

The friendzone.

The ultimate put-you-in-your-placer. A huge wince-inducer for the nation's single men.

It turns out that Asians know a little more about this *friendzone* than most other people. Asian men and Asian women occupy different sides of it: men as the most likely recipient of it, and women as the most likely to have to put folks into it.

First, the men. The two least-swiped on race-gender combinations on Tinder are Asian men and Black women. This is despite that out of all races, Black women are the most likely to be the breadwinners of their own household, and that Asian men actually earn higher incomes than *all* other races and genders.[8]

Clearly, attractiveness on Tinder is not solely determined by income, but by deeper, more primordial factors. There is a primal, physical component to romantic interest—it cannot be dictated by rationality alone. Courtship is about building a connection that is irreplicable in other aspects of the world. It is also one of the few arenas left in America in which explicit racial preferences are allowed in polite society. Grindr, a dating app for gay men, had an "ethnicity filter" until June 2020, while Match.com and Hinge (a more "relationship-oriented" dating app, according to its branding) have continued to retain their race filters at the time of this writing.

In this strange world where polite racial discrimination is allowed, Asian men lose out. OkCupid data from 2014—data corroborated by multiple other online dating sites—confirmed what Asian men already knew: They, along with Black men, are the "least desirable" race.[9] Asian and Black men had a significantly negative rating from all other races except their own, while Latino men had a neutral rating from white women and white men had a positive rating from all races except for Black women. (Interestingly, the *Huffpost* article reporting OkCupid's data wrote, "preferring to date someone of a particular race isn't in itself racist," while the 2020 *Washington Post* Date Lab opinion on the same topic said it clearly was.[10])

So, what's up? Why are Asian men getting the short end of the stick?

In short, it's not precisely Asian men's *fault* . . . but it does relate to Asian Americans' inability or lack of desire to actively combat the prevailing stereotypes of Asian people present since the Kearney era.

Royce Chen, a second-generation Taiwanese American student in North Carolina, thought he struck gold with his first relationship with a white girl—the type that commentator and author Wesley Yang describes Asian Americans as being inherently disadvantaged at pursuing. In his essay *Paper Tigers*, Yang discusses "Asian American disadvantage in the sexual marketplace," and one Asian American pickup artist's (a person skilled at seducing women) attempt to fix that in a class on pickup artistry for "robotic" Asians. Yang wrote:

> "Yes, it is about picking up women. Yes, it is about picking up white women. Yes, it is about attracting those women **whose hair is the color of the midday sun** [emphasis added] and eyes are the color of the ocean . . . "[11]

Well, Royce did get that kind of girl. She was petite, blonde, close in age to him, but with little dating experience. Their first date went well, and their second, and their third. But fractures soon started to occur. She wouldn't understand some of the jokes he made. Their dates became frustrating and loveless. And they broke up after six months. That was when Royce, a Bay Area college sophomore who had moved to North Carolina for college, considered the factors that led to their breakup. He began to mull over race.

"About midway through my sophomore year . . . I got into a relationship and I remember feeling I had a hard time communicating . . . there were a lot of conversations that felt kind of awkward, that weren't understood," Royce explained. "I never really felt like I had to try as hard to be understood or to try to be that courteous around people of my own race. I felt like I could be blunt with people of my own race and it wouldn't come across as uncaring or rude . . . I could make jokes and they would be interpreted the way that I wanted to . . . she and I didn't always have a lot in common. Like when we talked about our experiences of family, our experiences of churches and things like that, they just felt very, very different. That's when I first started thinking about my race . . . more in the context of close, close relationships. I feel like I can learn and even thrive in a world that is majority white, I could thrive in the business world, but I felt that the close relationships—my very inner circle—maybe those people have to have experiences that I have. Maybe they have to be Asian or they have to grow up around Asians."

Royce began to see dynamics at play in his relationships—racial or ethnic overtones. He told a high school friend about the relationship, and his friend said, "I don't date anyone who doesn't speak Mandarin." Royce had once thought "it was a very extreme stance but for the first time after dating this girl, I started to see value in his thought."

Bad breakups often lead people to question themselves in a way they would not have otherwise. (After ending a relationship with a woman, my dad took up tai chi and became an extremely disciplined exerciser, to the point where he could wall sit for nearly sixty minutes at a time.) But for many Asian American men—because of our culture's prevailing winds, and the weight of racially coded rejection weighing them down in their greatest ambitions and ideals—issues of rejection can often be traced directly to issues of race.

Mark Kahanding, an Army Sergeant who is a gay and Filipino man, sees overt anti-Asian bias play out even more in gay relationships: "The sexual stereotype of Asian men [is] as less dominant than other men . . . [on] dating apps, Asian men aren't seen as attractive . . . it's unfortunate . . . I'm friends with a lot of other Asian men, and it comes to the point . . . when they try to date people outside their other races." And what happens then?

Well, we could get into the "locker room talk" about why Asian men are perceived as submissive, but truth be told, we don't need to—the "polite company talk" is demeaning enough.

"I asked someone why they wouldn't date me, and word-for-word they said it was because I was Asian," Mark clarified.

Black women, who are similarly negatively rated on these apps, share concerns about inferiority with Asian men. In fact, one female dating coach said that at 50 percent, her Black clients were the most likely to exhibit a racial preference.[12] Yet, for Black women, this "[can be] based on who they think will like them. They often don't have the experience of being asked out by white men, so they assume these men aren't interested." Asian men mostly do the asking by virtue of their gender—and so they experience the rejection explicitly and in real time, rather than passively or by assumption.

So how did we arrive at this matrix with Asian men at the bottom of beauty standards, despite higher incomes and presumably greater stability? Maybe Asian men *are* test-taking robots with no personality. Wesley Yang says that perceptions of lack of charisma are "rooted in the way [Asian Americans] behave, which are in turn rooted in the way they were raised."[13] But I would have to disagree with Yang on this. Asian Americans are raised in such a way that reinforces stability—but many people crave stability. Whatever cranial node fails to connect an Asian man's projection in the mind of a white woman does not have to do with the Asian man but with the fidelity of the projection. Which is influenced by "particulates" of the culture, lingering racial stereotypes deeply ingrained in the American psyche. Kind of like pure light travelling through the atmosphere—corrupted by particulates before it hits our eyes.

These racial "particulates" have not yet been collectively resolved as a culture. And yet, they have consequences in more than the realm of dating. These are the racial stereotypes that allow Harvard to get away with its unfounded claims of Asian Americans lacking personality—the very claims that give it the cultural credence to discriminate.

Asian American men have not been able to present a successful counter-stereotype to this devastating line of attack on Asian attractiveness and charisma. We are still living in Kearney's world. And changing the world really does mean changing the culture.

THE OTHER WAY FOR ASIAN WOMEN

Asian women face a different, parallel struggle. Unlike Asian men, Tinder and OkCupid data show that Asian women receive the *highest* number of swipes compared to other minorities—equivalent to, and in some respects exceeding, white women. (Model minority, anyone?) Asian women are in fact the only race/gender combination to score positively with *all* races. This is odd, considering neither Asian men nor Asian women have much media representation. But American culture negotiates them separately.

To many Asian women, the expectation—it seems—is that they are docile, passive. Genevieve Nadal, a Filipina American who headed an Asian organization at her alma mater Florida Southern University, said: "There are stereotypes about Asian women as submissive. In the media they're background actors or if there are Asian roles, they'll be the love interest of a white man, so it's not a positive representation."

White-male and Asian-female actor/actress combinations are ubiquitous, especially in popular television. One 2012 culture article in the *Washington Post* shot off a list of ads played just in the recent years, including a Chevrolet commercial where an Asian woman cooed "Good job, baby" to her white husband while he sealed the deal on a new Chevy, and a Heineken commercial where a white man and Asian woman went "cavorting" in an exotic nightclub.[14] The white-male–Asian-female pairing is a powerful cultural trope. Such a partnership was first used in the early 1900s, when Asian women came to America often as exotic dancers—and were quickly objectified. This trope solidified during the Vietnam War, when many American soldiers came home boasting of their exploits with Vietnamese women. Those stories were then integrated in film and the idea of Asian women as accessories, often with emphasis on their "sexual availability," flourished.

Real-life matches between white men and Asian women also flourished. According to the Population Reference Bureau, 27 percent of white men's intermarriages were to Asian women—while only 9 percent of white women's intermarriages were to Asian men.[15] Jewish men seem to be especially attracted—and attractive—to Asian women, perhaps because of similar educational levels: According to Amy Chua, in liberal elite circles, Jewish-men–Asian-women circles are "the majority."[16]

There are some people who think this is a problem.

Krystal Lowe, a Jamaican, Chinese American woman studying medicine in Florida, says it's actually demeaning. "I've only dated Asian guys before because I don't want to just feel like I'm a fetish," she said.

I'm sure that most of the white men who marry Asian women do not have some kind of sexual fetish for them. But there is always the worry, and the suspicion of entitlement that springs from the sheer plenty of these couples. In *The Social Network*, the white, Jewish Facebook cofounder points at a gaggle of Asian girls and says, "It's not that guys like me are attracted to Asian girls. It's that Asian girls are generally attracted to guys like me."[17]

So what is it—chemistry or fetishism? Trends in matches naturally occur based on similar interests, educations, and goals—or stereotyped, warped fatal attractions are based on histories of exploitation and objectification?

The first mistake people make when analyzing racial dating patterns is assuming that those patterns—say, Krystal Lowe's suspicion of white-male–Asian-female combinations—are occurrences for which someone or something is at "fault." These are matches—not assaults. To assume that Asian women do not have a choice but to marry white men ironically abets the very stereotype of submissiveness often applied to Asian women.

But it's worth looking at patterns and gleaning all the information that we can. It's true: Many of these women were raised in conservative cultures, where rules were established—and no, not all of them solely to oppress women—that gave men headship over the family. Many of these women were raised with certain qualities that perhaps, to a cynic, look like docility—but in the eyes of those who are actually cultured should be seen as hospitality and humility.

But sometimes, among Asian American women who date white men, that docility boils over into a kind of suppressed instinct, and the *Americanness*, the hunger for recognition and individualism, comes out.

In the short story "Omakase" published by the *New Yorker*, a white, Jewish-coded American man and Chinese American woman (the archetypal "Chua" couple) go on a date in a Japanese restaurant. The Chinese American woman is at once impressed and slightly appalled by the white man's grace and easy cadence in the Japanese restaurant. There was status in dating a white man as an Asian American woman, according to her friends.

> "[Her boyfriend] met most of her friends, who afterward found a way to tell her how lucky she was to have met someone like him: single, American—an artist, no less—and her age. By 'American,' some of her Asian friends also meant 'white,' the implication being that she was somehow climbing the social ladder."[18]

At the same time, she wonders whether he just was dating her because she was "exotic":

> "What was [his ex] like? the woman asked, but really just wanted to know if she was Chinese. The man said that she was nice, though a little neurotic. But what was she like? the woman asked

again, and the man said, What do you mean? She was Jewish and tall."

Those tensions come to head when she announces in front of the chef and her boyfriend that she is "Chinese," responding to a comment from the Japanese chef that a previous restaurant from which he had been fired had a manager who was Chinese. The boyfriend grew tellingly embarrassed, thinking this was some kind of racial standoff; the woman became angry that the boyfriend misinterpreted her. She grew aware of the fact her boyfriend was merely trying to preserve his control over the ambience of the date, rather than defend her. That she was being negotiated into a submissive role.

It's an illuminating work of fiction illustrating the subtle negotiations that still go on in our discourse, between a generation of up-and-coming millennials striving to be cosmopolitan and one with a historical consciousness that remains residually racial.

"It's very ironic and weird that Asian males have that stereotype of being unattractive and Asian females are fetishized," Krystal Lowe told me. "There was a sign I saw in a museum once that said: *Exhausted not exotic*. And I thought that was a cool, succinct summary of the Asian female experience."

This whole dating game shows the stereotypes still infusing the negotiations of Asian men and women in American culture, often at their own expense—but not without truth. These stereotypes are weapons to be sold to the highest bidder.

And what higher bidder than Hollywood, California?

HOLLYWOOD CREATES THE SUBORDINATE STEREOTYPE—BUT IT'S UP TO ASIANS TO DISPROVE IT

"Asian characters are not good at acting," said Ye Z. Pogue, a Chinese-born, American-married, self-proclaimed liberal. "It makes me sick."

Ye was fuming over the movie that was supposed to be Asian Americans' world debut: *Crazy Rich Asians*. "A lot of Asians watch[ed] it to show solidarity," she said, "so there would be more movies that cast Asians even though we didn't actually like *that* movie . . . I don't know one Chinese [person] from China who liked it."

Crazy Rich Asians marketed itself as *the* monumental Asian-led comedy that would finally give Asians the recognition and acceptance they deserve in mainstream Hollywood. But did this fluffy rom-com really do that—at least, to the extent that *Black Panther* opened up a world of Black-led superheroes to mainstream fame and popularity?

No. And you can blame the acting.

Both lead actors in *Crazy Rich Asians* were bad—and not only inept at their craft but stereotypically represented in a way that only reinforces the worst assumptions about Asians in mainstream culture.

Let's start with the female lead, Constance Wu. She found minor stardom in B-list ABC television series *Fresh Off the Boat* (2015–20), an Asian-focused show that also served as a kind of affirmative action for Asian actors. (Restaurateur Eddie Huang, on whose memoir *Fresh Off the Boat* was based, said that the show was "pasteurized network television with East Asian faces."[19]) I say this because none of the other main actors on the ABC show ever truly broke out of the Asian TV-movie space—which had appeared to be bristling with promise when the show was released.

And judging by Wu's performance in *Crazy Rich Asians*, she too was clearly not ready for the silver screen. Her dialogue was ham-handed, her subtlety nonexistent. One scene in *Crazy Rich Asians* is meant to show Wu and her romantic partner's conflicting cultural tastes. In it, Wu approaches the mother of the obscenely rich man she is dating; the trick in this scene was to convey Americanness without seeming goofy, so as to take the viewer out of the suspension of disbelief in all successful romantic comedies. Wu missed the mark entirely. She bear-hugged the fragile Chinese woman, her potential mother-in-law, and squealed in off-putting delight—a break in manners so off-putting and out of line I laughed out loud when I saw it at the theater. The fact that the directors didn't immediately censure her and demand another take exemplifies the all-around lowering of standards necessary so that this movie could earn woke points for having an all-Asian directorship and cast.

Which brings us to the male lead, Henry Golding.

Golding's romantic performance, devoid of charisma and roboti-cally arranged, probably set Asian male romantic leads—already in the Neanderthal age—back to the Cretaceous Period. Seemingly trying to make up for decades of mis-portrayal, it appeared as if the director of *Crazy Rich Asians* sought to make the Asian male lead one-dimensionally perfect and therefore equally ridiculous and unsympathetic. Golding's rich-handsome guy trope is well-worn, but he managed to make an unfathomably wealthy Adonis dull as a rock. Even his engagement scene set in the middle of a crowded plane was delivered in a flatly monotone voice so devoid of passion, you would have thought he was entering an arranged marriage. "Rachel Chu, will you marry me?" was delivered so thoroughly unconvincingly that a random extra next to Wu had to squeal, "Yes, yes!" for the scene to have any ounce of emotionality. Maybe he was supposed to sound suavely monotone, as posh British accents do. But make no mistake: This was no James Bond.

This poor casting choice may seem like a moderate error—but for a movie that stamped itself not only as a public spectacle but as a political statement to revitalize Asian representation in the cultural mainstream, this was critical. It is so because of Hollywood's historically biased treat-ment of Asian men.

The history of the Asian male in film and television is not kind. The phenomenon of the "emasculated Asian male" is a trope almost as old as Hollywood itself, residual of the anti-Asian sentiment of nineteenth-century Californians.

According to Asian pop-culture magazine *Giant Robot* founders Martin Wong and Jerry Nakamura, two generations of Americans were introduced to two mainstream Asian characters that helped set the tra-jectory for Asian Americans in Hollywood culture today.[20] The first was Bruce Lee, martial artist and true unicorn. Bruce Lee "was an infallible polymath: a fashion icon, a philosopher, a cha-cha champion, a nutrition-ist, a street fighter, a teacher, and a revolutionary fight choreographer," Jeremy Berger writes for the *Ringer*. "Lee was also the ultimate underdog, an actor who fought for the working class in *The Big Boss*, and against Western and Japanese oppressors in *Fist of Fury*."[21] The question is not of

Lee's uniqueness; it is whether that uniqueness could leave a lasting legacy in cinema. Or whether Lee's unorthodox portrayal of Asian American men would eventually be betrayed by the forces of Hollywood.

Enter Long Duk Dong.

Long Duk Dong, played by Japanese American actor Gedde Watanabe, was a John Hughes creation. Yes, John Hughes—you know, the guy who made all those '80s movies about jocks and geeks, cool kids and kooks (*The Breakfast Club*, *Ferris Bueller's Day Off*). Great movies about characters pigeonholed into categories. In the John Hughes oeuvre, Long Duk Dong is the foreigner, who can be criticized in comedic fashion just like any other category of high school bit-player. He is hilarious in *Sixteen Candles*, which is probably why the movie became Watanabe's breakout moment—and a source of near-nonstop quotations among the pre-Internet generation. "Every single Asian dude who went to high school or junior high during the era of John Hughes movies was called 'Donger,'" said *Giant Robot* founder Martin Wong.

I'm not one to excoriate artists for crafting characters befitting their directorial styles just because they are politically incorrect, and there's no evidence to suggest that Hughes—the maker of so many innocent and beautiful movies—was racist when he made Long Duk Dong. But unfortunately, Hughes's unflattering portrayal of the foreigner trope went mimetic; it became the defining depiction of Asian Americans in the '80s and '90s. It was a static caricature that was really funny. But it was one-dimensional. Watanabe elaborated on his famous character thirty years later, not angry at his own portrayal (although he been much accosted for it) but rather to flesh him out:

> "He's lost some of his hair. He has eight or nine kids, I would imagine . . . lots of grandchildren. It's a mixed marriage. Probably married someone blonde so his kids are mixed race. Actually, he's probably been married a few times. And for someone who fell so in love with America, he's probably changed his name. Some of his kids are in the arts, one in a rock band, probably, some are teachers, a few doctors. I think he owns restaurants. They're kinda

famous. And he's kinda well known for it. And he's about to make a bid for the L.A. Clippers."[22]

It's not that you can't laugh at Asian actors for parodying Asian people. (Asians make fun of white people too much to disavow that happening the other way.) No, it's that Asian Americans have never had a fulfilling moral or character arc, a three-dimensional portrayal. Hollywood has never had the patience for fully developed Asian characters. This is partly the result of the lack of directorial direction, partly the lack of acting talent. But the result is the same: flatness, emasculation, diminution.

Asian viewers are well-familiar with the one-dimensionality of their Hollywood portrayals, when they get any attention at all. "Asians are demasculized compared to their white counterparts. It all depends on what the media portrays them as. Right now, we've gotten a little bit better, but we still get the horrible accent," Mark Kahanding said. "Regardless of what the media portrays us as, I know that it's completely untrue."

So what must Asian Americans do to overcome these forces stacked by the titans of Hollywood, to achieve the representation they crave and claw out from cultural inscrutability?

I outline three approaches: the Leftist/victim approach, the mainstream liberal approach, and the asymmetrical/entrepreneurial approach.

THE LEFTIST/VICTIM APPROACH

Asians could complain. And complain.

Not like they haven't been already. Complaining about the lack of representation in media is practically a cottage industry in Asian American circles. Search "Asian representation in media" and you will find millions of joyless articles on the subject. In fact, Asians have been complaining about their media treatment since they arrived in America. Take this particularly embellished complaint from *New York Times* movie critic Thessaly La Force:

> "Representation is about demanding more: more leading Asian American actors, more films in which we are allowed the

everyday banalities of our existence. The anxieties, the boredom, the simple gestures of affection. It's about showing that you are like us. Not the other way around. Not adjacent. Not other."[23]

In this demand, La Force tells of a world with Asian actors in every blockbuster movie, in every great film. La Force fantasizes having Asians in every nook and cranny of big cinema:

> "What if *Ferris Bueller* took place in Pasadena and not Chicago, if its projection of youthful freedom and dilettantish attention span—youth is now, and now is free—were something you could see played out among a well-to-do Chinese family? Or if *The Graduate* was about Mrs. Kwan, not Mrs. Robinson, a complex woman with whom we could understand the isolation of an empty marriage? Or if *The Breakfast Club* was about a young Japanese American woman in the suburbs of San Francisco just discovering the power of her sexuality?"

Yeah but, the thing is, these alternate fantasies don't exist. The auteurs of those films—great, coming-of-age works of cinema—deserve to have their vision. To co-opt those visions solely to achieve racial representation insults them. This is a socialist instinct: to take someone's work and subject it to a collective will, especially a *racial* will.

La Force is allowed to live with her fantasy. But part of the reason that the movies she cited *are* such classics is because the auteurs were able to cast the actors they wanted. Actors aren't interchangeable. Directors aren't interchangeable. Artistic visions must remain authentic to the artists who envisioned them. If such visions were deconstructed and melted down for the sake of something as lowly as an ethnic fantasy, we would truly be living in a post-art world, the kind of which Marxist art critic Walter Benjamin says:

> "The instant the criterion of authenticity ceases to be applicable to artistic production, the total function of art is reversed.

Instead of being based on ritual, it begins to be based on another practice—politics."[24]

THE MAINSTREAM LIBERAL APPROACH

This approach is all about working your way through Hollywood, carefully crafting your brand and image so as to appeal to its tastes—while taking full advantage of corporations' newfound interest in diversity to milk that angle as hard as you can for your career "on behalf of Asian Americans."

This approach is probably best exemplified by *Crazy Rich Asians*—the good and the bad. The good: It obviously advanced its lead actors' careers, especially for Constance Wu and Awkwafina (making more than $300 million at the box office tends to do that). Press carefully followed a "We're the breakout movie for Asians!" marketing script, and it worked, at least from a monetary standpoint. It is unclear how long that marketing technique can work. Eventually, Asian American acting will have to sell for reasons other than novelty. But it worked this time.

The bad: Relying on elite liberals and mainstream writers to advance your representation inevitably amounts to tokenizing yourself. Suddenly, you become the Asian actor, the person who gets strung along in the name of a narrative. You may wonder—what's so bad about being tokenized, if you get all this praise and opportunity? Well, sometimes it backfires on you.

Anna May Wong was the first Asian actor to achieve any form of mainstream success in Hollywood. A beautiful and graceful woman, she was born in Los Angeles and infatuated with cinema from a young age. While she was working at a department store in Los Angeles, a casting crew came around asking for three hundred extras for the film *The Red Lantern*. She volunteered and never looked back. Picture after picture, she climbed from various supporting roles to her first leading role in *The Toll of the Sea*. At first, she didn't mind being cast for the stereotypical evil foreigner and seductress roles; she felt lucky just to be working in the industry. Her star was pointing in the right direction—but for one fatal flaw. The antimiscegenation laws of the time made it illegal for any woman of color to be intimate or to marry white men. Anna May Wong could not, therefore, kiss a man onscreen—a terrible forbiddance that prevented her from ever becoming a leading lady in Hollywood.

Disenchanted with the stereotypical, subordinate roles she was forced to play, Wong left Hollywood at the height of her career and moved to Europe, where she became a star. When she came back to America, she started refusing the stereotypical "evil villain" and "seductress" roles she once took. However, the one role she coveted—that of O-Tan in the film adaptation of a bestselling novel about China, *The Good Earth*—was handed instead to a white actress with taped-back eyes wearing yellowface. When Wong learned of this slight, she left America distraught and went back to her country of ethnic origin, China, seeking to rediscover herself apart from our country's bitter racism.

Anna May Wong's story reveals resilience, but also great pain, at the hands of a society that put a legal ceiling on her prospects even as she burst at the seams with potential. It also reveals the enduring toxicity of race. Careers, lives, love are ruined because of the dichotomies societies have projected upon us. At least one—the eminently talented Wong—was driven to leave this country because of its racial toxicities.

In the film *Daughter of the Dragon*, Wong starred across the only Asian American star contemporaneous to her. Sessue Hayakawa was a Japanese-born University of Chicago grad who arguably had an even more successful career than Anna May Wong during his lifetime—albeit without achieving the level of critical attention his female colleague did. But Hayakawa, a bona fide sex symbol popular with—get this—white women, made a staggering $2,100 a week at the peak of his career and started a $2 million production company, partially to fight against being typecast into stereotypical villainous roles.

His success lasted until it became politically expedient for the American government to turn against Japan for World War I. Sessue Hayakawa found that the goodwill previously shown to him by Hollywood elites was erased in the span of weeks. Contracts bled dry, and the film and television establishment grew suspicious of him. In 1922, Hayakawa left Hollywood to pursue other ventures in Europe and Japan.

Or we could take a more recent example of how mainstream media's tastes for "Asian talent" sour at the spur of a moment. Connie Chung was a fast-rising star, a television host whose aggressive tactics revealed much about her guests. She was a dogged interviewer—which news networks loved—and skilled at what she did (Magic Johnson revealed to her that he was HIV-positive in 1991). But her ascension toward the top was affected by other factors. CBS desperately wanted a woman to anchor their prime-time programs.[25] And the fact that she was Asian American allowed them to add some color—literally—to their set. For a time, Connie Chung's voice was one of the all-star primetime voices on television. Then something suddenly changed. Broadcast networks previously high on her became less so. Her aggressive volleys of questions—previously seen as an asset— became a target. After she made comments perceived as sarcastic about the Oklahoma City Bombings in 1995, CBS stripped her of her primetime show. CNN cancelled the show they promised her. Chung went straight from superstardom down to the dredges in no time at all.

I'm not going to blame Connie Chung's downfall solely on her Asian identity, but her story is at least a warning that one's Asianness or "diversity" may be the foot in the door in modern Hollywood, but it is not a shield of invincible armor.

These stories lead me to view Hollywood's pledges for "diversity and inclusion" with more suspicion than maybe would register at a liberal cocktail party. I'm reminded that well-meaning liberals may indeed at first be well-meaning. But to accept being the token minority of liberal Hollywood is to put yourself at the mercy of a capricious and quick-shifting ideology of race. *Crazy Rich Asians* may have made Asian people more acceptable in Hollywood, but that could change in a snap of a moment. That could change as soon as a United States President decides that China needs to be exterminated, or as soon as the Left's obsession with taking down white men starts to bleed over to Asian men as well. Asians' tenuous place in the Left's victimhood pyramid makes me queasily wary that the positive attention for Asian talent may just be ephemeral instead of long-lasting.

I don't believe that conforming entirely to liberal expectations provides zero benefits to the people that manage it well. After all, you shouldn't fault Anna May Wong for doing what it took for a woman of her color—that is, typecasting herself—to make it in Hollywood. I just don't see this kind of conformity giving Asian Americans the *lasting* respect in Hollywood that they need to entrench themselves as a critical part of our American culture. Rather, the kind of representation Asians currently get is mostly confined to movies specific to Asian culture, but not to *A* blockbusters in which Asian activists are pining for representation.

I don't say this because I believe liberal Hollywood should ignore racial representation. I say this because I know the history of liberal Hollywood's capriciousness and how it makes any investment into the diversity and inclusion game a tenuous proposition at best.

THE ENTREPRENEURIAL APPROACH

If you've made it this far in the chapter, you are presumably sympathetic, as am I, with the goal of having more Asian Americans in media and Hollywood. But I don't want Asian Americans to gain superstardom on the basis of white liberals extending generosity to them. I want Asian Americans to demand recognition on their own terms, not someone else's.

So I want to talk about rap music.

Rap was born in Black culture. It is undeniably, historically Black. It is also American. You are just as likely to hear a white girl rap the words to Kanye West's "Monster" at a frat party as you are to hear a Black man freestyling. Rap is a lasting crossover, a product of entirely Black incubation and talent, that has come to directly impact our culture and enshrine Black sensibility in the mainstream.

Rap is one of Black culture's greatest achievements because it wasn't the brainchild of a corporate executive or a diversity consulate or an academic grant from the Ford Foundation. It was a genuine wellspring of creativity and work ethic from Black men and women, and so still shares the characteristics of its founders, good and bad. We can debate the moral legacy of rap, but we cannot deny its lasting impact. It's one of those mediums that was developed and fully, authentically articulated from Black culture, *and* became a crossover success. It also elevated Black personalities, ideas, and thought into a world of social respect that was extraordinarily limited before its introduction to the mainstream. It *changed the game.*

For Asians to leave a lasting impact in American culture, they must do so from the ground up. And doing so requires a level of trust—not in the Hollywood elite, but in ordinary Americans. Trusting that ordinary Americans really *do* welcome diversity when a product of it is presented interestingly and vividly, that Americans would buy a product that showcases talent from all parts of the world.

There is an emergent Asian cultural entrepreneurship that could potentially rival rap in its scope and influence in ten years' time. It is uniquely Asian in heritage and yet becoming more appreciated by American culture. It is the medium of *anime.*

It was dizzying to see *Avatar: The Last Airbender*, an anime targeted at eight-year-olds and originally premiering on Nickelodeon (2005–8) during this author's childhood, be revitalized by Netflix in the summer of 2020 and quickly gain an incredible crossover audience that topped it on the Netflix charts. An anime for *children* attracted one of the largest audiences Netflix ever had up to that time. An unapologetic homage to East Asian culture and thought—the four elements represented in *Avatar* are the four traditional elements of Japanese folklore (water, earth, fire, and air)—yet simultaneously universal. What a feat. What a triumph.

Anime used to be niche. But now people of all races flock to it. Cameron Laux of BBC wrote: "Anime and its sister printed art form, manga, used to be considered geeky (the Japanese say otaku) pastimes, but clearly they are moving into the global mainstream."[26] Why? Because Asian and Asian American artists piled their heart, soul, and craft into it for a sustained period of time, gaining first a critical mass with the Asian audience in America, then a more general "nerd" audience, then finally making a push for a broad audience across all backgrounds. That is: They sought to cultivate a smaller audience of devotees first, rather than attempt to try to catch onto a wave. *Spirited Away*, anime's "breakthrough" movie, was released in 2001; after twenty years germinating in American culture, millions of Americans now consider it a must-see classic.

And the best part of anime? It can exist—and in fact, has existed— totally apart from Hollywood's limiting rules and games. In fact,

Hollywood's own movies have been met with derision and shrugs from the anime community, self-confident in its ability to go toe-to-toe with the industry behemoth. Acclaimed anime director Moromu Hosada said about Hollywood: "I might feel this strongly because I'm an animation filmmaker, but I just think [with], say, [the live-action] *Beauty and the Beast* . . . [there's no] respect to the original filmmakers. I just kind of feel like they just did it for the money . . . They need to pay more respect to the original animations."

Could someone beholden to Hollywood executives make such a pointed critique? Not likely.

The entrepreneurial path to advance Asian recognition in American society is a daunting one. But it is also noble. A path that will help the Asian American community show who they are independent of elite help. To show the true strength of Asian American excellence and creativity. And maybe even break down a few stereotypes.

THE POSSIBILITY AND PERIL OF AN ASIAN AMERICAN RENAISSANCE

Cultural capital can be attained—and Asian Americans are approaching a window to attaining it, at the time of this writing. A more diverse society has created a renewed demand for multiethnic culture. Although the novel coronavirus has possibly inflamed anti-Chinese sentiment, there is actually opportunity in adversity; Asian and especially Chinese Americans can cast themselves as fully aligned with the American proposition of freedom and liberty, rather than the autocratic Chinese Communist Party's sensibility for control. As 2020 Presidential Candidate Andrew Yang wrote in the *Washington Post*:

> "We Asian Americans need to embrace and show our American-ness in ways we never have before. We need to step up, help our neighbors, donate gear, vote, wear red white and blue, volunteer, fund aid organizations, and do everything in our power to accelerate the end of this crisis. We should show without a

shadow of a doubt that we are Americans who will do our part for our country in this time of need."[27]

Yang does not write this because he believes that America is a perfect country and that everyone should conform to it—hardly so. In fact, much of the first half of his opinion piece laments the anti-Asian racism occurring in the streets during the beginnings of the coronavirus pandemic—racism that continues to occur in 2021 on the streets of Oakland, where an elderly Chinese man was pushed down by a city delinquent, and other areas of the country. But Yang understands that the solution to anti-Asian racism and stereotyping must come from Asian Americans themselves. There is no use crouching and whining for what you yourself cannot cultivate and create.

When you look at the Left's responses to Andrew Yang's editorial, however, you can't help but be depressed. One particularly nasty editorial came from Canwen Xu, a Columbia University senior (where else but the guilt-ridden Ivy League?) and TED Talk speaker, who accused Yang of being a "white-people pleaser." In her mind, Yang perpetuates the "decades-old myth of the model minority: that Asian Americans are the obedient people of color, the ones who are willing to uphold a system that is rigged against us by submissively working within."[28]

The crux of Xu's argument is this statistic: 33,000 Japanese Americans served in World War II, while 120,000 were interned in internment camps. Xu frames this as obvious proof that demonstrations of "Americanness" don't stop white people from suppressing and discriminating. But Xu also misses a critical part of the story: After the war, those 33,000 Japanese Americans who served greatly assisted in helping America normalize its relations with Japan, turning the former bitter contest into a pivotal friendship that reaped major benefits during the Cold War. And America signaled its gratitude towards these Japanese Americans by awarding approximately $38,000 (adjusted for inflation) in reparation payments per capita to interned Japanese Americans in the Civil Liberties Act of 1988. Those American soldiers of Japanese descent did not change stereotypes *immediately*—but their demonstrated love for their country paved the path for Japanese Americans to contribute at the highest level to America . . . and later be rewarded for it. Canwen Xu's Leftist attempt to alienate Asian Americans from the American narrative simply does not take into account the full spectrum of history.

There is a bitter fatalism in Xu's article, decreeing that no matter what Asian Americans try to do or show, they will not be rewarded. That is simply a false deconstruction of Asian American autonomy in American culture. Listening to Leftists like Xu peddle the "damned if you do, damned if you don't" narrative makes for an extremely depressing and paralyzing vision of America that gives Asian Americans basically no path forward, except as subordinate conduits to victim identity politics.

But Yang showed his belief in a vision of America where each culture it houses can position itself as something important to offer, something from which others can learn.

Sophia Chan was an administrator for the Los Angeles Police Department when the coronavirus pandemic hit in March 2020. Immediately, the shortage of masks impacted the police department's operations. "The LAPD assigned only one N-95 [mask] per officer, and there was so much great need," she said.

Chan decided she would help her fellow officers. Immediately she took to the Chinese social media app WeChat, where her Chinese American community had bought hundreds of boxes of masks before the virus ever hit US shores. When it became a national emergency, Chan organized a large-scale mask donation to her LAPD unit. "There are 10,000 officers. Everyone only has one one N-95. PLEASE help us," she wrote in one message. The immense gratitude of her LAPD branch led Chan to realize that so many other places—hospitals and law enforcement agencies—needed her help. She organized a mask donation apparatus around the country. "By the end of April, based on my calculations and community groups that I know of, we donated about 1.5 million pieces of PPE with a total value of $2.4 million."

Then, Chan noticed something: In the midst of these acts by members throughout the Chinese American community, not a single news journalist—not one—covered it. The stories they seemed preoccupied by were about other people, and the few times they ever talked about Asian people, it was only about anti-Asian racism.

Racism this, racism that—never stories about ordinary Chinese American—*American*—heroism.

Sophia grew frustrated—then determined. "We helped the nation survive that national shortage. Without Asian communities [and their] generous donations, [public institutions] would be waiting for masks to come in from China," she said, bothered that these ordinary heroic acts weren't being recognized. But instead of complaining, she decided to do something about it.

Sophia assembled a press list, nearly from scratch, of California beat reporters. She knew that unless she herself took action to rectify it, her own Chinese American community would never be recognized for the hard work they put into making their country a better place. She also felt a duty to help the world see that Asian Americans were patriotic, making their home in *this* land, not beholden to any other. People needed to hear these stories.

At first, the local media would not respond to her inquiries. But Chan was tireless. She sent emails regularly about Chinese Americans volunteering across the country. When emails went unanswered, Sophia called reporters. Eventually hits trickled in. Chan started to get California coverage of the heroic voluntarism of the Chinese American community. Finally, the local ABC station called. At her mask handout events, "ABC-KCAL 9 showed up three times," she said. Then FOX. Then NBC. Chan's actions—hustling for Chinese Americans on the front of culture—paid off and made the Chinese American response to the pandemic a television story that showed the goodness and patriotism of her community.

Sophia Chan wasn't a smoothly trained member of the public relations elite; she was no Connie Chung. But she embodied, in many senses, the greatest potential of the American spirit: self-starting, with great belief in the power of the individual to effect change in one's own small way. She embodied the great potential of the Asian American community to break into the culture, should it summon the willpower and desire to do so. If Chan, an immigrant who did not grow up in the States, can bring positive national attention to the Asian American community, then surely the community itself has the capability to respond to America's stereotypes and preoccupations with Asian people and *change the narrative*.

The reality is, whether Asian Americans can achieve a lasting imprint on this culture is solely determinant upon Asian Americans' own effort to train up cultural talent and assimilate themselves as people with something *important* to contribute to American culture. Will Asian Americans be able to define themselves in the American narrative—or will they let Leftists and identity politics peddlers do it for them? The former takes a lot of effort—but provides a long-term return. The latter allows for short-term passivity—but almost guarantees subordinacy in American culture for future generations.

If Asian Americans are going to achieve any level of political and cultural success, then they need to think long and hard about how they are being negotiated right now. And especially by the stereotypes of Asian Americans on which the identity-politics Left and liberal Hollywood still rely. There has been no real culturally cathartic challenge to these stereotypes in Asian American history, no tool like the Civil Rights Movement that forced people to see them in a different way. As such, the cultural capital that greets other minorities falls cold on Asians.

If Asian Americans should emerge as a cultural force, it will be after recognizing honestly where they are right now—and fighting back on their own terms, not on somebody else's. Fire with fire.

DIVERSITY AND EXCLUSION

Ning Zhou had seen it all in Silicon Valley. He had experienced the flush power of startup culture in the Bay. He had worked for several big tech companies for which millions of smart Americans aspired to work: Intel. Amazon. Ning sported a PhD from MIT and thought it would carry him to the senior ranks of company leadership. His career certainly started off in a good place—he was courted straight out of MIT to work in a technical role at Amazon. There, he put years of productive work under his belt.

Ready to make the leap to management, Ning struggled to find a position commensurate with his experience and talent. One interview sticks out to him in particular.

"After MIT, after Amazon.com, I went back to Boston and was in the building [of] a company for a senior job," Ning said. "The interview went very well. They had me talk to some of the engineers that I would be managing. After the talk, the director called me in . . . I asked him how the interview went," Ning said.

"Good!" the director said. Then the director paused. "The only thing is I don't know how our employees would be able to work with you because they never had someone *like you* as their boss."

"They never had a non-white boss," Ning clarified. "I didn't get hired. I DON'T WANT TO GO THERE," Ning said, his voice raised.

But in the progressive epicenters of Silicon Valley, Ning said those prejudices against his leadership talent remained.

"One of our partners at Intel was investing 2.5 billion in Dalin, China, to build a chip plant," he explained. "They needed someone with China expertise to join the core management team. They recruited me out of MIT to a senior position at Intel. I heard the same kind of crap." Ning's voice grew louder. "They were saying, 'Well, these Chinese guys are very sound technically. But they just don't have the management know-how.' This is actually a Western story. I've heard this for so long."

Eventually, Ning got tired of corporate-speak and trying to fit in. He quit and started his own company, an alternative to online art education called Courseart. "We're trying to build a global art community online," he said. "Professionals, designers, engineers, and students."

His platform took off. "Currently part of my partners are Chinese. I can tell you these guys have incredible work ethic and they're very competitive," he said , then slyly added: "Right now I make twice as much as I did in Intel." An ever-so-slight nod to the slights he received in his decades in the world of Big Tech.

Ning was never a Republican of any kind. "I like Andrew Yang," he said. But he grew tired of Silicon Valley's liberal posturing, the millions spent on diversity and inclusion when it was clear that these educated, intelligent liberals seemed to possess the same racial sliminess as the people they deplored in middle America—just couched in language approved by McKinsey & Company.

"This is exactly the same story when Harvard rejects an Asian applicant. They evaluate Asian applicants based on personality score," Ning said.

It certainly feels like a familiar story, doesn't it?

Harvard's personality scores were never just about personality. They are about what happens after all these Harvard graduates leave the elite job incubator and take their executive banking and tech jobs in places like Silicon Valley. The stereotypes and racial preferences Harvard inculcates within their brains at such an impressionable age impact their political and even social points of view for the rest of their careers.

Because as it turns out, when stereotypes are legitimized—and when people simply get the notion that the views they hold about others are actually *moral* and even *virtuous*—then they don't disappear: They perpetuate. And Ning Zhou saw that perpetuation up close and personal.

"I believe this kind of mentality is why Silicon Valley firms fail so miserably in China. And, of course, the Chinese tech sector has proven itself to be very competitive. They've proven America wrong," Ning mused.

He believes that there is a deep undercurrent of resentment and suppression of Asian and Asian American achievement in Silicon Valley. He sees it in his own life. And in a way, he understands why this is the case.

"Anyone who goes into Intel [for senior management], the average time you last is 3 years. The reason is you don't grow up in Intel. If you're an outsider, you come in at a senior level, it can often be very hard. There are very few senior level positions, so don't expect anyone to give you any favors. Everyone is going to use *whatever resources they have to compete for any senior position* [emphasis added]."

And those resources include whatever weapons they can use against you. Racialized weapons. Stereotypes. Little bits of gossip. Anything to get you off their tail.

■ ■ ■

Silicon Valley runs on Asians. This is a banal fact of the tech world in general, but especially of its elite sector. In 2010, Asian Americans became a simple majority, 50.1 percent, of all tech workers in the Bay Area: software engineers, data engineers, programmers, systems analysts, admins, and developers.[1] In contrast, white tech workers made up 40.1 percent. Other races made up, in total, less than 10 percent.

Leon Zhan is a twenty-four-year-old Facebook product manager fresh out of the University of Virginia. He interacts daily with teams of software engineers at Facebook, coordinating and leading projects and getting them in line. Among the four teams of five or so software engineers he works with on a daily basis, Leon told me that *fifteen out of the twenty* are Chinese. "I don't mean Chinese American," he clarified. "I mean Chinese-Chinese, like from China." These Chinese people largely speak Mandarin as they romp on the Facebook keyboards, making the company billions writing lines of code with their machine-gun-like efficiency. Leon put it more bluntly: "We're at an American social media company surrounded by Chinese [speaking people]."

(In case you were wondering about the other five out of the twenty: they were Asian American. Leon said, "I think I might see one or two white software engineers here and there. Not a single Black or Hispanic [engineer].")

I will state again the Asian skew of Big Tech just to reinforce how weird this is when put in context. Where else in America, besides NBA basketball, maybe, are you going to find a field so insanely dominated by one minority race? And furthermore, just like basketball players are the core of the NBA business, software engineers are *the core* of Facebook. The company can survive without marketing managers or HR staff. At the least, we can all concede that marginal increases in a marketing manager's merit will lead to marginal increases in Facebook's profit—that are probably much, much less than the marginal increases in a tech lead's merit would be.

In short, Big Tech rises and falls with the quality of its technicians. And the technicians that Leon Zhan works with at Facebook are the world's best—and nearly all of them are Asian or Asian American.

At surface level, you could spin this as a triumph of diversity: Attracting truly the best of the world's talent, the American system welcomes people of different races to contribute to American business and American society. The narrative of Asians making a difference at a huge American company like Google or Facebook could be portrayed as a great feat, a show to the world's greatest talent of the American Dream at work.

Yet that is not what happens. In press briefs and company images, I am not treated to examinations and profiles in how talented a tech team—*the core of their skyrocketing profits and market dominance*—they have, how it represents both the company's and the country's highest aspirations.

Facebook's online Diversity portal, with their racial and gender break-down, features nine stories.[2] There are three people who appear to be Black and two who look distinctly Latino. Only one looks to be an East Asian person. His name is Henry B.

Little did Henry B. know that he would be the only East Asian person featured in any of the diversity stories, racially representing half of all Facebook technical employees. Every other employee's story has bright lighting, full smiles, and gushing reports of how much they cared about Facebook's diversity platform. Henry B. has the shortest of all the stories and a dimly lit photo of himself. You can't imagine he chose this path or this portrayal. Perhaps he just wanted to get the photo over with. But the camera always matters, and Henry B. did not realize what a dimly lit representation he would be presented as when he accepted Facebook's invitation to be "featured." He alone represented his entire pack of Asian engineers—the pack that kept the company running, that made *every-thing* work at Facebook.

Asian Americans have really become a sort of unfun topic in Silicon Valley corporate life. In fact, they embarrass the diversity-obsessed gurus at Google and Facebook.

One would think that diversity and inclusion, now the dominant cultural ideology in progressive epicenters like Big Tech, would benefit Asians. But as with that assumption about elite colleges, one would be wrong.

Asians are not considered "diverse" in the progressive tech world—despite unequivocally being a racial minority as only 6–8 percent of the total American population, and yet representing 40-some percent of the world's population by heritage. In fact, Asian Americans represent 41.8 percent of Google's workforce. Yet in Google's 2020 Annual Diversity Report, sponsored and written by Chief Diversity Officer Melonie Parker (yes, these are well-compensated, professional positions in modern cor-porate life, with average salaries close to $127,000 a year, according to Glassdoor), Asian Americans are barely mentioned.[3] Instead, the report comments on Google's "increase[d] representation for women globally, and for Black+ and Latinx+ employees in the US. We saw the largest increase in our hiring of Black+ technical employees that we have ever measured," Parker gushed. The report's focus is near exclusively on bringing more "Black+" and "Latinx+" people into Google . . . not to mention Parker never even defines what a "Black+" person is. In Melonie Parker's and Google's diversity wonderland, the terms are "Black plus" and probably "Asian minus."[4]

To be clear on who Google welcomes as part of its diversifying efforts, *Forbes* diversity writer Ruth Umoh wrote, "Google released its seventh consecutive diversity report on Thursday, revealing modest gains in representation for women and people of color, and a disproportionately white, Asian and male workforce."[5] Since when did Asian people occupy the same space as white people? Weren't many of them fleeing Communism with no money to get to America just fifty years ago? And now *Forbes* chooses to lump them *in* with white people, as if their historical experiences are at all similar?

Why is it that diversity-obsessed Google and its related media do not care about and even rail *against* the number of Asian Americans at its own company? It's as if Asian people—the people who keep Google and Facebook running; who allow their CEOs to gobble up extraordinary profits and make San Francisco the city with the third-most number of billionaires in the world—are embarrassing, secondary assets that should be kept in the dark, as far away from recognition as possible. In fact, they are the *primary assets* of these companies.

Contrast this with the treatment of the corresponding primary assets in the sports world, largely Black basketball players, who are pampered like royalty to play on the courts. Stephen Curry. LeBron James. Are these people hidden in the dark, nameless and status-less like Henry B.? No. They sign $40 million a year contracts and become the faces of their franchises. Good for them! They deserve every penny, given how much revenue they generate for their teams.

But now do the math for a Facebook software engineer, tech's elite of the elite. The NBA of tech! A Facebook software engineer's average starting salary is $150,000 a year. If you go to a more senior level, you can make maybe $500,000 a year. $150,000 may sound like a lot. Outside of San Francisco, it's probably equivalent to around $50,000 a year. And it's pennies compared to how much these people are worth. They should be making *millions*, because they are making their companies *billions*.

Don't believe me? Let's make the most conservative estimate we possibly can of how much a Facebook software engineer is worth. First, take Facebook's annual revenue in 2019: $70.7 billion dollars. Then take the number of employees at Facebook: about 20,000. The number of employees at Facebook who are engineers is about 1,000. Let's say, therefore, that they are collectively responsible for at least one-twentieth of Facebook revenue, near $3 billion dollars. (This is a ridiculously low estimate, but we're underestimating the revenue for which engineers are responsible for the sake of being conservative.) That means each software engineer is worth, at the very *least*, $3 million per year.

They make $150,000 to $500,000.

There are a couple reasons why Facebook and Google software engineers are so vastly ignored and underpaid—and each is directly related to race and national origin.

One: Asian software engineers are often imported from other countries— China, in particular—through the H1-B Visa application process. It mandates that to come to this country to work, you must be sponsored by an employer. The employer can revoke its sponsorship of you when it feels like it, and then you must get another job or leave the country. This means that companies like Facebook and Google have extreme leverage over the puny software engineer, and can therefore artificially depress their value; and not only their value, but the value of other people—Americans—who work in your field, simply by threatening your visa status in America. As long as Facebook and Google continue to import engineers the way they do, everyone in the software engineering department gets artificially screwed because the employer holds the cards to something much more important than money: your ability to live in America.

Two: Silicon Valley PR and business execs effectively exploit Asian stereotypes to limit their exposure and train Asian software engineers to view themselves as less valuable than they actually are. "The Asians are made for the backroom." "They aren't born leaders." Blah blah blah. Harvard's rhetoric.

There is a scene in *The Big Short*, a movie about how stockbrokers completely ignored the oncoming Great Recession, wherein actor Ryan Gosling, playing fund manager Jared Vennett, breaks the fourth wall to talk about stocks. To illustrate an example for viewers, he suddenly introduces an Asian financial analyst into the scene. "Look at him," he says. "That's my quant." (A quant is a slang term to describe a person primarily specialized in quantitative analysis, like a financial analyst.)

A greasy-haired Chinese-looking guy comes out with his shoulders hunched and a bewildered look on his face. "His name is Yang!" Ryan Gosling exclaims, as if to prove a point. "He doesn't even speak English!" "Yang" just sits there with a glazed look. And then, while the head honchos are talking, "Yang" does his own fourth-wall break. "Actually, my name is Jung, and I do speak English," he says privately, in perfect English, to the audience. "Jared likes to say I don't because he thinks it makes me look more authentic." It's hilarious. And a brief view of how elite liberal business execs basically view themselves in relation to Asian software engineers: as kings overseeing little worker rats, to be put down when they decide they want to have a voice.

Unfortunately, this strategy of keeping down Asian talent works. By the time these data guys realize their true value, when they maybe even get enough chutzpah to complain about it, they are fired or on their way out. A new naïve Asian tech guy comes in to replace them. The average tenure of a Google employee is 3.2 years—and that's on the high end. Google is not a place for Asian tech guys, the one who probably spend college trying to master their craft and get into Silicon Valley companies to build careers. It is a place where they are inevitably discarded.

I have saved the most sobering statistic for last: According to publicly available 2020 data from the company itself, Asians make up 44.5 percent of Facebook's total positions and 53.4 percent of what Facebook calls "technical roles." (Reminder: Technical roles include both the hardcore "software engineer" roles that are almost exclusively Asian and the softcore "data scientist" roles which have more white people.)

But Asians make up 25.4 percent of what Facebook calls "leadership" positions. That is a nearly 50 percent depression in terms of Asian employees who start in the company and move up to leadership roles.

No other race is as depressed between entry level roles and leadership as Asians are. Black people have 3.9 percent of all roles at 3.4 of leadership. Hispanic people have 6.3 percent of all roles and 4.3 of leadership. White people? Forty-one percent of all roles, and 63 percent of leadership.

Asian employees: 44.5 percent of all roles. 25.4 percent of leadership.

Think about this: When we measure whether a company has an *inclusive* climate, what are the statistics that we really should be measuring? The percentage of people of various races who come in and start working for the company? Or the percentage who actually advance, who become leaders and drive the company's focus and culture? The latter would surely be more revealing of how inclusive a culture really is. Presumably, more inclusive cultures would mean more people of different races see better paths to success.

If this statistic shows anything, it's that Facebook is not the dream work environment for technically-oriented Asians as is presupposed by the Asian people flocking to its campuses for dream jobs from which they don't progress. They either get fed up and leave, or they stay and work the same backroom job with some minor increases in salary, but no increases in prestige—or, for that matter, social respect.

I don't mean, of course, that none of the limited opportunity is due to Asians' own lack of ability to negotiate and break their own stereotypes. As we discussed earlier, Asian people come from different cultures—that's why they're called *Asians*. These cultures do not speak English as their primary language. Their attitudes are very different. Would a lack of English skills and cultural fluency impact one's ability to negotiate for top dollar? Well, would the lack of a mouth impact one's ability to eat?

Maybe that is the best explanation for the lack of Asian progress up the Facebook and Google ladder. But if culture and values are the ultimate explanation for that lack of progress, can we not also attribute culture and values to the lack of Black and Hispanic "representation" in these tech fields too? You see the bind that diversity and inclusion types have when seeking to advance the argument that Asian culture is primarily responsible for Asian Americans' inability to climb the corporate ladder. So they prefer to ignore them.

THE SPECTACULAR ASIAN BLASÉ ABOUT THE WHOLE THING

This absolute devaluation of Asian talent in Silicon Valley should set off a five-alarm fire in every Asian tech aspirant's head. It should lead every Asian American to question the diversity and inclusion machine—a machine that does not seem to genuinely care about them and their problems. Every Asian individual in America should feel compelled to demand their wages and their worth—or at least prompt a deep discussion about what Asian Americans in Big Tech need to do to demand their voice be heard in the hiring and promotion process. If every single Asian software engineer walked out of Google and Facebook right now, not only would the site crash but Google and Facebook—trillion-dollar companies—would never recover. CEOs basking in their gold bathtubs would go back to driving Ubers for a living. One Hacker Way, Facebook's namesake street, would become a wasteland. Mark Zuckerberg would be laughed off Half Moon Bay, a complete technological meltdown and business failure in his wake.

Indeed, Asians' true worth is so obvious that the only way Asian Americans would not recoil in horror at Google and Facebook's anti-Asian culture and exclusive diversity ideology is if the Asian tech engineers were somehow brainwashed to buy into their own inferiority.

Conversations with several Google and Facebook tech engineers reveal, unfortunately, that diversity and inclusion has done precisely that. Four to ten years at American universities followed by a couple years in Big Tech, the progressive epicenter of America (alongside Hollywood), wreak havoc on the Asian American mind.

A 2009 study by the Pan-Asian Collective in Silicon Valley revealed that in surveying Asian executives, most acknowledge that the problem of suppressed Asian success is real, but they are either too intimidated or too overworked to figure out how to handle it. "The Asian reaction has been, 'I know that I am one of the few Asian execs here, but I am too busy to try to change the system,'" the report concludes. "Because there appears to be a profusion of successful mid-level Asian managers in the professional workplace in these companies, the dearth of Asian executives is really a problem hidden in plain view."[6]

Perhaps the advent of diversity and inclusion and its subsequent corporate takeover lead Asian aspirants to feel like they have someone on their side. These Asian aspirants are wrong, but might be comforted nevertheless by the diversity industry.

I talked with Tian Yu, a Google Cloud engineer for three years, about Google's diversity and inclusion programs. Tian Yu moved from China to the United States in 2008, enrolling in Duke University's graduate school for electrical engineering, then switching to software engineering to have a better chance at getting a job. His entire life in the US, he worked in the corporate world—first at Bank of America until a switch to Google in 2018.

Tian has a soft heart. He loves America, believing (rightly so) that it is a land of opportunity. "I feel the kindness of this country. I feel very appreciative of the opportunity I was given," he said, with a soft innocence you don't see much anymore. I'm normally thankful for people of this attitude. They are not embittered, like so many native-born Americans are, by narratives of systemic oppression. Tian is exactly the opposite; like many immigrants, he is a romantic. You come to this country and you leave everything behind, because in some sense, you do love this country's ideals. You are a romantic, and you choose to believe.

But unchecked, soft hearts can be manipulated. They can be stretched to defend things that really shouldn't be defended.

For eleven years, Tian Yu lived his life hopping between enclaves—a graduate school program, Bank of America, and finally Google. As such, he was immersed in each of these institutions' diversity and inclusion ideologies from the moment he stepped foot on American shores. He was schooled in diversity apologetics, day in and day out. When I interviewed him, he gave stock answers that could have been appropriated straight from a McKinsey handbook to every question I asked.

What is the advantage of a diverse culture? "People coming from different backgrounds can share different ideas and people look at things differently."

How does diversity help a business? "The customer is diverse. Our staff has to be diverse to accommodate a diverse customer base."

What percentage of Google is Asian? "About 50 percent from what I've seen. In some places, it's lower. In some places like data or computer science, it's higher."

How much higher? Around what percent of software engineers are Asian? "I don't have a number off the top of my head."

Then I asked whether he, as an Asian employee at Google, *felt included in Google's diversity and inclusion practices.* Tian did not answer. Instead, he deflected to a more negative point about his Asian coworkers. "The Asians usually refer their Asian friends for the job. If in that case, the team will have more people coming from the same background. There should be a policy from top down saying we can't just have people from the same background."

This response struck me as odd. Asking Tian about whether as an Asian he felt included in Google's diversity ideology, he turned the blame around to Asians for their complicity against Google's diversity ideology.

It's that subtle turn, the nonanswer, that gets me. I believe Tian knows implicitly that Asians are not part of the diversity and inclusion ideology. In fact, they are subliminally told to blame themselves for Silicon Valley having too many of them. Do some Asians recommend their Asian friends to get hired at Facebook and Google? Sure—*just like every other ethnic group.* It is not the responsibility of the software engineers to self-police hiring habits. Rather, it's the responsibility of hiring managers to choose applicants meritocratically.

Do Black NBA players police front offices to make sure other races are represented on their basketball team? Do white estate owners police the country club to make sure enough nonwhites join? No. And yet Tian Yu worries about too many Chinese employees at Facebook.

Tian Yu's mind reflects a sort of shame in his Asianness that could only have been cultivated from years in diversity schooling. If a Google diversity officer tells a crowd of engineers that they want the engineering department to "look like America," and everyone in the room is Asian, it's no wonder that some of those 50.1 percent of tech workers in Silicon Valley might feel a little shame too. They shouldn't. If you really deserve to be there, you should be proud. But Tian Yu wishes for "racial balance." For fewer people who look like him.

■ ■ ■

Christina Qi is a serial entrepreneur, the founder of several data-related finance and tech firms that have propelled her to incredible success—and the cover of *Forbes* magazine—before the age of thirty. Christina's story is unique. After a horrible internship at a Wall Street firm ("They made us grab coffee for them, in five minutes, or you had to do pushups"), Christina eschewed the corporate finance world that her MIT education had prepped her to enter. Instead, she started her own company with two partners—out of her dorm room in her junior and senior years of college. "We weren't friends," she described them, although they eventually became friends. "We had almost nothing in common. One was a software engineer from Apple, another was a mathematician and physicist. He was more of a quant background. I was the finance person."

The three friends—Christina and two men, Luca Lin and Jonathan Wang—set off on their own to gain financial independence from the big-city firms. They designed a trading algorithm that specialized in high-frequency trading (yes, the kind of trading of *Flash Boys* fame). Their company, Domeyard, rocketed up the food chain with the help of a few angel investors, and Christina's three-person team found themselves in need of more talent. That's when Christina made one of her biggest mistakes.

"My two cofounders were Asian American, and I was Asian American, so we thought, 'Let's hire people who are much older with gray hair, who have a lot more experience.' So we tried to hire people with that kind of background who kind of looked like Warren Buffett," Christina said. "It flopped, our strategies weren't working, it was really terrible, and we had to go back and evaluate—like, what's going on in here?"

According to the same justifications that diversity and inclusion devotees would have you believe, Christina thought she needed more "diversity" of background, age, race, which in her case meant hiring more old white people who had "experience." She was, in other words, hiring on background for the sake of hiring on background.

That didn't work. "I realized they were stuck on their old ways," Christina said. The old guys refused to budge on their lifetime strategies, and her company was bleeding money. The hires said to her, "[This strategy] made $100 million dollars in 2008." But "five years later, it's not going to work," Christina said. So she pivoted, firing the Warren Buffett lookalikes and hiring young guns who understood the game-breaking nature of what Domeyard was trying to do. They had fresh perspectives that represented innovation, not staleness. And that's when things started working for Christina.

It makes sense: Surrounding yourself with different people of all kinds of skillsets is pretty helpful. But different backgrounds don't necessarily correlate to race. Christina and her two partners were very different; one was skilled in math, the other in computer science, and she in finance. But looking at the team of founders on a bulletin, one might say, "Wow, they're just a bunch of Asians." Yes. They're a bunch of Asians. But they are so much more than that.

Christina Qi was uniquely suited to understand how odious hiring on the basis of background and "looks" could be—especially when that framework focused on things like race, age, and gender. I asked her what she thought about the fact that 45 percent of Facebook technical employees were Asian but only 25 percent of leaders were. Christina paused. When she spoke next, her normally excitable voice meandered. "Oh, yeah, at a certain point, that's not a coincidence," she said. "There's a lot of, uh, factors, at play that impact all of us as a whole."

It was unclear whether Christina thought Big Tech's exclusionary diversity and inclusion policies were contributing to those factors, so I asked her directly: "What do you think about the state of diversity and inclusion?"

Here Christina began to gush. "[The] Black Lives Matter movement came around, and first off, the Black and African American community has done so much for Asians, you never even realize. Because of *Black Panther*, you have [the Marvel movie] *Shang-Chi and the Seven Rings*, and all that . . . you have [venture capital firm] Andreesen-Horowitz, you have Sequoia donating to racial justice."

Christina spoke glowingly of the diversity and inclusion industry, but only for certain underrepresented groups, like Black and Hispanic people. I wanted to push her on where she saw *her own race* on this issue. "Do you think Asian Americans are a full part of this diversity and inclusion effort?" I asked.

Here Christina paused. "Tech companies get a huge proportion of Asian applicants . . . Asia is such a diverse group of folks. Affirmative action would hurt them even more."

I asked her about Google's diversity and inclusion policy that gives a plus to Black employees but not to Asians.

"We shouldn't compare the racial narratives of different groups. Yeah, there's a lot of Asians who apply to Google, and that's fine, that's great. [But many] never go anywhere for promotion . . . We should care about underrepresented minorities. Doesn't mean we should ignore the Asian American narrative. That Harvard lawsuit . . . there's a lot there. You can't compare the trauma of one group to another."

Christina's knee-jerk response when asked about diversity and inclusion was to discuss Black Lives Matter and racial justice, not to talk about herself as an Asian person. But when she was pressed, and began to open up, Christina began to acknowledge contradictions in diversity and inclusion ideology.

And yes, there are difficult narratives with which each racial group must contend. But that doesn't mean that a company like Google or Facebook has the right to judge between narratives. To *prefer* one narrative to another.

Yet it is an implicit reality, even to those who've bought into diversity and inclusion like Christina, that in practice, Asians are ancillary pieces of the diversity equation. D&I supporters, either as a matter of principle or simply to signal its benefits, simply downplay the Asian angle or focus their advocacy on attacking white people. Diversity and inclusion is about increasing the percentage of minorities in elite corporate life— specifically, increasing the percentage of Black and Hispanic minorities. Racial preferences of the Harvard variety. Nothing new here.

DIVERSITY AND INCLUSION: AFFIRMATIVE ACTION GOES TO WORK

The diversity business is one of the fastest growing in the nation. As Diversity, Equity and Inclusion (D.E.I.) becomes part of corporate life's standard protocol of, those who position themselves as leading experts on systematic oppression reap windfalls, UC-San Diego's head of Diversity and Inclusion makes $250,000 a year.[7] D.E.I. job postings on Indeed went up 25 percent between 2018 and 2019. It is a skyrocketing industry making a few of its adherents rich. Therefore, it's an industry that some people have a vested interest in working to prop it up.

It seems odd—sinister, even—that a word like "diversity" (the principle that nigh every American, aside from a few far-right nuts, believes is a strength of our country) is immediately used to specifically justify *racial* and *gender-based* policymaking. After all, isn't it innate to the word "diversity" that it is has many forms, not limited to race or gender, narrow categories that reflect political alignments more than anything else? Diversity of intellect, talent, personality, value system, perspective . . . many of these categories seem more relevant from a hiring, "what do you bring to the table" perspective than race, or, to a lesser extent, gender.

So how did the business intelligentsia settle on diversity of race as the predominant form of diversity to be measured and enacted in the first place?

Let's start the story where it begins: the '60s.

In 1964, Congress passed the Civil Rights Act, formalizing a new era of race relations in America. Middle schoolers learn about the Civil Rights Act as the first piece of legislation that totally banned racial discrimination in all sectors of American society. But reality was, the Civil Rights Act's wording and execution was a much larger project—leaving it open to exploitation, primarily from the government. The Civil Rights Act achieved a number of great things, like banning segregation in public facilities, schools, and businesses. It also became the gateway to all sorts of expansive visions of how race should be applied in daily American life that went far beyond the text of the law. Some of those visions were entrenched under liberal governance. Particularly that of President Lyndon B. Johnson, successor to President John F. Kennedy.

When Johnson signed Title VII of the Civil Rights Law, which laid out guidelines for nondiscrimination against people due to their race or sex (and sexual orientation or gender identity, with the 2020 *Bostock v. Clayton County* decision), he set out to do more than ban discrimination from public facilities and businesses. LBJ wanted to utilize Civil Rights Law for his own special purposes.

President Johnson did this by taking advantage of the political capital afforded him by his predecessor, John F. Kennedy. In 1961, while Johnson was vice president, President Kennedy appointed Johnson to lead the President's Committee on Equal Employment Opportunity, tasked with developing an approach to ensuring companies would not discriminate on the basis of race in hiring. When he stepped into the office of the presidency after Kennedy's death, Johnson saw an opportunity to institutionalize the work he did on the former president's committee into American government. He created a new bureaucratic agency in the same vision of his former post, but now of a permanent nature—the Equal Employment Opportunity Commission (EEOC).

Crucially, Johnson didn't want the EEOC to just be a sounding board for discrimination complaints. He wanted it to pressure companies into setting racial targets for employment. First, he ordered the EEOC to require large companies to submit race and ethnicity data on its hires to ensure compliance with racial goals for hiring Black and Hispanic employees. Noticeably not considered—and for understandable reasons, due to their miniscule percentage of the population at the time—were Asians.

If the numbers were unsatisfactory in the eyes of the EEOC, compliance officers could knock down a company's doors and conduct an audit, checking all the hiring records to make sure that management met the requisite quota of Black and Hispanic hires recommended by EEOC guidance. Although the EEOC could not press criminal charges, civil penalties for noncompliance were often severe enough that companies' hiring practices met the EEOC's affirmative action guidelines just for fear of its officers' wrath—even if that meant sacrificing a more meritorious candidate.

The EEOC created many rules, including the 80 percent rule. Corporations had to hire at least 80 percent of each racial group's national labor force proportion to avoid being targeted for an audit. So if Black people compose 10 percent of the current national labor force, a company must hire at least 8 percent Black employees to avoid an audit. It is where we get the modern-day rhetoric about company workforces needing to reflect the demographics of the national labor force.

Yet rules like this added to company pain, and many struggled to keep up with the regulations. Many companies grew fearful of legal crackdowns for alleged discriminatory practices. To further counter-act potential action against them, many big companies hired their own EEOC/AA (AA being "affirmative action") compliance consultants to weather potential lawsuits for discrimination in hiring or promotion.[8] Those administrative officers became an embedded part of company culture, encouraging the development of specific goals in the hiring of women, Black, and Hispanic employees. By 1976, more than 70 percent of employers reported employment plans that included such hiring goals.

Then, in the 1980s, the Reagan administration cut the regulatory power of executive agencies—the EEOC included. EEOC/AA officers, originally placed to help companies conform to existing EEOC enforce-ment, faced a sudden crisis. If the companies they worked for were no longer heavily pressured to comply with affirmative action, why would they need their compliance officers? *Gulp.* Job rationales for compliance officers were in danger.

But if there is one thing government officials are good at, it is perpet-uating themselves. And they did so in the most ingenious way.

Race preferences were instituted as a matter of giving underrepre-sented communities—that is, Black and Hispanic communities—a leg up. But as the rationale for affirmative action started to fade, the EEOC/AA officers and related industry members came up with an ingenious way to not only justify their positions but to expand their reach. They called it *diversity*, and they made an argument outlandish for its time: Diversity would *help* the company bottom line.

The first arguments for diversity were in the *Regents of California v. Bakke* case and were reserved for college admissions. But compliance managers plucked those arguments directly from the Supreme Court decision and simply repackaged them for the corporate world.

In the *American Behavioral Scientist* article, "How Affirmative Action Became Diversity Management," Princeton University researchers Erin Kelly and Frank Dobbin chronicle how EEOC officers in the 1980s quickly adjusted to the times with a completely new tactic: switching from *compliance* to *efficiency*. Kelly and Dobbin wrote:

> "EEO and AA offices and activities survived [during the Reagan administration], we argue, because EEO/AA specialists did not respond passively to Reagan's cutbacks in enforcement. At first, they touted the efficiency of formalizing human resources management through such antidiscrimination measures as grievance procedures, formal hiring and promotion system, and systematic recruitment schemes. Later, they invented the discipline of **diversity management** [emphasis added], arguing that the capacity to manage a diverse workforce well would be the key to business success in the future."[9]

In short, Equal Employment Commission Officers reformulated their purpose by inventing a new rationale for their existence—creating "diversity." They commissioned studies that attempted to show the value-add diversity brings. Most fundamentally, they sought to create a company environment in which diversity became an overarching *moral* requirement. Diversity sounds good, doesn't it? Let's make it an imperative. By merging their own jobs with the diversity movement, they could survive the regulatory rollback and keep their positions.

Here was the other trick: EEO had to specifically align diversity with *large, profitable* companies to achieve the prestige that granted legitimacy. First they aligned with management consulting operations, which advised big corporations on business practices. Then they went for large, technologically oriented companies like the Digital Equipment Corporation (a big get in the '90s). Soon other companies joined in: Avon, Corning, Digital, Honeywell, Highest, Merck, Procter & Gamble, and Xerox. By the early 1990s, diversity initiatives had been adopted by 70 percent of Fortune 500 companies. Once settled into these big companies, they adopted all the standard proto-D&I business practices—putting on conferences, publishing articles and briefs in business journals, and hosting training seminars that predated today's industry of diversity consultancy. In short, diversity managers survived the curbing of formal affirmative action practices by becoming corporate animals: aligning diversity ideals with the cultural practices of big business.

The modern zeal you see for "diverse" workplaces and businesses is a product of nearly forty years of grandstanding, an ideology that clawed its way out of deregulation by completely wedding itself to corporatism and managerialism. The consequence is that diversity has become a corporate luxury term—that is, a way for corporations to show off their status and progressive bona fides without having to compromise their status quo to any meaningful degree.

Diversity is a bureaucratic ideology—invented by bureaucrats to secure their bureaucratic positions—that has secured its future by becoming an expensive moral ideology. For companies that can afford it, investing in the diversity bureaucracy helps from a PR perspective, potentially allowing the Left to go pick on some other corporation while leaving yours alone. But let's be clear: Diversity ideology did not form because scientists went out and statistically tested the performance of diverse versus nondiverse companies and concluded that diverse companies were better suited for profit and growth (and virtue, clearly). The diversity ideology came first. The studies and economic cases and showboating came with the goal of perpetuating it.

ASIANS PROP UP THE DIVERSITY CASE

The diversity industry was never built around the status of Asian Americans, or any minority that didn't happen to be "underrepresented," for that matter. But that is not to say the industry didn't eventually find a use for Asians . . . for themselves.

Highly educated and skilled Asian immigrants began coming to the United States in earnest in the late '80s and '90s—which happened to line up with the time that affirmative action compliance managers started embracing the diversity ideology in earnest. How convenient for them. To agenda-driven diversity managers, highly educated Asian immigration was a goldmine of great data.

Why? Because defining Asian immigrants, who follow meritocracy and tend to add high levels of value to whatever companies they join, as a "minority" would make it much easier to build an economic case for "more minorities" in high levels. Asians could be used to greatly inflate D&I ideology's economic case that they could sell to corporate executives: "Boss, look at how much *Diversity and Inclusion* is helping your corporate profits!" But in fact, it isn't the diversity and inclusion practices that help the company, but the inflow of highly skilled immigrants who happen to be of a minority race.

One of the most prominent examples of this intellectual gaslighting is a 2015 McKinsey study, "Why Diversity Matters," that states that businesses in the first quartile of ethnic diversity in senior leadership are 35 percent more likely to financially outperform businesses in the fourth quarter of ethnic diversity.[10] But does this justify the whole diversity and inclusion industry's economic case? It may be true indeed, for example, that companies who utilize diversity and inclusion programs tend to be more profitable. But it may also be true that companies who are more *profitable* tend to simply be more racially diverse for reasons with no link whatsoever to the kinds of diversity and inclusion programs that consultants often justify with these studies.

I took a look at public diversity data from 2015–6, the year after McKinsey published its study, from Fortune 500 companies to compare their senior leadership breakdowns to statistics cited in the McKinsey report. In order to have diversity data published, a company fills out a form with the EEOC called Form EEO-1.

Most companies were reluctant to share their diversity data. According to *Fortune*, 3 percent of Fortune 500 companies did so in full in 2015 and 2016. That is seventeen firms.[11] Thirty-four more Fortune 500 firms pledged to release their diversity data in Spring 2021, not yet available at the time of this writing.[12]

These seventeen firms are top of the line organizations—Apple, Google, Costco. White people were a vast majority of their senior leadership. But in second place were Asian people—in *all seventeen of these firms*. And with only the most miniscule representation were Black and Hispanic people.

What this data conveys, then (if McKinsey's profitability statistics are to be believed), is not that "diversity" helps companies' business performance—it's that more Asians do.

I don't relish stating these facts. I wish there were more Black and Hispanic people in senior management. Out of all the arguments for them having greater representation in any field, this economic case is more sympathetic than others; the percentage of senior leaders who are of these races is just ridiculously small.

However, I keep going back to what Ning Zhou told me about his time in Silicon Valley: "Everyone is going to use *whatever resources they have to compete for any senior position.*" To get to the senior level—and to maintain your position—takes a combination of raw skill, political maneuvering, and a tenacity that most others simply don't have. You must be prepared for a brawl for those limited senior spots. And expect no favors. No one will give up their seat for you just because you are any kind of minority.

I see the economic case for Black and Hispanic representation as a mirror image of what happened with Asians in media. The dearth of Asian Americans in TV, movies, and popular culture is influenced by anti-Asian stereotypes, yes—but at the same time, Asians were never able to build the kind of cultural talent that would engender a substantial number of A-listers. Getting more "representation" onscreen through affirmative action may ostensibly help in the narrowest sense by driving Asian talent towards the elite mainstream rather than the underground, but it may also unwittingly restrict the flourishing undercurrent of Asian talent that could change America. Remember, it was from the underground that rap and hip-hop, born from African American culture in Harlem and suppressed from the mainstream for years, completely changed the landscape of American culture and the world.

Which brings us to another reality: Black and Hispanic communities have faced many obstacles and challenges to build business success in America, and affirmative action may be hurting them by driving rising talent into bloodsucking corporate cultures rather than into entrepreneurship.

Black and Hispanic communities also failed to catch onto the technological revolution that brought prosperity to those who caught on early—disproportionately Asians, who cultivated computer skills. As Malcolm Gladwell describes in his book *Outliers*, "what truly distinguishes [successful people] is not their extraordinary talent but their extraordinary opportunities." And Asian people with better training in math and science happened to be better positioned during the computer revolution, which allowed them to capitalize on the flush of wealth it produced for those positioned to reap it. You could say they were the most merited for the job at the time. This does not mean Asians and Asian Americans were better than Black or Hispanic Americans. But it does mean they were better situated for the technological tasks at hand during the time of the great computer and Internet boom.

WHAT ASIANS STAND TO LOSE

Asians are in a unique position of having the meritocratic spirit pushing them to advance flattened by diversity ideology, which is then propped up by the economic case for its use, through the example of Asian success. They face the diversity double standard.

But this also puts Asians in a position to use this experience to speak out for truth—truth so politically incorrect to articulate, most would lose their careers over it. But to allow diversity ideology to fester within a company is to ask for its eventual death, and in due course, the death of the country.

Diversity and inclusion types get one thing right: Company hierarchies are often clubby. People hire among their friends and social networks before they hire a stranger. Longstanding and largely white "social networks" and "country clubs" act as the corporate equivalent of legacy admissions, rewarding the privileged few over the wannabes. If business hierarchy reform is justified, it's likely in terms of more merit-based promoting and hiring rather than through connections and buddy systems.

Merit happens to be the most prized value at any well-run business. Yet diversity and inclusion was normalized based on shoddy consultancy frameworks, which provide limited evidence that the presence of more minorities in leadership would boost profits alone.

But over the past ten years, D&I has wormed its way into nearly every major Big Tech corporate center in the country. Without serious opposition, it will run roughshod over merit.

We know intuitively that this is wrong. *Asian immigrants* would have never been hired into these companies—often needing sponsorship and lacking critical language skills—except for their merit. If merit is racist, why would a company extend themselves so far to hire from a completely different culture, enduring all of these hurdles?

When admissions and hiring is meritocratic with clear guidelines, Asians tend to benefit. This is because Asian American communities in the United States typically focus on skills building, on generating value that is difficult to reproduce without the strong work ethic and educational background emphasized by Asian culture.

Diversity and inclusion, on the other hand, is anti-meritocratic: It specifically emphasizes the hiring of *less qualified* candidates for the sake of racial inclusion or political tradeoff. In the past, that tradeoff was affirmative action compliance; now, it is based on shoddy economic cases like McKinsey's report. However, the political winds give diversity and inclusion advocates an advantage, allowing them maximum leverage with which to put forth their demands. Asians in business, who tend to emphasize low-supply, high-demand skills-building as opposed to vocality and political alignment/leverage-building, will lose out in the diversity and inclusion ideology if it is allowed to continually gain power and influence.

Indeed, everyone should be concerned as diversity and inclusion worms its way further into the corporate bedrock—but no one has more of a fundamental reason to be frightened than Asian Americans.

The problem for Asians, however, is that they rely *so much* on their meritocratic ethos—their skills and talent—that the D&I storm will affect them disproportionately and in severe ways compared to every other cultural group.

Asian Americans don't have the country club networks that privileged white people have as enclaves to weather diversity and inclusion. They don't have the victim capital that ambitious Black and Hispanic people can use to demand representation as a matter of morality (or political leverage). And when the percentage of *total* American labor force is used as a benchmark for diversity and inclusion ideologues who demand reform at a senior level, as it was in McKinsey's study and in the EEOC's reasoning, Asians Americans are often *extremely* overrepresented in the firms in which they congregate—meaning that they will be targeted in the great diversity culling. Take a look at the Bureau of Labor Statistics' table on the racial composition of the national labor force:

Bureau of Labor Statistics 2018 total labor force composition by race/ethnicity:[13]

White Non-Hispanic:	63 percent
Hispanic, any race:	17 percent
Black:	12 percent
Asian:	6 percent

Six percent! That is the acceptable percentage of Asians in senior management according to the McKinsey study, which demands representation in the US labor force according to population make-up, and others like it.

In many of these companies, Asian representation in senior management has already far exceeded the composition of Asians in the labor force—despite that as a percentage of *total Big Tech employees*, Asian leadership is significantly underrepresented, potentially even suppressed. But according to the very simplistic measure of total American labor force composition, they are "overrepresented." Never mind the 50 percent penalty at Facebook between Asian talent and Asian leadership. By the D&I industry's measure of racial acceptability, the percentage of Asians in senior management at Facebook is already unacceptable—and needs to be balanced further.

Chilling.

WHAT COMPANY HIRING SHOULD REALLY BE ABOUT

Back when Google was a garage startup just trying to stay afloat, their first twenty-one employees were 70 percent men, and every single one white or Asian.[14] This is not to make any statement on the worth of competent underrepresented minorities in tech. This is simply to say: Diversity was not one of Google's concerns back then. Hiring the best employees, regardless of who they were on the race and gender spectrum, was.

And we're lucky that Google didn't worry about things like that early on. Its team of ragtag engineers—domineering, absolutely visionary brains—created what is still the world's best search product, giving billions of people access to untold riches of knowledge they would never have attained before. Then they mapped a good portion of the world and posted it publicly so people could reach any destination at the touch of a button. Yes, they made your life better. (Or worse. But they affected your life.) And it would not have happened if they didn't have the engineering world's cream of the crop, a synthesis of great minds. It would have been an absolute loss to interrupt with bromides about diversity and inclusion.

Truth is, Google didn't need diversity then. Google needed the best—period. So why does Google need it now?

Now Google is a behemoth, to the point where even its founders, Larry Page and Sergey Brin, could not handle the incoming questions about its organizational monopoly. The *New York Times* describes their 2019 exit from the helm of the company: The issues facing it "are not merely technical problems or scientific problems." The problems "are very much corporate lawyerly types of policy issues, for which historically they have not been enthusiastic."[15] As current CEO Sundar Pichai put it, "technology doesn't solve humanity's problems."[16] And while some might applaud Pichai's zinger, many are concerned. Why should we trust a tech company to solve humanity's problems? Why would a CEO lay out a company's mission like this? Google doesn't exist to "solve humanity's problems," nor should it. Google exists to solve certain, specific problems. The paucity of online search engines, for starters. Maybe the problem of smartphones or computers or GPS systems. But not the problems of "humanity," religion, law, race, or politics.

Today Google genuinely views itself, like Harvard and Yale, as a purveyor of morality and status to the world. This is distressing to hear—and reminiscent of the cosmic arrogance that permeates the halls of Harvard and Yale.

That cosmic arrogance is why Big Tech's attempted solutions to the real problems of racial strife in America are so ineffectively milquetoast. At the deepest level, Google understands that it *can't* solve these problems of race and diversity in America without compromising the core purpose of its mission. No matter how many bones it throws at grasping underrepresented minority hands, no white executive is ever going to step down to let a Black woman or a Hispanic man take his place. Why? Because he believes he deserves to be there. And so he is.

■　■　■

In the late '80s, when everyone else at UC-Berkeley's Business School was hobnobbing their way into Wall Street firms, Peter Wachtell read a math finance book, *The Binomial Options Theory*, and promptly made $108,000 selling stock options from the lessons he learned. "Options were pretty new," Peter said. "Most traders were old-style traders. I was one of the only guys who were more quant in nature."

When Peter was twenty-two, he set out on his own as a businessman. "I began to bid on the dregs that on one else wanted. A savings bank in San Diego. We would buy the stuff at a discount. We securitized streams of cash loads . . . I was young and had nothing to lose." Year after year, Peter bet and mostly lost —but when he won, he won big. Soon, Peter became a multimillionaire.

Where others would follow fads and trends, Peter followed the data. He applied his contrarian philosophy to everything in his life—including his hiring. Peter specialized in finding talent that nobody else saw. "[My business] created the land of misfit toys," he said. "These were all people who were smarter than their bosses at Capital One. They would listen to the directions and think three steps ahead. When they presented their projects, they should have gotten recognition and a promotion. Instead, they got reprimanded for not following directions."

In many ways, Peter pounced on the hiring disparities between what was *perceived* to be valuable and what was *actually* valuable—and oftentimes, those failures in perception took racial overtones. "A lot of these people [overlooked by their employers] were non-US, were Asian; some were adjacent to the autistic spectrum, but were very capable," he said. "An autistic guy doesn't look you in the eye." But he can sure as hell figure out market inefficiencies.

In many ways we should not overlook his use of the term "Asian" to describe the people he has hired who were traditionally overlooked. Asian people *do* tend to be overlooked in the business world, especially in Big Tech promotional environments. Their lack of cultural capital in America absolutely affects them in a negative way. But Peter's nontraditional approach to finding talent also accomplishes a nobler goal: reducing the impact of personal and racial bias in hiring and decisionmaking by giving people overlooked for reasons other than merit the opportunity to find professional homes elsewhere.

In other words, the free market, combined with the culture of entrepreneurship that fuels free-market values, smooths out racial inefficiencies in labor markets. And people who built skills in different backgrounds and talents in different areas aren't overlooked solely because they lack a certain personality, or—god forbid—conformity to a certain race or ideology.

Good business leaders implicitly understand that diversity that matters represents far more than race. Race isn't even the tip of the iceberg— it's the storm current that distracts, that *pulls you away* from the real iceberg.

This is the society we want: one where people are rewarded according to their merit, disregarding their ancillary characteristics. It is the direction that our biggest tech competitor, China, is moving towards while our culture of excellence drifts away. Which direction will fuel a national advantage in ten years?

Austrian economist Friedrich Hayek believed unplanned spontaneous order would allow for the greatest proliferation of diversity because everyone would be free to utilize their diverse talents in the ways they wished. There is a "division of knowledge" in society, Hayek argued, and the greatest way to allow diverse knowledge to flourish is freeing people to pursue their own ends instead of trying to chart the course of their paths or artificially interrupt the unplanned shuffling of their talents. He wrote: "The value of freedom consists mainly in the opportunity it provides for the growth of the undesigned."[17]

Catholic tradition, especially under twentieth-century Pope Pius XII, stresses the organic nature of human development in all its diverse realms and how that diversity must necessarily be "the unplanned, natural character of formations."

Hayek and Catholic thinkers saw diversity as a *natural outgrowth* of policies of openness and subsidiarity—the process of letting people and small communities make their own choices about what is best for them.

When that process abounds, it is absolutely certain that some communities will gravitate to particular areas than other communities will gravitate to. What is most important about this process is that we must, in the openness of our spirit, *allow* it to happen. We must not try—even with the best intentions—to interrupt people making their own choices on their paths to success. In doing so, we prevent people from enjoying the fruits of their own choices. True openness requires a humility of spirit. It requires accepting that humankind's diversity means the priorities of others may not immediately seem as valuable as the priorities *we're* pursuing. This is true diversity, deeper than the surface level—one that is rich because it represents the whole of not only one's background but the choices one makes in light of that background.

This is the kind of diversity I would imagine is envisioned by the majority of Americans. A blend of cultures, all choosing to go on their own paths, all finding something to contribute to society. All finding success and pride in their own contributions, and most importantly, all *tolerating* the paths that others take so long as that path is orderly.

Diversity and inclusion, on the other hand, propagates a version of diversity that does *not* mean what is envisioned in the eyes of most Americans. Diversity and inclusion puts people who do not choose the same path as others artificially put on that same path in order to make it more representative of the population. That is not open and inclusive. That is enforced sameness.

America *is* diverse—in all respects, racially and otherwise. The trick is to learn how to appreciate not only the diversity of background that people bring, but also how one's background informs one's choices; and to allow people the freedom to choose branches that diverge from their backgrounds. This would mean not arbitrarily assuming a narrative based on one's background. Not thinking, all high and mighty, that you have all the answers because of how someone first appears to you. That is not diversity—that is conformity.

SHUT UP ABOUT THE TEST

THE AMERICAN DREAMS OF THE NEW YORK CITY CHINESE

Tatsu Ramen, tucked away in a crevice on New York City's 1st Avenue, serves the meatiest ramen soup in East Village. It is where Charles Jin, class of 2008 Stuyvesant High School graduate, went every month to get his noodle soup fix.

I met Charles at Tatsu Ramen, where we ate outside on an angled sidewalk turned into outdoor dining to protect from the coronavirus. He is a skinny, pasty Asian guy with a mop of jet-black hair and wire-framed glasses. Charles talks reedily, as if through a straw—not exactly the stereotypical bark of a New York native. But he is a local. Charles never knew a city other than New York: "I emigrated from China to the United States as a young child."

After an early childhood education in the Big Apple, Charles went to Stuyvesant High School, then Baruch College (a City College of New York). Two years in, he transferred to New York University to pursue music. Instead, he graduated with a computer science degree, found shelter in New York's tech scene, and bunked as a software engineer for a New York City health services company where he presently works.

Charles sees his opportunities not simply through the lens of America. He sees them through the lens of New York City. This is the only city he has ever known. This is his world.

Charles grew up with an ambitious father who nevertheless could never get it together. Although his father was able to obtain an American business degree, his career in finance "didn't work out." He settled for IT. But this wasn't the typical middle-class family contented with average. This was a family with an education and an aspiration to be better than what their place on the socioeconomic ladder dictated. How to be better? To study.

So Charles studied. For the big day—the Specialized High School entrance exam. He scored among the top two hundred and got into Stuyvesant High School, the most famous and highly reputed high school in New York City.

Wait. Let's back up a moment.

Charles scored among the top two hundred scores on a single exam . . . and got in? That's it? No arcane interview process? No mysterious, "holistic" admissions policy determining "character" and "fitness" for an elite school? What an outrage to the chattering class!

"I've heard those criticisms," Charles said. "I heard Upper East Side 'progressives' say we were gaming the system, that our success on the test was because we were 'coached' rather as a result from years of rigorous studying long before we actually took the test."

Granted, Charles could have applied for one of those New York screened schools that take more factors in consideration—teacher recommendations, extracurriculars, "personality." There were plenty of those prestigious schools in New York City, like Beacon and Millennium High School, that go for more traditional factors for admission. But there was a reason why he went for the Specialized High Schools—and it had nothing to do with their prestige.

"We liked the Specialized High Schools because we knew they didn't discriminate against Asians. How could they? Admissions is solely based on one objective, race-blind test."

One test to get in. A remarkable admissions process in a sea of "holistic" judgments of fitness. That test, the Specialized High School

Admissions Test (or SHSAT), solely determines entry into New York City's eight "Specialized High Schools," of which Stuyvesant is the top.

In 2018, Asians made up 73 percent of Stuyvesant High School's student body.[1] In New York City, 62 percent of Asian American middle schoolers at the top end of the seventh grade English and math exam distribution enroll at a Specialized High School like Stuyvesant, Bronx Science High School (64 percent), or Brooklyn Tech High School (61 percent). This is the highest among all ethnic groups—even when controlled for academic performance. For example, only 20 percent of Hispanic middle schoolers who scored in the same top range as the Asian middle schoolers ended up at a Specialized High School.[2] So indeed, academics alone weren't the only influence in these Asian students' decisions to choose the Specialized Schools, or vice versa—the decisions of the Specialized Schools to choose these Asian students.

But still, I pressed him. "Surely, you didn't put at least some aspect of prestige on your radar? Maybe getting into Ivy League colleges?"

"Most of the kids who got into schools like Stuyvesant and Bronx Science end up attending New York state colleges or city colleges," Charles replied. "And besides, Harvard has a quota for Specialized High School kids anyways. Every year, roughly twenty kids from Stuy get into Harvard. And it's nearly always roughly ten whites, ten Asians, with a handful of other minority students."

This is true. In an article on the Specialized High Schools, Wesley Yang describes how a Stuyvesant assistant principal, Casey Pedrick, broke down emotionally when asked to describe why this distorted ratio of admissions persists at Stuy. "Because these numbers make it seem like there's discrimination," she said through tears, "and I love these kids, and I know how hard they work. So these just look like numbers to all you guys, but I see their faces."

"You should check out that article," Charles told me.

To many, these world-renowned schools represent distasteful things. The Specialized High Schools are often seen as representative of the horrifying competition culture from which upper-middle-class liberals shirk. They are seen as exclusive outlets that systematically exclude Black and Hispanic students—a claim sparked by the idea that the test for entry itself, the single goalpost that makes or breaks admissions onto these campuses, is racist. To people of differing viewpoints, these Specialized Schools may represent such things. But to Charles Jin, New York City's eight Specialized High Schools represent something different.

"They are the last form of pure meritocracy in the United States," Charles stated with a bold sense of finality, a confidence resembling that of a pure New Yorker.

■ ■ ■

To a largely poor Chinatown population lacking wealth or connections, New York City's Specialized Schools are exceptional opportunities for kids of shopkeepers and restaurant managers to receive a quality education that enables them to attend a good college and become successful. In the 2012–3 academic year, 46.8 percent of people accepted to these Specialized Schools were on free or reduced lunch. These were not rich kids. These were the sons and daughters of aspirational parents who banked on education to help give their kids a better life.

Yiatin Chu is a mother and first-generation immigrant from China. Her own mother and father arrived in the United States with her when she was just eight, during the first wave of mid-twentieth-century Asian immigration: in the early '60s to '70s, after an amendment to the Immigration and Nationality Act allowed more access to Asian immigrants. Yiatin's parents were educated in Taiwan; her mother was a teacher. But when they came to America, they started over. "They had no language skills," Yiatin explained. "Everything had to be built up again."

A typical day in Yiatin's crowded Manhattan apartment was full of manual labor. "We'd be stringing beaded necklaces for five cents apiece," she said. "We would make batches . . . you would get a batch and have all the beads and the owner of the factory would bring that home."

Yiatin's mother had high aspirations for her daughters, rooted in her own aspirations to better herself in society. "My mom started off in a sweatshop," she said, "but ended up in an office job." Eventually they were able to move to the suburbs. Yiatin's mom—despite her broken English—placed a strong emphasis on education in her family, and Yiatin eventually attended the Bronx High School of Science (Bronx Science), a Specialized High School. Despite facing racism for her lack of initial language skills upon entry into America, Yiatin studied, with the encouragement of her mother, and got into Bronx Science—today still one of the "Top 3" Specialized Schools in New York City.

Yiatin has daughters now. She thinks about the opportunities she is able to open up to them because she speaks English fluently, because she is well integrated in the New York City social milieu. One of her daughters got into the Anderson School, a local gifted and talented middle school program. Another daughter was eligible for Anderson based on scores, but did not get in. Yiatin didn't despair, but she empathized with the impoverished families that would have. Unlike her less well-connected friends, Yiatin had knowledge of New York City's inner educational workings from decades of living in the city. She was able to find a small, dual-language, English/Mandarin school on the Lower East Side and placed her daughter there. She is thriving and having an excellent academic experience, Yiatin said.

Not every child in New York City is as lucky to have Yiatin as a parent. Many of the poor Chinese parents in the city barely have English-language knowledge, let alone that of the complex social and political structures that underpin the educational bureaucracy in New York. "They rely on the Chinese newspaper," she said of her Chinese friends. "The SHSAT is on the Chinese newspapers every week."

But the New York Specialized Schools didn't just randomly become name brands. They became the prize of the New York City Chinese community because they represent more than a pathway to success—they represent a kind of meritocratic opportunity that *they*, as low-income, non-English speaking parents, could aspire to for their children. An opportunity that was open to people like them, regardless of their social connections.

Why? Because although the SHSAT is notoriously hard—covering a wide range of subjects and requiring hours of studying—*it's just one test*. "The test is hard, but the process is very easy," said Yiatin. "The Specialized High Schools are simple in that you take a test, you score high, and you get a spot. If you live in South Brooklyn, Flushing, you have a shot."

And for those who doubt the efficacy of a school system built entirely on a single test, the Specialized High Schools prove the skeptics wrong again and again, every year, becoming some of the greatest incubators of homegrown American talent in the country. Nobel Prize-winning physicist Steven Weinberg and biochemist Robert J. Lefkowitz, economist Thomas Sowell, actor Tim Robbins, sports journalist Mike Greenberg, politician Gary Ackerman, grocer magnate John Catsimatidis, and politician and convicted sex offender Anthony Weiner are all Specialized High School alumni. Bronx Science has produced eight Nobel Prize winners, the most of any secondary school in the world. Stuyvesant High School has produced four Nobel Prize winners, tied for second in the world. Manhattan Institute thinker Heather Mac Donald commented that the Specialized High Schools "have nurtured nine Nobel laureates, hundreds of Westinghouse Science Talent Search winners, award-winning biologists and astrophysicists, astronauts, inventors, and captains of commerce."[3] She is right. They have justified their status as factories for New York City's excellence.

"National Security Centers," Chien Kwok called them. The New York-raised businessman went to Brooklyn Technical High School. After a stint in the record and music rights negotiating business, Chien lived in Hong Kong for sixteen years, where he met his wife and had kids. But after sixteen years in a foreign country, Chien felt the call of home. And there was one event that pushed him to come back to New York.

"My son got into a gifted program in New York," he said.

Chien is grooming his sons for the educational path he took . . . through the Specialized Schools system he went through. He moved back to the United States to provide his son that opportunity. That is parental dedication—and the ultimate affirmation of worth to a promising young teen of the education the Specialized Schools can provide.

As a matter of truth, New York City's Specialized Schools accomplish two great objectives that America needs today: They train the best and brightest minds in our society to accomplish their full potential, and they economically uplift some of the nation's poorest immigrant communities in the process.

It's a good deal, and it is accomplished by one foundational idea.

THE F—ING TEST

In the early-to-mid twentieth century heyday of New York City's mega-expansion, a Jewish Polish science teacher named Dr. Morris Meister noticed that the Bronx needed a school to train the bright kids he encountered on the street of his borough in math and science. He and the New York City Board of Education founded the Bronx High School of Science under the following premise: that the school would be open to all New York boys who achieved a top result in a competitive entrance exam engineered by Columbia University's famous Teachers College.

We cannot ignore Dr. Meister's Jewish background, here, and the historical context of this test's development. In an era when Harvard, Yale, and Princeton colluded to systematically exclude Jews from elite colleges, the Bronx Science single test for admissions flatly eliminated the possibility of human error in judgment. In an era when Jewish Americans struggled to find placement in schools and jobs worthy of their skills, the Bronx High School of Science offered an opportunity to escape prejudice and be graded on a very empirical standard.

It was not like the Bronx High School of Science was "pro-Semitic," or something like that. The test wasn't a test of Hebrew or of the Torah. It was a straightforward math and reading exam that mirrored the public curricula of the day. But admissions solely based on a single test was a huge upgrade over the anti-Semitic "tests of fitness" and "character" that plagued striving Jews in this time. Jewish Americans and many other groups flocked to this school and made it their home. They gave Bronx High School of Science the reputation it now retains, in New York City and across the world. A place for excellence of all stripes.

The tests for admission to Stuyvesant, Bronx Science, and Brooklyn Tech were later standardized to become the SHSAT. And as the three schools rose in influence and fame, the prestige associated with them rose correspondingly.

But so did unwanted attention on the selection process. An undercurrent of resentment was beginning to form against these prestigious schools that mirrored the often racially divided restlessness of the late 1960s. In 1971, the local school board of Manhattan's largely Black and

Hispanic District 3 Borough called the SHSAT the abettor of "a privileged educational center" and compared it to an "intelligence test," proposing that students should be admitted solely on the basis of teacher and administrative recommendations.[4]

Nonetheless, by then there were enough Specialized High School alumni in influential positions in the city; when liberal New York City Mayor John Lindsay signaled deference to the Left-dominated school board's charges, Specialized School alumni revolted. They pushed the passage of the 1971 Hecht-Calandra Act, which permanently enshrined the SHSAT as the sole measure of admissions to these factories of excellence. The defiant reaction of SHS alumni, who otherwise trended liberal like most New Yorkers, is telling. Even at the height of social upheaval in the '60s and '70s, educated people understood that some things were worth preserving after all.

The SHSAT has since become a blot on the social visions of the educational Left. It has been called the emblem of New York's educational "segregation."[5] It has been labeled as "racist" and lambasted as the epitome of "buying your way in." Let's examine this claim in its simplest form. This is a snippet of an SHSAT template widely used to mirror SHSAT questions:

The SHSAT tests two capabilities: English and Math. An example question of the type of problem found on the SHSAT would be:[6]

English: Read the following sentence. Which edit should be made to correct this sentence?

The newly constructed athletic complex features a myriad of amenities multi-purpose gymnasiums, an elevated jogging track, squash courts, and exercise studios.

- O   insert a colon after "newly constructed"
- O   insert a colon after "complex"
- O   insert a colon after "amenities"
- O   insert a colon after "multi-purpose"

Math: $x + x \cdot y + y =$

- ○ xy
- ○ 2xy+y
- ○ 4xy
- ○ x+xy+y

One of the major ideas behind the SHSAT was that it would be a differentiator between groups of excellent students. For example, if every student who applies to a certain school has an A average (as many of the applicants do), how do you choose who to admit? The SHSAT is designed to do this very differentiation. It does so by mixing in different levels of questions on its reading and math programs. The test's originators know that standardized eighth grade exam questions would be too easy for the majority of the high achieving test-takers in New York City. So they add a few ninth-grade, even tenth-grade level questions into the mix. This way, they are able to make distinctions between groups of high achieving students.

This is the concession one makes for excellence. To launch a school truly aligned with the standards of the best and brightest, one must necessarily reject most people who apply. But how to most clearly separate out the best and brightest? Dr. Meister's radical idea was that eliminating human error as much as possible was the key to fairly delineating. Allowing only the dispassionate analysis of standardization was best. You may call it cruel. But this vision of judgment as separate from prejudice has the root of its necessity in an even crueler history. For American Jews, the experience of prejudice is perhaps more salient than most. Better to decide on the basis of hard empiricism, uncontestable logic than on the basis of human preference, tests of character and fitness, prone to all the things to which humans are prone.

The blows against the SHSAT for "being racist" could only stick if standard English was racist, if basic algebra was racist. The Left-dominated public education system is increasingly willing to make that concession, but that is a discussion for another time. In any case, the SHSAT has weathered its fair share of criticism, producing the best-prepared academic and research talent in graduating class after class, without fail, doing its job to maintain factories of excellence.

WHAT THE TEST REVEALS ABOUT NEW YORK

By 1973, Stuyvesant High School was 90 percent Jewish. Other minorities were represented as well. By 1982, Brooklyn Technical High School was 55 percent Black and Hispanic. Then, in the late '80s and early '90s, something happened. Brooklyn Tech's Black and Hispanic population halved in nine years. Bronx Science's went from 20 percent to 11 percent. Stuyvesant, which was always low in Black and Hispanic students, went from 8 percent to an even more miniscule 5 percent. Now, numbers are even starker. A dismal 14 percent, 9 percent, and 4 percent Black and Hispanic students were admitted to the class of 2017 at the Big Three Specialized Schools.[7]

All the while, Asian Americans began to flood admissions into these schools. Stuyvesant went from 20 percent Asian to 40 percent. Then 50. Now, 70 percent.

What happened? Aside from minor revisions, the test never changed. But something else did: the composition of New York's intellectual high performers.

New York City once had an extremely robust gifted and talented citywide program that tracked high aptitude kids at every public school and placed them in courses matching their strengths. In 1990, The *New York Times* claimed that "virtually all of New York City's school districts have gifted programs."[8] The *New York Post* described gifted and talented programs "in nearly every city school in the '70s and '80s."[9] These programs "tracked" students—which is to say, judged their ability and put well-qualified students in local accelerated programs with teachers and courses that catered to their intellectual ability.

But in the 1990s, progressive activists' vendettas against differentiating by aptitude were finally realized. One example was in 1993: A progressive educator, Irma Zardoya, gained power in the Bronx's 10th District. She immediately pushed for an end to the district's "homogenous" gifted and talented programs, calling them pathways of privilege rather than opportunity. Throughout the '90s, gifted and talented programs started disappearing across that district and the rest of the city. Ten years later, District 10's Specialized High School admissions is down 80 percent, even as the population of the district has increased 25 percent.[10]

Today, ten out of thirty-one school districts with 88–96 percent Black and Hispanic enrollment have only one K–5 gifted and talented program or none at all. Most Specialized High School students enter through a corresponding feeder program in middle school—and the elimination of those programs in these predominantly Black and Hispanic communities for the sake of "leveling the playing field" has robbed these communities of the level of success they once had in Specialized High Schools.

■ ■ ■

Lack of Black and Hispanic achievement on the highest level in New York City is a complex problem. Specialized High Schools admits were 4 percent self-described Black and 6 percent Latino for 2019.[11] When *New York Times* education reporter Eliza Shapiro noted that in 2020, only ten Black students got into Stuyvesant High School, some people—maybe even Shapiro—may have thought she was pointing out a flawed or racist test. Reality is, she was pointing out problems embedded much deeper in New York City's public education system (which is two-thirds Black and Hispanic) than a single "racist" test.

In reality, admissions of Black and Hispanic students did not suffer in the years following the SHSAT's 1971 enshrinement as the standard for admissions; they climbed. When the Hecht-Calandra Act passed, Brooklyn Tech was only a combined 25 percent Black, Hispanic, *and* Asian.[12] Bronx Science was 90 percent white. In 1973, Stuyvesant was 90 percent Jewish. Five years after standardizing admissions under one test, Black and Hispanic enrollment climbed in both schools; Black and Hispanic enrollment in Brooklyn Tech and Bronx Science went to 38 and 25 percent of the admitted class, respectively, by 1976.[13] Brooklyn Tech's highest percent Black and Hispanic admission was in 1982 at 55 percent—eleven years after the SHSAT was introduced.

Take that in: One of the three most prestigious public schools in the entire city—possibly the country, at the time—had a makeup of 55 percent Black and Hispanic students.

Black and Hispanic representation at the Specialized Schools remained high until about 1996. Then began a horrifying, mesmerizing decline, from the perspective of those concerned about the welfare of New York City's Black and Hispanic communities. Fourteen percent, 9 percent, and 4 percent Black and Hispanic enrollment for the class of 2017 at the Big Three Specialized High Schools is a far cry from the 55 percent of 1982.

Is this a problem? Yes, a huge one! If Specialized High School admissions are proxies for New York City's public school system's ability to create excellence in local communities, then we are witnessing a gigantic crash of Black and Latino excellence in the city! A massive chasm in the ability of students to receive first-rate educations at New York City public schools! This is a startling indictment of the educational performance of the city's public school system and its disservice to low-income Black and Latino communities over the past fifty years. It's yet another data point showing why the city's charter school industry piles on expansive wait lists and New York, the richest city in the world, can't provide for its neediest citizens.

And there are other distressing data points: New York City spends more, at over $28,000 per student per year (2019 data), than any state average in the nation and almost single-handedly moves the state of New York to highest in per-student spending in the entire nation.[14] (By contrast, the national average for student spending per annum is $11,762.) And what does the Big Apple have to show for it?

According to the *New York Times*, "About 46 percent of the city's third through eighth graders passed the state math exam, a three percentage point increase from last year, and just over 47 percent of students passed the English exam, up about one point compared with last year." Less than half of New York City students demonstrate proficiency in math and English by the eighth grade. And although public school defenders are keen to point out that the 46–47 percent proficiency is higher than the state average (of 45 percent English and 46 percent math), the city's public school results are also significantly less than the results of its charter schools (54 percent English and 59 percent math).[15] This is despite the fact that charter schools (which by law cannot have selection criteria for its incoming students) receive only $16,343 per pupil—less than 60 percent of funding available per capita to public school students.[16] Almost 93 percent of NYC charter school students are either Black or Hispanic.

The New York City Board of Education, unfortunately, has a tool to obfuscate the real issues facing these students: grade inflation. Disreputable schools can move students from grade to grade without adequately investing in their actual learning. In some of these schools, grade fraud runs rampant, and the number of students in the city who pass math classes but fail basic math performance tests is high. Over 140 of its high schools have grades with 90 percent state math exam failure rates, according to the *New York Post*—but implicit "no-fail" policies allow them to pass their students anyway.[17] The *Post* reports:

> "At highly rated Maspeth High School in Queens, students know they can play hooky, skip course work, flunk tests—and still pass. They call it the 'Maspeth Minimum,' meaning everyone gets at least the minimum grade or score needed to pass or graduate, no matter what. Whistleblowers call it fraud. The secret to the school's 98 percent graduation and 90 percent Regents pass rate, they say, is simple: 'Cheat!' Four teachers told *The Post* that the 2,100-student high school—awarded a prestigious National Blue Ribbon in 2018 by the federal secretary of education—has an unwritten but iron-clad 'no-fail policy,' even for kids who repeatedly don't do the work or even show up."

In fact, 80–94 percent of students in some NYC public middle schools passed their math classes while in those same schools 2–15 percent passed their math exams.[18]

And finally, despite both grade inflation and extremely high per-student spending, the graduation rate at New York City Public Schools is still a miserable overall 65 percent—lower by far than the national average.[19]

New York City public schools can do much better, especially given their pool of funding. It will be difficult; all education reform is. But while reform happens (or does not happen), education-oriented parents, exemplified by the New York City Chinese community, will not sit and wait for schools to catch up to what—and who—is already excellent.

No wonder conscientious Chinese parents in New York seem so desperate to get their kids into a Specialized High School.

DE BLASIO COMES OUT AGAINST THE TEST

But these are not problems that New York City's administrators are willing to stare in the face. Instead, they prefer to blame Asians.

"I heard the Upper East liberals say we were gaming the test, we were being coached," Charles Jin said. He is referring to the snide and crude remarks from town halls where he was forced to hear racism directed at people like him. "I've heard [people on the Right] engage in anti-Asian racism like saying I spread the China virus, 'Go back to your country,' 'Know your place,' 'They are taking up our resources,' 'They are gaming the system,' et cetera . . . but people on the Left do it too, just more subtly."

Sometimes it isn't as subtle. New York University Professor David E. Kirkland said: "We've known for some time that the exclusion of Black and Brown students from the City's specialized high schools and the kinds of opportunity hoarding enjoyed by more privilege[d] racial and ethnic communities were in fact de jure consequences of lingering legacies of racism and white supremacy." He effectively denigrates the majority-Asian students at Stuy and Bronx Science as "opportunity hoarding" people of "privilege."[20]

The use of the term "opportunity hoarding" is telling here. It hearkens to a popular 2017 book, *Dream Hoarders: How the American Upper Middle Class is Leaving Everyone Else in the Dust, Why That's A Problem, and What to Do About It*. In it, Brookings Scholar Richard Reeves argues that the "top 20 percent" hoards opportunities by coaching their kids to take advantage of self-reinforcing networks such as college legacy admissions and inbred job networks—giving them unmerited advantages in the game of life. Kirkland's use of the term comes from Reeves's idea that the upper-middle class engages in "anticompetitive 'opportunity hoarding'" that actually limits the lower and middle classes' opportunities to move up the social ladder.[21]

Reeves's argument is interesting and worthy of debate. But David Kirkland's description of Asian students at the Specialized High Schools as opportunity hoarders is an entirely fact-free insult. May we be reminded that nearly half of Stuyvesant students receive free or reduced-price lunch? These are not children of privilege. Whatever societal "opportunities" they earn are hardly given to them. They work for their spots, spending lonely weekends in enrichment classes, striving for a better life through education. To denigrate them as upper-class hoarders is perhaps the *inverse* of the truth.

But for some reason, this narrative lingers like a scab, painting Asians in a sinister light where they happen to not only be enriching themselves but also sapping opportunities from the "truly underprivileged."

New York City's famously socialist-sympathizing mayor, Bill de Blasio, and his top educational lieutenant, NYC Schools Chancellor Richard Carranza, sincerely believe the admissions exam advantaged the privileged over "the genuinely needy." "For thousands and thousands of students and neighborhoods all over New York City, the message has been these Specialized Schools aren't for you," de Blasio said at a Black and Latino advocacy group in 2018. "So, the solution is simple: The test has to go."[22]

Then said Richard Carranza: "I just don't buy into the narrative that any one ethnic group owns admission to these schools."[23]

Nativism. That's how the liberal community in New York City responds to Asian success in these schools. The narrative is the same one Denis Kearney used so effectively to drive Chinese Americans out of California goldmines. It's the narrative of foreign invasion, of aliens coming in and "taking over" American institutions.

"The test was borne out of racism, and it has achieved its objective, and that is to keep *us* out of these high schools," said Charles Barron, a Black New York City assembly member who championed cutting the SHSAT from admissions.

De Blasio and Carranza also subscribe to the narrative of the racist test—the idea that the SHSAT and other tests like it perpetuate systematic discrimination against the Black and Latino communities. Those who defend the test, then, must be equivalent to those defending racist and white supremacist superstructures.

Of course, there is a political motive to painting these Asian students as privileged, opportunity-hoarding racists or racist enablers; it is not at all surprising to see why even liberals would do this. By demeaning the studying habits of Asian kids, the intellectual and political Left deflects discussion of *real* failures of opportunity brought about by the government's treatment of Black and Latino kids in New York City today.

Such as the day of Mayor de Blasio's fateful announcement: his intention to dismantle the entirety of the SHSAT, immediately.

On June 3, 2018, in front of a crowd of activists and supporters with signs emblazoned "ALL KIDS DESERVE A CHANCE," de Blasio said, in soaring overtones: "The status quo is broken. We have to make a major change. We have to make sure the very best high schools are open to every New Yorker. Every *kind* of New Yorker. They need to look like New York City!" Raucous cheers abounded.

At that press conference, de Blasio introduced his plan to rid the city of the scourge of the SHSAT. His plan would replace the SHSAT with a "by school" approach, automatically awarding the top seven percent of each class at each New York City middle school admission to a Specialized School. The effects of this proposal were obvious: It would increase the number of Black and Hispanic students in each school while lowering the number of Asian students, since the latter made up a lower percentage of the city public than either of those communities and also since they tend to congregate in a narrow range of schools. A NY1 article explained:

> "Earlier this year, a study by the city's Independent Budget Office said the elite schools would change under de Blasio's plan. The study found that the percentage of Black students accepted would jump to 19 percent from 4 percent and the percentage of Hispanics would more than quadruple, to 27 percent from 6 percent. The percentage of Asian students would drop in half, to 31 percent

from 62 percent. The number of white students would remain about the same."[24]

Those are the racial effects. The other relevant effects: Given the vast disparity in public middle schools' performance, doing away with the SHSAT would lead to student bodies vastly disparate in talent; students from highly outperforming high schools sitting in the same class as students from difficult or challenged backgrounds would make it hard for a teacher to educate both communities of people at the same level.

If de Blasio's policy changes go through, no longer will schools be composed of the best and brightest according to the SHSAT. It will be the best and brightest of *each* school according to each school's own grading metrics. Of course, these New York City institutions compete at greatly varying levels, raising the question: Which is a better measure of who truly is the best and brightest, the most excellent student?

WHAT THE TEST REVEALS ABOUT MERITOCRACY

The local debate over the SHSAT parallels a larger discussion in America today—the relevance and endurance of standardized tests. The same arguments are made on a national level: The SAT, the largest national college entrance examination, is too easily gamed; it tracks privilege, and it does not capably determine the true merit of a student.

But Duke University economist Michael Munger challenges the notion that the test has nothing to say about a person.

"The SAT saved me twice," Michael said. "First, it brought me to Davidson [College in North Carolina]. Then it made my [college] advisor hold me to a higher standard, saying 'You can clearly do this.'"

Michael Munger grew up in rural Florida. "My father worked at a lumberyard, and my mother stayed at home. We lived on an orange farm, so much of my work when I was at home was [on it]."

The economist describes his child self as "lazy." "I attached no value to intellectual things." He had Cs and Ds in most classes. But a standardized test—a ninth grade state test that all Florida students were required to take—identified him immediately as an outlier. "We took this test, and the principal of the school came in and said, 'Which one of you is *Munger*?' I had the highest grade in the school. And then they said, 'Why are you in this class?'"

Michael was immediately transferred to an upper-level class where he promptly did better and received higher grades. "I started doing the homework," he said. He took the PSAT (the Preliminary SAT) and was awarded a National Merit Scholarship, which put him on the map to recruitment to selective colleges. With an excellent SAT, Michael was awarded a scholarship to the highly selective Davidson College, where he—the son of orange farmers—would study the great classics and eventually be put on a tenure track as a Duke University professor.

"This is arrogant of me to say . . . but I, with no preparation, went to Davidson [and] had a mean, terrible person who was my advisor, who said, 'Looking at your test scores,' meaning my SAT, 'you're just lazy! So you have to take Calculus-based physics and Calculus.' And I did, and I ended up majoring in Math, because it's true—I was able to do it. Because I was a Math major at Davidson, I was able to get a PhD in Economics."

To him, the SAT wasn't a destructive experience; it was his biggest opportunity yet. The SAT, a nationwide test administered the same way for every student who takes it, forced colleges to seriously consider a boy from a high school that selective colleges never touch. It showed the world that Michael Munger was capable of competing with other students at the highest level.

"I went to my fortieth high school reunion: Ten of the guys I graduated with are dead because they drove tractors in the [orange] groves, putting out insect spray without respirators . . . I escaped that program because of the SAT."

Think about that: One might even say the SAT saved Michael Munger's life.

■ ■ ■

The argument, then, is that tests are able to be gamed, students coached to higher grades. This is a myth and a stereotype. The effects of coaching are low. Is it true that you can test-prep your way to higher SAT and ACT scores? Sure. But the effect of commercial test preparation, so to speak, is rather low—about 13–18 points on the SAT mathematics section and 6–12 points on the verbal. That's a lot of work for fairly little external benefit.[25]

"There are two things [the SAT] measures: one is innate ability, and the other is preparation," Michael said. Michael had no preparation—but he had ability. Some students don't have innate ability, but they prepare hard. And here is the rub: For the purpose of college admissions, *both characteristics are meritorious*. We can agree that innate ability is good for college preparedness, and that preparation is good for college preparedness. Ergo standardized tests are productive measures of academic excellence.

If we can agree that the SHSAT at least is a *productive* measure of academic excellence, then an exam evaluation is likely both the simplest and fairest measurement of excellence, i.e., the least prone to human error and bias. Standardized test scores may not be the sole valid implementation of meritocratic thinking—on that, de Blasio makes a valid point—but one must acknowledge that it is clearly the simplest and perhaps even the most objective. Standardized tests have the potential to be what Charles Jin called an oasis of "meritocracy," one of the last of its kind possibly in the entire United States.

It's not out of the question to say, therefore, that a single test is the simplest—and likely most cost-efficient—method of evaluating an applicant. No need to spend time and money interviewing applicants or combing through detailed research on their backgrounds. The score is "win and in." That simplicity is part of the appeal to the nonconnected immigrant community.

A single test may not sound fair, but consider the alternatives: grades, extracurriculars, performance on interviews, essays, teachers' recommendations, and so on (and on). Each of these are prone to human error—worse, *arbitrary human error*. That is, unsystematic error. If one answer is misstated on a test, for example, at least it is misstated for everyone. Grades, teacher recommendations, and interview performances can vary between teachers, interviewers, and recommenders. Heck, an interviewer could be having a bad day and screw over a person's application just because he was feeling disgruntled over his own personal life.

And grades also vary depending on teacher and intention. "Often teachers are not in agreement among themselves as to how to interpret grades from each other," wrote Kristie Waltman and David Frisbie in a seminal educational policy article. "Teachers state they rarely use the grades assigned to students by other teachers as information they can rely upon due to low levels of validity between teachers' grading practices." In fact, Waltman and Frisbie stated it flatly, as found in their study: "50 percent of teachers surveyed indicated their grades reflected both achievement and non achievement factors."[26]

But there's another layer to this that pseudo-socialists like de Blasio, wedded to the activist Left who believe the test is racist, do not acknowledge: Standardized tests are potentially the most *equitable*.

If we look at median scores on the SAT, it is true that students whose family incomes are greater than $200,000 a year perform about one hundred points better per test section than do students whose families make $20–40,000 a year, according to 2013 data.[27] But it is also true that the standard deviation of these bell curves is the same—one hundred points. That means that for every four randomly selected wealthy students compared side-by-side to a random impoverished student, one student in the latter group will do better on the SAT than his rich-parented peer.

At a college like Davidson, Michael Munger's alma mater, that range of achievement would be considered highly equitable. Only 16 percent of Davidson's Class of 2013 were students coming from the bottom *60 percent* of the population, according to the *New York Times*.[28] If Davidson admitted students strictly and completely on the basis of SAT scores, they would have significantly more poor and middle-class students than they currently do—not fewer.

That's because the SAT and other standardized tests capture characteristics absent from face-to-face evaluations of a student. They put a spotlight on a marginal student with mediocre grades and a poor work ethic, but who clearly had the intellectual potential to succeed in this country—Michael Munger, and all others like him.

When measurements privilege arbitrary human error, as in the cases of evaluating based on interviews or teacher recommendations, they privilege the ways people can be manipulated to prefer one person over another for reasons other than merit. The *recognition* heuristic, a "fast-and-frugal" one that informs decisionmaking, is the preference we give towards people that we know. Wealthy, well-advantaged Americans can take advantage of the recognition heuristic far more easily than impoverished people. Measurements that privilege personal connections, such as extracurriculars or interviews, are intrinsically exploitable by the socially connected—the wealthy, liberal, Upper East Side parents who often despise standardized testing.

Even grades are more impacted by a teacher's perception of the student—which is therein affected by social aptitudes that are disproportionately mastered by society's well-to-do rather than its hardworking yet unconnected.

The worst thing for the educational industry would be people who are wealthy, socially well-connected, and politically powerful gaining opportunities in the system that they do not deserve. It would be sickening to see a mediocre but rich Upper East Side kid get a spot over a brilliant but disadvantaged kid from Chinatown or the Bronx.

■   ■   ■

Yet, as it turns out, the whole enterprise of "holistic" admissions seems to inherently privilege the privileged and socially connected, the ones who can send their kids to Europe to find themselves and "become more well-rounded." How do you measure "well-roundedness?" It's unclear. At Hunter College Elementary, a New York City elementary school with 1,500 applicants for forty-eight spots, admissions officers tried holistic portfolios one year and then quickly abandoned them. The *New York Times* reports:

> "Although school systems in Texas, Virginia, Maine, Iowa and elsewhere are increasingly considering 'student portfolios' among their criteria for entrance into gifted programs, Hunter discourages it. 'We tried it one year,' says Nancy Goldman, an educational consultant at Hunter. 'Little Jimmy sent in his tape and little Betty sent in her picture, but we couldn't figure out any way to quantify it, so we dismissed it.'"[29]

The advantage rich kids have in gaming the holistic admissions process is revealed to be even greater by the *Students for Fair Admissions v. Harvard* dataset. Peter Arcidiacono, who did additional research on Harvard's prized holistic admissions process, found that "within racial groups, [Harvard's] holistic admissions criteria favor advantaged applicants. They benefit from the particular criteria Harvard uses to evaluate applicants, and they receive an additional tip in admissions decisions conditional on those criteria."[30]

Poor kids don't have the luxury of navigating the labyrinthine social cues that make someone "well-rounded." You pick one thing and run with it. As New York City's Chinese students prove, for many, that thing is the standardized test.

Luckily, standardized tests usually *do* measure what they seek to measure—the aptitude of the student to compete with others, achieving academic proficiency and excellence. In 2013, New York City's Board of Education commissioned a consulting group, Metis Associates, to do a study on the relationship between the SHSAT and other common performance metrics such as GPA, performance on subject-area tests, and performance on AP exams.

The study didn't exactly conform to the narrative de Blasio wanted to exert on the viewing public when he said that the Specialized Schools were poor metrics of student merit and ability. The Metis Report confirmed that due to its strong correlations with other important metrics, the SHSAT is an appropriate measurement of student aptitude. Students were found to have SHSAT scores "strongly correlated" both to first year GPA and performance on key subject tests. Metis Associates reported: "The fixed effects of the SHSAT predictor for ALL outcome variables presented in [key subject area exams] are positive and statistically significant with a p-value < 0.001."

Surprisingly, de Blasio's administration didn't release the study to the public until 2019, even though it was conducted and released to the board of education in 2013. Just another spit in the face of the many immigrant Asian parents who see these Specialized High Schools as their gateways to generational opportunity.

Which brings me to my last point about standardized tests, perhaps most salient in the context of de Blasio's failed educational administration: Standardized metrics are key to reversing the corruption and politicking that begets the hiring of political appointees in the United States. This is why one of Chinese Premier and Mao's successor Deng Xiaoping's first moves post-Mao was to restore the standardized exam for college admissions. He sent a message: You want to join the governing elite? Prove it by merit—not by partisanship. And he was right to do so: There was a legacy of corruption and Mao worship in the highest sectors of public service, eating away at China's culture of excellence. Today in America, when one party wins power, they install their cronies into the vast gamut of appointed positions in the government system. Then, when another party takes over, they install *their* cronies to replace them. Friends, connections, corruption, and race and diversity ideology—they all play their hand. But merit increasingly isn't.

Ask yourself this question: Would our government run better or worse if a standardized test was made to separate the competent from those completely incompetent to run our public schools, our transportation authorities, and our various economic agencies? If our leaders needed to explain why they brought in their friend, who failed a basic civil service exam, to run the local agricultural authority and make decisions on who gets access to land? Would that be too much to ask? Perhaps America's stomach for meritocracy has grown so weak that we are not even be able to swallow the banal idea that some people really are *too stupid* to be appointed to run our government.

SPIT IN THE FACE

De Blasio's proposed policy change to Specialized High School admittance set off a momentous, rollicking battle, with a rollout against which New York City's Chinese community instantly and unprecedentedly mobilized. Just days after de Blasio set his intentions to phase out admissions exams, Chinese Americans with no previous experience mobilized in a political nanosecond to defend what they see as the sole measure enabling their children to advance in society and bear fruit to the sacrifices that they made coming to America.

Asian American parents protesting de Blasio's decree to regulate the Discovery Program and SHS admissions somewhat hearken to a traditionally conservative position: suspicion of the government's motives, even in the service of so-called laudable goals like "diversity" and "equity." We know these government buzzwords are often used and abused for political ends. The general public has a right to be skeptical.

But these immigrants aren't exactly Tea Partiers—in fact, they aren't even Republicans. These are parents who are also socially concerned with the increasingly sordid state of public education in New York—perhaps the reason why they are so desperate to get their child in a dream school like Stuyvesant or Bronx Science, to begin with.

So these immigrants revolted.

In the period after de Blasio announced a replacement of the SHSAT, immigrant activists produced more than 1,000 articles on the measure, turning it into national news. They organized a streak of daily rallies across city hall. One rally, organized just two days after de Blasio's June 2018 announcement, featured throngs of protesters at Brooklyn's Sunset Park who carried signs emblazoned with "I Have a Dream" and "Keep SHSAT" in all caps. "The mayor is pitting minority against minority, and that's really messed up," said one protester, Kenneth Chiu of the New York City Democratic Club.[31] "He never had this problem when Stuyvesant was all white. He never had this problem when Stuyvesant was all Jewish," Chiu said. "All of a sudden, they see one too many Chinese and they say, 'Hey, it isn't right.'"[32]

Even local Democratic Chinese American politicians, previously supportive of the mayor's agenda, couldn't tolerate the blatant replacement of one race with another. "I also take issue with reported comments made by the chancellor about one ethnic group owning admission to Specialized High Schools," said Representative Grace Meng (D-NY6). "I am insulted, and these comments are false. Asian Americans aren't trying to own admission to these schools."

De Blasio's progressive push, in short, was not exactly received with open arms.

Feeling the pressure, the mayor tried to stage a well-choreographed "sounding board" event at Gracie Mansion (the official residence of his office), inviting Yiatin Chu, one of the leaders of the group opposing de Blasio's SHSAT cancel campaign, to present her case.

"De Blasio was getting a lot of heat for not having engaged with the Asian community at all," Yiatin said. "There [were] a lot of discussion as to: Do you go, do you not go? Is he using this as a photo op, just to check a box? Anyways, I agreed to go."

Maybe she shouldn't have gone. What Yiatin saw at Gracie Mansion disappointed but did not surprise her. "I would say there were probably four regular parents, no affiliation. And the other twenty parents were from CBOs, community-based organizations . . . you had every possible Asian organization[that] was probably getting funding from the mayor."

CBOs, as Yiatin described, are organizations formed to serve constituent communities. They can be as large or as small as is their ambition; CBOs often receive money from local and state governments to conduct their mission, whatever it may be. The issue with community-based organizations, of course, is that their complete reliance on government money in many ways beholds them to government agendas. You can be sure that de Blasio leveraged that to his advantage in this meeting.

But Asian Americans did not stop rallying. They made the SHSAT a campaign issue. In diverse Queens and Manhattan neighborhoods with high concentrations of Asian constituents, candidates could simply not ignore the issue anymore.

On May 1, 2019, de Blasio held a public hearing on the impending SHSAT elimination, supposedly to take into account the local community's input. Yiatin, a foremost full-steam-ahead Asian American voice to protect the standardized exams, sought to organize as many members of her coalition as possible to attend and raise their voices on this matter. They were promised a chance to speak and make their opinions known as ordinary parents and citizens.

"We got to city hall, and we all want to speak, and the media was all there," Yiatin said. "It was a scene. We're like regular parents signed up to speak." City hall was packed. Eliza Shapiro, education reporter for the *New York Times*, was there along with representatives from nearly every news station and newspaper affiliate in the city. There was a ton of buzz—not only from Asian Americans. New York City is a diverse place with diverse views. Ideological lines don't run as cleanly as they might elsewhere.

At first, Asian parents awaited expectantly to present their opinions on the issue, like football players waiting for their names to be called on draft night at the NFL.

Then, Yiatin remembered, a nightmare materialized. "The elected officials started calling up these groups," she remembered—and video footage of the public hearing confirms. "[Social justice activist and 2021 Mayoral candidate] Maya Wiley . . . [and] diversity groups . . . started talking about racial equity and social justice and nothing else.

"At around 2:30, the crowds started thinning out. The media and cameras were being packed up." The diversity groups were given full attention. But Asian parents continued to wait their turn on the sidelines. They were facing what so much of American culture had historically levied upon Asian Americans since their entrance into this country: invisibility, rejection of their voices, dismissal of their desperate wishes to contribute to a society they travelled ten thousand miles to reach.

Yiatin continued: "It wasn't until 5:30 [that] they started calling up regular parents. The whole room was basically empty except for . . . Asian parents, other parents. All that is on video," Yiatin added, to clarify her story is substantiated.

"At 6:30, my turn came. And I had to make a snide little remark." Yiatin's voice rose with mirth. "I said, 'I see how inconsequential the local government [looks] on the small little voices.' . . . It took so much bravery to speak when you barely knew English." And yet the Department of Education basically treated Asian parents like trash.

"I have another thing to add," Yiatin said. "All the reporters had left except for Eliza Shapiro and Nikole Hannah-Jones from the *New York Times*. But they didn't bring their laptops or anything. Eliza Shapiro had her hair back . . . The job part was over. It was at best observation, at worst entertainment. To make parents wait the entire 8, 9 hours to have their two-minute public comment. And it was going to be different, they told us."

Yiatin spoke with earnestness and feeling. "It was emblematic of a lot of things you see around me. How the established organizations across the gamut get a presence and a priority."

Politics is a dirty game. These Asian immigrants believed—perhaps naïvely—that they would be given a fair shot to contribute to the discourse the way others would in this country. Because this isn't just any country. This is *America*. To have their hopes dashed so flippantly through the extraordinary contempt of the de Blasio administration and media so established as the *New York Times* frazzled them. "That was a big wake up call to see how the city viewed us," Yiatin said.

The immigrants were frazzled. But they did not give up. With nonstop demonstrations in front of city hall, coordination with Specialized High School alumni (an influential bloc of New York City's elite), and a level of sophisticated political organization unprecedented in the history of New York's formerly quiet Chinatown, they organized one of the most interesting and distinctly *American* revolts against the system that the de Blasio administration had seen in its tenure so far.

After almost a year of protest and unfair treatment from the progressive administration, New York City's immigrants began to see some progress. The state legislature, which had to approve de Blasio's plan, simply ignored it—seeing it as politically untouchable due to these activist Asian parents and students. "The legislature has proven apathetic or openly hostile to the mayor's plan," said a New York *Chalkbeat* article.[33] Still, as late as June 2019, de Blasio vowed to fight the entrance exam. "Mayor de Blasio has spent the last year fighting to end the outdated practice of letting a single test on a single day dictate a kid's future. There's no other system like it in the country," Will Baskin-Gerwitz, a spokesman for the mayor, wrote. "He won't give up the fight until we have a more equitable system."[34]

The battle remained in gridlock for about a year. Then the mayor suddenly folded.

On September 25, 2019, more than a year after his first announcement, de Blasio reversed his decision to cancel the SHSAT: "Our plan didn't work."[35]

De Blasio vowed to figure out more ways to increase racial diversity in the Specialized Programs but acknowledged that scrapping the test didn't have to be a part of that calculus, saying, "Some would argue that there's a way to do it while keeping the test, and you have to have that dialogue, too."

Credit Asian American activists for their arduous journey to maintain the integrity of the tests amidst Department of Education-sponsored cries of racism. And the influential alumni of these selective schools who fought to keep the test. In the end, a combination of Asian American grassroots voices, aligned with the alumni base, persuaded even Democratic politicians in the New York City legislature to criticize de Blasio and Carranza's proposal to scrap the test.

"Diversity in schools is a worthy goal, but it must be attained in the context of educational excellence," said Democratic Assemblymember Bill Colton. The member of de Blasio's own Diversity Advisory Group had previously discussed not only scrapping the test but scrapping the whole of gifted and talented programs.

Truth is, the mayor's proposal—a scorched-earth Leftist policy—was never that popular with a legislature who answered to the actual, diverse citizens of New York City, particularly because of the perception that de Blasio was advancing this proposal in service to his Leftist base rather than to the constituents he represents. Mark Treyger, Coney Island representative, said that "Mayor de Blasio needs to move on from this issue and focus on the real systemic, pressing issues facing our entire school system."[36] Bill Colton suggested figuring out how to expand the number of and slots within the gifted and talented programs instead. It seems like a pretty good idea. After all, if these schools are in such high demand and so selective, would a proper solution not be to create more opportunities of admittance to these highly reputed schools?

De Blasio was willing to step away from the issue, facing pressure even within his own party (yes, there are many differing views among New York City's full slate of Democrats).

Meritocracy is not a party issue or a race issue. It is an *American* issue. It was what made New York City into New York City—the belief that hard work and personal character, not background, is what truly matters. One of the world's most ethnically diverse cities, it is a true melting pot; the idea of its competition and fair play is what drove so many to seek American shores. Asian Americans happen to be the victims of the mayor's anti-meritocratic proposal, but if it was another group that majorly attended these kinds of school—like the Jewish Americans who attended selective schools in the '70s—you can bet they would be fighting back too. The difference is that the Left uses vicious racial stereotypes to paint these Asian Americans as vicious, selfish, tiger parents, and therefore dismiss the validity of their activism.

The Asian American community won a key battle to protect the tests in New York City. But they were defending more than school slots. They were defending the very principle of objective meritocracy upon which this country became a global powerhouse of excellence.

THE RULES ARE CHANGING

CRITICAL RACE THEORY

D r. Martin Luther King Jr., was one of the greatest public moral intellectuals of the twentieth century. But that doesn't mean Dr. King was not exposed to other ideologies—ones that exuded charisma and hopes of revolution, of separating from the American nation-state.

Some Black leaders were aggressive in their rhetoric. Black and Muslim leader Elijah Muhammad said of white people: "Your entire race will be destroyed and removed from this earth by Almighty God. And those Black men who are still trying to integrate will inevitably be destroyed along with the whites."[1]

Malcolm X, a Black activist operating the same time as King, stopped short of advocating for violent revenge, but he did advocate for separation based on racial identity. In 1963, he said, "Twenty million ex-slaves must be permanently separated from our former slave master and placed on some land that we can call our own. Then we can create our own jobs. Control our own economy. Solve our own problems instead of waiting on the American white man to solve our problems for us."[2] He advocated for independence, believing that Black separation from white people was the appropriate response to the national harvesting of Black labor and livelihood for centuries.

The truths in Malcolm X's ideas are seductive. He points out "white liberal" failures in integration and welfare programs. He excoriates white people for turning Black people into "tokens," using them for the sake of arbitrary diversity ideology.[3] He talks presciently about the white real estate agent who urges the Black family to move into a white neighborhood, only to have the exorbitant prices drive the Black family out and leave only the white real estate agent to profit. His stories would get anyone angry at all forms of white impositions, but also make it very difficult to see a light at the end of the tunnel for coexistence and even love.

Dr. King Jr. only once met Malcolm X, but he was aware of—and contemplated—the separatist's ideas. They would tempt anyone oppressed by a country's laws and practices. But King advocated for the welfare of something larger—not only of his children and grandchildren but of the nation as a whole, in an attempt to heal, to forgive, to not only live together but love each other. The welfare of America and America's highest ideals.

In doing so he had to reject the critique perfected by leaders like Malcolm X. Even without violence, the critique rested on the same notion on which today's identity politics critique rests—that the races live in a state of natural disharmony, that no true reconciliation can ever occur between them, and so the best course is to separate. To contend. And then, when provoked, to fight. Marx and Mao would be proud.

America today faces a philosophy, critical race theory, that began in the 1960s and '70s as an academic discipline stemming (symbolically, at the least) from this ideological conflict between Martin Luther King and Malcolm X. Critical race theory is the view that "the law and legal institutions are inherently racist and that race itself, instead of being biologically grounded and natural, is a socially constructed concept that is used by white people to further their economic and political interests at the expense of people of colour."[4] The division of people into empowered and disempowered groups—privileged white people and oppressed Black people—is the fundamental assumption of American critical race theory.

From critical race theory we get the concept of systemic racism, the idea that laws and power structures remain stacked against Black people and "people of color." (Asians largely not included.) From systemic racism, we get the idea of racial equity, i.e., equality of outcome based on race. American University Professor Ibram X. Kendi defines it in this way in his bestseller, *How to Be an Antiracist*: "Racial equity is when two or more racial groups are standing on relatively equal footing." Creating racial equity, then, logically entails treating individuals differently in order to correct for racial disparities in outcomes. Kendi continues: "An example of racial equity would be if there were relatively equitable percentages of all three racial groups living in owner-occupied homes."

Currently, the hottest word in the critical race theory dictionary is the Kendi-popularized "antiracist." According to Kendi, you can never be "race-neutral." You can only be either racist or antiracist. An antiracist is "one who is supporting an antiracist policy through their actions or expressing an antiracist idea." (Kendi uses circular definitions a lot, giving him the advantage of fitting every policy opinion he has into his hermetically sealed ideology. If Kendi doesn't like a policy, he calls it racist. If he likes a policy, he calls it antiracist.)

Kendi also distinguishes between two types of discrimination: racist and antiracist discrimination. Discrimination is only racist if, Kendi argued, it leads to "great inequity":

> "The defining question is whether the discrimination is creating equity or inequity. If discrimination is creating equity, then it is antiracist. If discrimination is creating inequity, then it is racist."[5]

In Ibram X. Kendi's America, discrimination can be a *good* thing if it is antiracist—that is to say, creating greater racial equity. This is the full circle ideology that justified whacking the Asian American population at Thomas Jefferson High Schools, which you might remember hired Kendi to speak the summer before they changed their admissions policy. And this grand narrative of privilege and oppression, critical race theory, provides the backdrop for the racial battles going on in this nation today.

Think about how anti-excellence and anti-Asian antiracist ideology is. As Asian Americans continue to be overrepresented in the fields of tech, medicine, and education, antiracist ideology dictates that Asians should be shoved out to make room for minorities considered "underrepresented"—in the name of equity. Goodbye, meritocratic entrance exams. Hello, racial quotas, or "holistic" admissions and hiring of the Harvard variety.

What happens in Kendi's America? Asian American effort and achievement, which buoy them in a country where they do not have social privileges and networks to buffet them, will be suppressed for equity. Kendi would see us sacrifice meritocratic excellence for unmerited equity in a heartbeat.

Because it is moral to do so! It is *antiracist* to do so! And in case anyone doth protest, may the diversity consultants and school administrators remind us that to be Asian is to be complicit in white supremacy by virtue of a desire to work and study hard. We should feel good about suppressing their excellence, chastising them for "white adjacency," and diminishing their efforts in the name of artificially boosting the underqualified and underrepresented.

Once again, Asian Americans are the inconvenient minority in Kendi's boxed-and-marketed critical race theory ideology. And because they are inconvenient so, too, will they be inconvenienced.

Asian Americans are thrust into the middle of this battle, whether they like it or not. In fact, they are one of its main players.

EQUITY MONEY

First of all, where there is discrimination against Asian Americans, there are likely greater problems beneath the surface.

In Montgomery County, Maryland, a suburb of Washington, DC and one of the most diverse and immigrant-heavy counties in the nation, the local school board is run by the richest and whitest liberals you have ever seen. (Three out of the county's nine city council seats are in the famously old-money liberal Takoma Park neighborhood, which borders DC and contains less than 1.8 percent of the county's total population.) It passed a proposal that would create more "diversity" in the school's—where else?—gifted and talented programs by greatly lowering the standards for entry and choosing attendees based on "local norms." I.e., similar proxies for race to those used by David Card in his defense of Harvard's discrimination policies. In two years, the percentage of Asian students in these gifted and talented programs fell 20 percent, while the percentage of every other race—Black, Hispanic, *and* white—went up.[6]

Classic discrimination case, right? A moderate person might be tempted to stop here and make conclusions—that the school board is racist towards Asians, that they are using the color of a student's skin to determine their destiny.

But don't be moderate; don't stop here. The reality is even worse. And it's worse for every minority—not just Asians.

"EQUITY AND EXCELLENCE" reads the banner of the Montgomery County Public Schools (MCPS) system. The unofficial slogan, adopted in 2015 under new Superintendent Jack R. Smith, was meant to unite the county by "provid[ing] all students, regardless of their learning needs, race, ethnicity, or socioeconomic status, with options and choices upon graduation."[7] It is an honorable message. But read between the lines and you'll find deep dishonor within it.

To illustrate their initiatives, MCPS officials showed this graphic at a 2016 community meeting to demonstrate the difference between equality and equity.[8] "Equity" is on the right:

According to Montgomery Public Schools, Black students stand on the rightmost box of the left half of the graphic, lowest on the racial totem pole, and Asian students stand tallest, highest in the status quo. How does MCPS know this? They point to a so-called "racial achievement gap." It measures the discrepancy in performance between the district's Black and white students; the Stanford Educational Opportunity metric pegs the Black/white achievement gap score at 3.09, and the Black-Hispanic/white-Asian gap even higher. This means that the average white or Asian eighth grader in Montgomery County scores more than three grade-levels higher on standardized performance exams than the average Black or Hispanic student.[9]

Now, this sounds quite high. By the standards of the Montgomery County Public School (MCPS) system, the racial achievement gap is nothing short of an educational crisis, a profligate systemic failure. Current MCPS Superintendent Smith wrote in the *Washington Post*, "For 50 years, the achievement gap in Montgomery County has grown in the shadows while many of our county's schools and students garnered well-deserved praise and earned awards . . . This disparity in academic outcomes is a crisis in our community that must be addressed."[10]

But the racial achievement gap statistic is not what it seems, nor does it indicate the true state of the district. Compare MCPS's record of achievement and public school growth with that of neighboring Prince George County, Maryland. Although, Prince George, a primarily Black county (one of the highest-income Black counties nationwide, with a median Black household income of $89,000 per year), has a Black/white achievement gap score of only 2.06 compared to 3.09 for MCPS. Its Black students score 1.1 grade levels below the all-race national average—which is worse than MCPS, whose Black students score about 0.5 below the national average. If you were a Black parent deciding where to send your child, where would you pick? The system with the lower achievement gap—or the system with better outcomes for Black students?

And what's more, the "achievement gap" between *Asian* students and white students is 1.63, meaning Asian students score 1.63 grade levels higher than white students. This, however, apparently does not imply "systemic" issues within the white group in Montgomery County.

Never mind these nuances, though. Facts must be forsaken in narrative pursuits, and the narrative MCPS was pushing was that Montgomery County was an absolute wreck for Black Americans because they scored so much lower than these white and immigrant kids. Of this gap, MCPS Councilmember Jill Ortman said in 2016: "In our country, we have experienced decades of horrors and atrocities against our African American families," fueling a distinctly racial spin to these community education issues.

What was the purpose of advancing this narrative? To crusade righteously on behalf of Black Americans and find real solutions to their problems?

No. It was to get state funding.

Jack Smith, Montgomery County Public Schools superintendent, is a balding, rosy-cheeked white man with a likeable, almost cloying demeanor. But he has presided over one of the greatest misuses of taxpayer money in Montgomery County history.

Using the racial narrative as backup, Smith solicited and then spent $124 million of state and federal money on programs targeted at low-income Black and Hispanic Americans.[11] A purpose of this spending was to "advance racial justice and cultural proficiency by interrupting systems of bias (implicit and explicit), oppression, and inequity in our policies, practices and procedures," per the school's Equity Initiatives Unit website.[12]

What did Smith spend it on? A fact sheet from MCPS is a revelation— he brought in "diverse teachers." Smith said at a local NAACP meeting in 2019: "We are about 58 percent students of color, students in poverty, or students of color in poverty. Yet, our teaching force is about less than a quarter of individuals who represent those students."[13] (What he means is that fewer than a quarter of teachers are Black or Latino. This is, of course, a sly insult to America's well-meaning white and Asian teachers, who would like to believe that they can "represent" these students as well as teachers "of color.")

Smith "introduced mandatory cultural proficiency training for all educators." He sought to reduce class sizes (one of the most expensive ways you can try increasing achievement; lower class sizes directly led to a need for more teachers to be hired and facilities to be operated). He expanded free summer enrichment programs, which is nice but also expensive. Smith threw cash willy-nilly at a lot of different things—some unlikely to help low-income children, some perhaps able to help at a very expensive cost— but without a clear goal in mind, except for this word "equity."[14]

Did this incredibly expensive undertaking help?

A 2019 study by the county's Office of Legislative Oversight (OLO) says no: All that money did not improve the achievement gap between MCPS Black/Latino and white/Asian students. OLO states unequivocally, "A review of the data evidences a wide performance gap that has not diminished by race or ethnicity among a majority of the metrics reviewed."

Look at these damning findings on the lack of progress to close the Latino gap (i.e., the difference in performance compared to Asian or white students) in Montgomery County:

> "Widened across seven measures—Dropouts, ELA 6–8, ELA 10, Graduation, AP/IB Performance, SAT Performance—English, and SAT Performance—Math; Remained unchanged for four measures—School Readiness, Math 3–5, ELA 3–5, and Algebra 1; Narrowed for one measure—Math 6–8."[15]

How could you spend upward of one hundred million on your low-income community of students, coming out to $1,600–2,000 for compensatory education per K–12 student per year, and make zero progress in closing the achievement gap?[16]

Because your efforts don't work. Mandating teachers be of certain races doesn't actually help students, it only distracts teachers. Cultural proficiency training, as with previous iterations of "implicit bias training" developed by the diversity and inclusion industry, pad résumés but don't actually improve teaching. Your equity and excellence initiatives produce neither equity nor excellence. Go figure.

Now, these results didn't matter to the rich, white liberals manning the MCPS School Board. Why? Because it's *not about the results*. It's about the money. Equity money.

In 2019, MCPS got $700 million in funding from the state's equity program, Bridge to Excellence—which, when passed in 2002, greatly increased the state tax burden on Marylanders to serve the program's equity ideals. Or rather, the ideals that "all students regardless of race, ethnicity, gender, disability, or socioeconomic background can achieve."[17,18] Twenty-five percent of MCPS's *total educational budget* dedicated to pursuing lofty ideals of equity, that liberal buzzword.

In 2020 Jack Smith asked for an additional $450,000 for good measure, specifically to conduct an "anti-racist audit" of its school system to determine how else they could ask for money for their equity and social justice programs.[19] (No, that's not what they actually said. But it's what's going to happen.)

Why would anyone in their right mind give a single more cent to a clearly ineffective outfit like the Montgomery County Public Schools' equity and excellence program, which just spent hundreds of millions of dollars and nearly five years on bringing "diverse curricula" to the public schools—without serving an ounce of the purpose that they set out to?

Look how the name of racial justice has been tarnished with antiracist dribble. Look how Black and Hispanic victimhood is used to push for strategies that don't help low-income Blacks and Hispanics. And look how, when things don't turn out like they seem, liberal elite politicians go right back to the well for the same equity and inclusion initiatives that failed their students before. Look how they give it—and have the gall to ask for more.

The cherry on top: In an effort to create a racial distraction, Smith, just like fellow liberal NYC Mayor Bill de Blasio, went after gifted and talented programs. He wrote a memorandum to the school board detailing that he sought "more equitable access to specialized programs." The new field test that came out of his redesigned admissions system lowered the percentage of Asian Americans of the overall student body at these gifted programs by 20 percent, instantly, raising the number of Black, Hispanic, *and* white students at their gifted programs. Of course, at the expense of these Asians.

How did they do it? In similar ways to de Blasio, except that rather than eliminate the test, they "made [it] a lot easier," said Charlie, a test-prep school owner in Montgomery County who has been following the developments for years. "The test [for third graders] used to be on Math and English," Charlie said. "Now it's 'non-verbal' and 'verbal.' You don't need to have any particular knowledge of math . . . the test does not allow someone to demonstrate actual ability." A greater pool of students entered the qualifying pool of applicants, giving the school board more discretion over who to cherry-pick for the gifted and talented programs.

They took from those who worked hard and play by the rules to artificially grant spots for their preferred races.

Real problems cause these yawning achievement gaps at MCPS, which has a high percentage of first-generation immigrants (from Asia and Central America) and English as a Second Language (ESL) learners. Many ESL students have different needs than the rest of the school population. One student survey suggested there would be increased retention and interest in class if these students had "instruction that feels relevant, more career pathways, teachers to slow down and after-school clubs for socializing, getting homework help and learning to navigate their schools and communities."[20] Former Education Secretary John B. King Jr., said of MCPS: "We can help kids have experiences after school, in the summer, or as part of the high school curriculum, that give them a connection to what they are doing after high school."[21] A relevant education, a career-building education—that is what is sought by the district's low-income Black and Hispanic kids.

Notice what was not said. These students were not asking for anti-racism audits, artificial elevation into gifted and talented programs, or enrollment in classes with more white or Asian people or even teachers. But that's what the county has been spending its equity money on—and it's not helping. Rather, it's taking away spots from the county's hard-working Asian Americans in the name of equity and serving the county's Black and Latino kids.

Eva Guo, a Montgomery County parent, has had enough of this nonsense. "Many MCPS parents, including Asian American parents, expressed strong opposition to the gifted and talented reform; however, the Montgomery County BOE completely ignored the public comments," she said. Eva got together with a group of parents. She and her newly founded civil rights organization, the Association for Education Fairness, sued the district with the help of a public-advocacy organization called Pacific Legal Foundation. As of 2021, the suit is moving through the courts.

But the school board's policies triggered a backlash from the other side against the county's immigrant Asian American population. Byron Johns, a chair of the local NAACP (which represents some of the county's Black leadership), believes Asian Americans are at fault for taking up too many spots in the gifted and talented programs. "You have a suspiciously high number of Asians, who are 13 percent of the population, but they make up 35–40 percent of the magnet schools," he said.

The use of the word "suspicious" is troubling. It implies that Johns is blaming Asian parents for trying to get their kids into these magnet schools. It also shows a fractured racial culture in one of the most diverse districts in the nation, where four ethnic groups—white, Black, Hispanic, and Asian—all comprise at least 15 percent of the county population.[22]

All the while, the Black and Hispanic communities do not benefit from these "equity and excellence" policies. When Superintendent Smith visited the NAACP Education Council in 2019 to hobnob with Black county leaders, he talked about adding more racial data to determine the severity of the "racial achievement gap" in his county. He talked about "culturally competent schools." But he did not talk about the returns of his spending spree.[23]

The culprit is neither the Asian parents nor is it the Black parents. It's the Montgomery County Public School system's racialized policies that infected the water of a district and turned people against each other for all the wrong reasons—all while letting an unaccountable school district spend and spend for ineffective and useless "diversity" policies and ask for more money for those same purposes.

Who wins in the zero-sum game of racial identity politics? The government.

THE ASIAN AMERICAN POLITICAL RENAISSANCE

The rules are changing. America faces an increasingly aggressive critical race theory complex that threatens everything about our meritocracy. Millions—no, *billions*—of dollars and our culture of excellence are at stake, if you just claim the proper victim status and sacrifice the proper morals to the racial narrative. A single county, MCPS, claimed $150 million in federal government money to prop up a racial equity ideology that did not even serve the people it purported to. But districts keep doing it in the name of equity, diversity, antiracism—whatever be the fashionable moniker of the day—because Americans are too gullible, weak-willed, or politically correct—whatever you want to call it—to do anything about it as a nation. And this critical race theory complex will take and take, until the rules of meritocracy are finished, and the rules of critical race theory reign supreme.

Who can stop this machine?

Enter Wenyuan Wu.

Wenyuan, a soft-spoken first-generation Chinese American woman (and Georgian) with thin-framed glasses, is always busy: "I work all the time. Fourteen to sixteen hours, but that's just me." On every Zoom call, she is mostly muted—because she is likely doing some other call or interview. The PhD and MA in international studies is up at ungodly hours, working every job she thinks could help the cause. As such, her requests—always predicated with a "Thank you!"—are short and to the point. Here is our agenda, she says, and lays it out in numbered form.

Meeting Agenda:

1. Progress quick updates.
2. Actions to reach out and mobilize Asian American communities and conservative voices in California.
3. Identifing [sic] key legislative members & actions to influence legislative members, lobbying,letters/email, phone calls.
4. Actions to take on the national level: petitions, alliance building, awareness building, public opinions.
5. Other matters.

When Wenyuan casually noted that the upcoming meeting will be about mobilizing Asian Americans and conservatives in California, the largest state in the Union; identifying legislators to influence; *and* commissioning petitions and alliances at the *national level*, the intellectual heft of this small Chinese American woman with an understated personality became apparent. Columnist Tunku Varadarajan of the *Wall Street Journal* identifies Wenyuan as "outspoken about freedom in the classic American way, yet deferential . . . in a manner that's unmistakably Asian."[24]

That list is from a March 25, 2020 email that Wenyuan sent to a few influential Californians about a new bill, Assembly Constitutional Amendment 5. ACA-5 would strip the state of California of a defining constitutional protection, one that would have—until 2020—banned racial preferences from the state forever. Constitutional protection Proposition 209:

> "prohibits the state from discriminating against, or granting preferential treatment to, any individual or group on the basis of race, sex, color, ethnicity, or national origin in the operation of public employment, public education, or public contracting."

ACA-5, a 2020 constitutional amendment advanced by California Democrats in the wake of the killing of George Floyd, would repeal the above statement of civil rights.

There's an interesting story behind Proposition 209. It was the brainchild of a Black businessman named Ward Connerly. Born in the segregated South but eventually rising through the ranks to become a successful businessman, Connerly was appointed to the Board of Regents of California in 1993. Was his race a factor in his appointment? We can never know for sure, but for the elites who sought a polite adherent to diversity ideology and token minority, Ward Connerly turned out to be the wrong pick.

Connerly vehemently opposed racial preferences of any kind at his school, despite being Black. He saw that the people who endorsed these racial preference programs did so mostly out of a sense of guilt rather than an actual study of the consequences. "You realize that race occupies just about every bit of attention of the universities that they're in," Ward said.

Rather, Connerly was convinced by data presented to him that white and Asian students with greater actual merit were being denied admissions that went to less qualified students solely because of their race.

After successfully convincing the UC system to drop preferences, Connerly expanded his activism to the entire state. Having convinced the state governor, Pete Wilson, of the issue's importance, Connerly called for a statewide referendum on racial preferences as a constitutional issue. He successfully conducted one of the most shocking campaigns of the 1990s, enshrining a ban of race preferences in hiring, admissions, and public contracting in the constitution of the most liberal state in America. The vote was 55 percent in favor, 45 percent against. It made Ward Connerly a legend. Sixty years old at the time of his Proposition 209 initiative, Ward felt triumphant. "Racial preferences are dead," he said after the proposition's passage. "The only question is to give them a decent and honorable burial."

In 2019, I asked Ward to elaborate on whether things have changed in the twenty-five years after he passed Proposition 209. Ward elaborated with a No True Scotsman: "Racial preferences *are* dead . . . " he said, "according to the American people."

Well, Ward's prediction was about to be tested. Again. In the same state where he had originally passed the proposition.

It's hard to say what the long-term effects of the era of civil unrest after George Floyd's death will be. But the short-term effect, at least in California, was to spark a bevy of racially charged bourgeois laws that include instituting corporate mandates of racial and gender diversity, establishing a study board of reparations, and requiring a social justice course for all students at California public universities. None would be as ultimately consequential as this constitutional amendment to repeal Proposition 209: ACA-5.

State Legislator Dr. Shirley Weber, a Black progressive legislator who worked closely with Democratic colleagues, introduced ACA-5, which would repeal Proposition 209 and allow for race preferences to once again be used in the California system, on the California House floor on May 5, 2020, with sweeping broadsides on systemic racism in America. "Members of the world watched in Minneapolis the symptoms of a much larger problem. And equally disturbing was an officer with his knee on George Floyd's neck. As well as the officers who stood by and were complicit in allowing this to happen," she said on the assembly floor, introducing this bill. "There is an urgent cry for systemic change."[25]

This is the same playbook that Princeton University President Chris Eisgruber used to enshrine racial preferences in his own admissions system: Spin a wide narrative of systemic racism in America and especially in his own university. Then pass a law that actually *discriminates* on the basis of race to compensate for that narrative.

Clearly, Weber had been waiting many years for this moment; she had been an Africana Studies professor at San Diego State for forty years with a PhD in communication. Amidst a national pandemic clouding potential undesirable coverage of her pet issue, and with a newly minted Democratic supermajority in the California General Assembly that would do the progressive wing's bidding, she saw her opportunity—and did not hesitate to deliver the striking blow.

ACA-5 would become a constitutional amendment under two conditions: one, if both houses of the State Assembly passed the amendment with a two-thirds vote; and two, if California voters ratified it in a public referendum with a majority vote.

It seemed a sure bet that in this climate, a more progressive California citizenry would ratify the amendment if it was put in front of them via ballot, so all Weber had to do was get it through the assembly and the Senate. She came prepared. ACA-5's public hearing in the Labor Committee, just days after the California Legislature reconvened post-COVID shutdown, was accompanied by nearly one hundred on-script Leftist California organizations calling in to say how "strongly" they supported ACA-5, despite the legislature having not debated the measure yet.[26] To anyone watching, it was clear that Weber was a formidable foe—politically gifted, and the first Black woman elected south of Los Angeles for a reason.

Of course, the fact that the California State General Assembly was 60 Democrats to 19 Republicans and the Senate was 30 Democrats to 9 Republicans helped. Shirley Weber's sailing to get her bill through was so smooth that even a few Republicans, such as State Senator Scott

Wilk, considered voting for her bill out of political pressure. The days of Connerly's crowning achievement banning racial discrimination seemed numbered.

Wenyuan Wu and the state's furious Asian Americans watched anxiously as ACA-5 continued to make its way through the California Assembly and then the Senate. Wenyuan, who formed a committee hoping to overturn the measure in the legislature, contacted a state lobbyist, Vietnamese American Jacqui Nguyen, to help push for her side. "Jacqui [is] to work on getting the opposition to speak at the Appropriations Committee as an invited witness against ACA-5," she wrote. Jacqui began to organize testimonies during the public hearing portion of the debate. Witnesses were allowed to speak for no longer than a few seconds; their name and "I *strongly* oppose this measure" was all they were allowed to say. But Wenyuan and Jacqui brought hundreds of those witnesses. Weber, of course, brought her force of liberal organizations to express support with the same script. The public hearing, where witnesses each offered just a single sentence, took longer than three hours in total.

Even after the clear expression of controversy within the public, the Democrat-dominated Appropriations Committee seemed dead set on passing ACA-5. "After much virtue signaling, this bill is about to pass in this committee," Wenyuan said the day of the committee vote. And she was right. ACA-5 went onto the assembly floor and passed with flying colors. The final vote was 60–14 aye, with five Republicans abstaining.

Finally, ACA-5 reached the Senate floor. Wenyuan waited patiently for the results. She wasn't optimistic. The roll call came in. Republican State Senator Scott Wilk crossed over to the other side. The final vote was 30–10 aye: ACA-5 was going to the public.

■   ■   ■

As Shirley Weber celebrated, confident voters in California, one of the most Democratic states in the nation, would ratify the repeal of Proposition 209, Wenyuan reflected on what appeared to be her doomed effort. "Sometimes I feel that our unending fight is like David vs. Goliath," she wrote privately days after the vote. "The cultural bourgeoise and intellectual elite are on a 'winning' side that constantly monopolizes victimhood and injustices to sell what? It is politics, in the end. And the supposed 'bright' minds are just brainwashed tools. History will remember our cause more kindly."

Wenyuan withdrew to a dark place after the vote seemed to confirm that race preferences in America would be a reality moving forward. Her friends reminded her that California was the most liberal state in the nation, and that there would be other fights. But Wenyuan's heart was invested in this one. She wrote in a text:

> "I cringe every time when these entitled and truly privileged ideologues talk about socioeconomic biases and structural stigma. It is gaslighting. When they do, I think about Asian kids whose parents toil in Chinatown with low pay and broken English. I think about myself and many others who studied hard in a foreign country [without] any prep for a fair opportunity to come study here."

What would Wenyuan do about the seemingly inevitable fact that California Governor Gavin Newsom and State Senator Shirley Weber intended to create a legacy of racial discrimination in their state, home to the largest cohort of Asian Americans in the nation? After ACA-5 (to be presented in front of the voters as Proposition 16) inevitably passed, Asian Americans would face government discrimination in college admissions. Public employment. Public contracting. An Asian-led business trying to contract with the government, with equal or greater value than a similar Black-led business, would be arbitrarily shafted just because the head of the company was Asian American. Asian kids in universities would face discrimination. As would Asian adults in public employment. Poor Asian kids in California, who studied hard and played by all the rules, would be shafted because they were the wrong color.

Wenyuan thought about all that. And she decided that she was going to change the inevitable. She would challenge ACA-5, now Proposition 16, in the court of public opinion. She was going to run a campaign.

■ ■ ■

First, Wenyuan had to recruit the most adept man in the field of race preferences to join her in her fight. Ward Connerly was enjoying retirement in Idaho. Coaxing an eighty-one-year-old out of retirement is not the easiest proposition. Ward was rehabilitating from a bit of triumphalism about race in America. As late as 2019, he said to me, "The election of a multiracial man, the reelection of that man," shows that "Black people are not powerless." And it is true. They're not. "You look at commercials on TV, which is a sign of where Black people are. Black people are in a very strong position and they know it," he said. And while that may be true, the narrative in America was also being reshaped before Ward's eyes. The concept of systemic racism has been percolating in the cultural mainstream for the past five years. Race as victimhood was becoming its dominant conception in some educated circles.

Fortunately, Wenyuan had an ace in the hole that she knew could convince Ward. She was an Asian American fighting for Asian Americans, and Ward greatly respected the Asian American population. "Here you have these Asians who follow all the rules and all the rules of the market, which is to say merit, who are being artificially suppressed from the most prestigious universities," Ward said. "I want to do whatever I can to help Asian Americans to get over that divide in our society. I think this is a more serious matter than any of us realize."

Wenyuan installed Ward as president of their newly founded organization, Californians for Equal Rights, and they immediately set out campaigning under the banner of the "No On 16" campaign. Ward and Wenyuan established an organization in a matter of weeks and brought on Arnie Steinberg, a Republican campaign operative, to helm the campaign. The newly created Californians for Equal Rights boasted the heft of Connerly's presence, the political instincts of Steinberg, and the network of Wu—all barely a month after ACA-5 passed the California Senate. By the time Attorney General Xavier Becerra put Prop 16 on the California ballot in August 2020, Wenyuan's organization, the No On 16 campaign, had already raised $500,000, mostly from the Chinese American community. By October, No On 16 approached $1,000,000.

You might think that is a lot. But just to show you what these Chinese Americans were up against—consider that the Yes On 16 campaign raised $13 million. *Thirteen* million!

Still believe race preferences is an issue that only Asian Americans who want to get their kids into prestigious colleges care about? Out of that thirteen million dollars raised, $5.5 million came from one individual, M. Quinn Delaney (the white wife of a Black real estate investor); $3.5 million from Educators for Equity (a composite of teachers' unions); $1.5 million from Kaiser Health; $1 million from Patricia Ann Quillin (wife of Netflix billionaire Reed Hastings); and $1 million from Microsoft cofounder Steve Ballmer, for a total of nearly $11,000,000 from less than ten individual entities. As it turns out, just a few really rich, really liberal people want to make it harder for Asians to get good jobs, good contracts, and into good schools.[27]

Ironically, the $5.5 million Delaney donated to the Proposition 16 campaign would, if Prop 16 passed, directly benefit her husband; By repealing the ban on race preferences in public contracting, the head of a real estate investment company would be awarded privileged access to government contracts solely because he is Black.

How much more conspiratorial can you get? Yet the Yes On 16 side cast this issue as all about racial justice. Please.

But it's this kind of contrast that shows the effects of Proposition 16 are not limited to race. It affects everything. Racial considerations apart from merit affect a deal signed with the government, which affects the quality of work that is done for the government.

UC-Santa Cruz Professor of Economics Justin Marion compared expenditures on highway construction contracts pre- and post-Proposition 209, setting the dependent variable as the expenditures on highway systems relative to federal government expenditures. Marion found that contractors in high-minority areas simply cost the government (and hence the taxpayer) more than contractors in other areas. After Proposition 209 was passed, highway construction contract prices went down 5.6 percent.[28] Scripps College Professor of Economics Sean Masaki Flynn found that if we were to extrapolate the additional cost from Proposition 16 in highway construction *alone* over a ten year period, the California taxpayer would be burdened with an additional $7.3 billion dollars because of its racial skew towards less-qualified and higher-cost construction businesses.

Wenyuan and Ward believed that if they got this message out, and focused broadly on the theme of equal rights for all while explaining the economic effects of racial preferences, they could win their audience. But it wouldn't be easy to get their message across in California.

Firstly, the deeply liberal Attorney General Xavier Becerra, a Kamala Harris disciple who succeeded her after she left to become California Senator, created a ballot title for Proposition 16 so blatantly biased that a sixth grader could point out the obvious skew. Here it is:

> "Allow Diversity as a Factor in Public Employment, Education, and Contracting Decisions. Legislative Constitutional Amendment."

Wow. *Allows Diversity.* As if California had never allowed diversity during this "miserable" era of Proposition 209, which prohibited discrimination on the basis of race.

But Becerra knew what he was doing. Americans oppose race preferences in college admissions *and* in the workplace by a margin of three to one when the question is accurately posed to them: "Race preferences."[29] But they support the general idea of "creating diversity" by a ratio of three to one. Becerra capitalized off the most positive reading of what Prop 16 was attempting, even though that reading doesn't actually explain the issue at stake. The issue isn't *diversity*, but how to create it—by using racial preferences, or in a more race-neutral way?

No On 16 tried challenging Becerra's wording through the courts. But the deferential judicial branch kept the wording, leaving the No On 16 with a skewed ballot to kick off the campaign. Not a great start.

Next, the Yes On 16 campaign started reeling in endorsements from California's high-profile elites. First it sought the endorsement of the University of California system (they didn't have to ask twice), and then that of state's most prominent sports teams. They got them. *Seven* major league sports teams endorsed Proposition 16: The San Francisco 49ers,

Oakland Athletics, Golden State Warriors, San Francisco Giants, San Jose Earthquakes, Oakland Roots, and the San Jose Sharks.

No, you're not the only one to catch the irony in these endorsements, given that sports are one of the last islands of true meritocracy in America today. A No On 16 campaign volunteer, Jason Xu, started a viral Change. org petition that played off the sports endorsements, reading:

> "[We] **DEMAND** that Warriors, Giants, A's, SF 49ers, Earthquakes, Oakland Roots, and SJ Sharks allocate **15 percent** roster spots for Asian Americans (California Asian population) starting in 2020–2021 season, and guarantee no less than **15 percent** of total game time [emphasis added]."[30]

And it kind of strikes a chord, right? The NBA is 75 percent Black, and the NFL is 70 percent Black. What about diversity for Asians in sports? "Where's *my* representation," Jason Xu said to the stuck-up elites endorsing Proposition 16.

But this is the kind of thing you do when you're a campaign outspent 13 to 1: You find creative ways to turn the opponent's biggest strength into its biggest weakness.

That's what Wenyuan and her seasoned campaign consultant, California Republican operative Arnie Steinberg, did: They reframed the battle as being of the grassroots versus the elite. They hounded Attorney General Becerra over the misleading wording. Ward Connerly went on widely known anti-elitist Tucker Carlson's FOX program to excoriate Becerra for being "corrupt," calling him "a plague on our democracy."[31] No On 16 pounded their opponent for amassing its great campaign war chest from a small, elite few, repeatedly mentioning the "two people who contributed a million dollars apiece" in their materials and messaging. When Connerly went on Tucker Carlson, he signaled to the world that the No On 16 campaign had become, in short, a grassroots anti-elite campaign.

While Ward worked the spotlight, the California campaign core—led by grizzled state strategist Damien Fussel—pushed for loud car rallies in every big city. Asian Americans turned up in force, with signs, speeches, and honking cars, forcing the local media to pay attention. One campaign volunteer, Sophia Liu, "learned to use the media to our advantage," despite its often biased viewpoints and unreliability. Sophia abided by the old adage: "Good press is better than bad press. And bad press is better than no press." "Every rally, we were able to get coverage," she bragged to me.

All the while Wenyuan was working the inside angle, devoted to a strategy of targeted, free media outreach to make up for deficiencies in paid advertising. She hired a little-known hothead named Kenny Xu to handle initial media outreach for the campaign.[32] He was able to score a few editorial board endorsement interviews with the state's most liberal papers, the *San Francisco Chronicle* and the *Los Angeles Times*.

At the interview, conducted over Zoom a few weeks before the vote, *Los Angeles Times* reporters confronted the No On 16 campaign with smug eliteness, none more so than the *Times* opinion page editor, Sewell Chan. The Harvard graduate, Marshall scholar, and child of Asian immigrants spoke as expected of someone with this kind of pedigree—properly deferential to the elites while castigating his own race.

"I was very lucky to go to Harvard," Chan said, for some reason. Then: "We live in a heterogenous society. Is Asian Americans opposing [racial preferences] contributing to carving up a small and elitist pie?"

Richard Sander, the author of *Mismatch* who was invited to the debate, replied: "Well, Jewish quotas were morally wrong." Or were Jews, too, just carving up an elitist pie, selfish grade-grubbers trying to gain greater privilege?

Sewell Chan did not respond. "The point is that it is imperative that Black and Latino representation continue," he pivoted.

Ward Connerly stepped in. "We should not be embedding race even more deeply into American life," he said. "We are so naturally diverse. If we allow people the freedom to pursue whatever they want to pursue, we will eliminate the barriers that exist, then people will compete in an effective way."

It is in this virtual confrontation between the pugnacious Marshall scholar and the hardscrabble businessman-turned caped crusader that you see Ward's vision perhaps most clearly. Of an America that could actually succeed in its goals to be a land of opportunity. Of an America where people are free to make their own choices; where hard work, competition, and the fortitude that competition produces enables anyone to climb the ladder, chart their own success, and build their life in a country that rewards them according to merit, not race.

Then you saw Sewell Chan's vision for America: A country that will continue to hold up Black and Hispanic Americans to the point that he deems them "represented," dividing Americans into racial blocks and pitting them against other races till the end of time.

"Why is it so *morally wrong* that an Asian has to score more than 250 points higher to get into Harvard?" Chan asked.

Ying Ma, communications director on the No On 16 campaign, spoke up. "My argument is that it is *wrong* to discriminate on the basis of race," she said simply, leaving it there.

The endorsement decision from the *Los Angeles Times* came out two weeks later. YES ON PROP. 16, the decision read, BECAUSE THE US IS NOT A MERITOCRACY.

The headline reminded me of a discussion I had with Hillsdale College Professor of Government David Azerrad. "It is less clear to me that Americans have the stomach for meritocracy," he said to me. "This country has grown too soft and compassionate."

Azerrad put it even more bluntly: "Harvard can't bear to see a system with too many Asians."

You can add Sewell Chan, an Asian American, to the list of those who are—for some reason—uncomfortable with a system that admits "too many" Asians because of merit. Maybe Chan is uncomfortable realizing that the answers to life aren't as simple as, "Put a Black person here, a white person there." That it is not the fault of those who get in that others did not. That someone *deserved* something, rather than "got it by luck," as Chan would explain his own Harvard admissions story.

So, of course the US isn't a meritocracy, Sewell Chan. The question is: Could you bear it, if it becomes one?

■ ■ ■

On November 3, 2020, Election Day, Proposition 16 came to California voters. And voters rejected it. Completely. Fifty-seven percent of California voters voted no to Proposition 16. So thorough was the shellacking, the margin was higher than the first time the constitutional amendment, Proposition 209, originally arrived at the hands of voters twenty-five years ago.

Ward Connerly was vindicated. So was his primary political legacy—and his optimism, his faith in the American people's resilience. "We get to race not mattering by practice, practice, practice," he said at the editorial board interview with the *San Francisco Chronicle*. When it comes to racial politics, Ward believes that hard work and a spirit of "forgiving the sinner" will lead to a victory for the campaign and new era in this country. The American elite drags its feet, but it appears as if the American people are willing to move right along with him.

As for Wenyuan, she glowed in triumph. Interviews came from all sides—people wanted to know the secret to how she was able to run such a masterful campaign. Wenyuan, humble as ever, deflected the praise to lesser-known heroes of the movement: "Nearly all of our funds came from 7,000 Chinese American donors of modest means," she said in a *Wall Street Journal* interview.[33]

But this did not mean that Wenyuan would settle for one victory, brilliant as it was. She had a greater vision, not only for America but for her own cohort of upstart immigrants. "Our victory is a more decisive indicator of political awakening or political coming of age of Asian Americans," she said in a call with the Asian American Coalition for Education merely a month after her impressive victory.

It's true. The difference between Ward Connerly's first push to end racial preferences in the '90s and the joint effort to banish Proposition 16 was undoubtedly made by the state's newly mobilized Asian Americans. Asian Americans led car rallies. They led the communications and lobbied senators. Their participation in the political process in this way was unprecedented in the history of the United States.

And they're just getting started, Wenyuan thought. But it's going to get harder.

"Sweeping reforms on critical race theory are being adopted in our curriculum," she said. "[Now there's a] bill to require ethnic studies to K–12 high schools in California." In a private meeting with top Asian American leaders in the country, she spoke as if she was a field marshal, surveying the depth and strength of the enemy for a future attack. The odds seemed long.

But they were long before the Asian American political awakening caught everyone off guard and on their heels.

Make no mistake: The next decade, especially under a Biden or Harris administration, will be a great cultural reckoning between the woke diversity ideologues at the top of the elite liberal institutions of America—Big Diversity, as Wenyuan calls it—and meritocracy.

Meritocracy won round one with a little help from the American people. But the other side is dusting itself off. They are further entrenching antiracism into colleges and our public schools. Kamala Harris, who may be on her way to becoming the most powerful vice president in modern history, is on the record as a fully ritualized and purified woke propagator. This is what she said, days before the November 3 election:

> "So there's a big difference between equality and equity. Equality suggests, 'Oh, everyone should get the same amount.' The problem with that, not everybody's starting out from the same place. So if we're all getting the same amount, but you started out back there and I started out over here, we could get the same amount, but you're still going to be that far back behind me. It's about giving people the resources and the support they need, so that everyone can be on equal footing, and then compete on equal footing. *Equitable treatment means we all end up in the same place* [emphasis added]."[34]

With a woke ally in the White House, the challenge couldn't be bigger. But neither could the importance. So Wenyuan gets back on the computer, in search of the next grind-your-teeth David versus Goliath matchup to sweat out. She, of course, is David.

MORE IMPORTANT THAN DIVERSITY

Asian Americans are not fighting housing, segregated facilities, poll taxes, and Jim Crow, like the civil rights activists of the '50s and '60s (in a movement some argue continues today). But they are fighting a sinister and insidious takeover of the American mind, which erases the moral progress made under the Civil Rights Movement. The sentiment of racial harmony—all people of all races being treated according to their individual excellence, without consideration of their race or background—is the central modern grounding of the American Dream. It's what draws so many immigrants to these shores.

Asian Americans who stand up for their rights in the fields of education and business risk dismissal or even outright snobbery from the intellectual class. There is even a term, the "self-flagellating Asian"—the Asian American, the Sewell Chan, usually second or third generation, who fancies attacking his own race in place of standing up. These are the risks and pains that Asian Americans must carry on their journey for equal respect in elite parts of our society, full of people who encourage Asian Americans to castigate themselves so they won't have to do it.

Hasan Minhaj, Netflix actor and second-generation Indian American, called the Asian Americans standing against Harvard "the worst kind" of American. The same kind of self-righteous attack on Chinese Americans is reflected in Yale undergraduate Eileen Huang's "Anti-Blackness is deeply rooted in my community" line.

Besides being hit with the accusation that they are somehow racist or complicit in white supremacy, Asian Americans who stand up for their rights risk being called selfish. Minhaj said of Yukong Zhao, one of the sponsors of the Harvard lawsuit: "Is this really about civil rights or your kid not getting into Harvard?"[35] In other words, in the name of social justice, Asians are being asked—or coerced—to share what they've earned, while other groups are given license to take and take.

But Asian Americans are vulnerable to these charges, because with no cultural capital, they can be easily dismissed. It is too easy to take an initial look at the Asian Americans' lawsuit against Harvard and roll your eyes. *Of course* Asians would sue Harvard . . . because they're obsessed with Harvard. *Of course* Asians wouldn't care about politics . . . until it affects the prestige of the university to which they would send their kids.

But problems are noticed when they first appear in one's community. Would it be right for us to demean women who fight sexism at their companies because they're already making money? Or to demean scientists whose work is being censored because they're simply lucky to have their prestigious positions?

It is perfectly reasonable for Asian Americans to notice cracks when they first appear in the diversity ideology in college admissions.

But a few college spots are endemic of a larger problem. The problem is the ideology of critical race theory, most conveniently manifested in the college admissions process but which emblemizes other conditions of the way these schools view individuals—as cogs to fit in a racial wheel. Ward Connerly said at that *LA Times* editorial board meeting: "Once you start using race, you can't stop using race. Race becomes *the factor*." And he's right. We've seen it over and over again.

Asian Americans need to buckle down and keep fighting. And since Students for Fair Admissions pushed to sue Harvard University, Asian Americans began slowly developing a political identity that pushes beyond their own self-interest to something bigger. Something at the root of the word political—*polis*—meaning "city." Meaning a multitude. Something that resembles the fundamental suppositions of civil rights.

■ ■ ■

Lin Yang was one of Edward Blum's first allies and an early supporter of Students for Fair Admissions. A mother and chemical engineer from Connecticut, she initially joined the movement out of motives that were concerned primarily with her children's welfare. "My daughters were freshmen and sophomores in high school," she said. "We took all the usual college tours." What college tours? "You know . . . Harvard, Yale, Princeton."

Lin Yang went on to host the rally at Copley Square that brought together hundreds of Asian American parents to descend on Boston and demand concessions on race preferences from Harvard. It was at the rally where Lin saw something different. This was bigger than just Asian Americans and college admissions.

At that moment, Lin realized that Asian Americans couldn't be the only ones getting the short end of the diversity ideology. Other people, in other places, were getting the short shrift, too. Whomever liberal race ideology excludes under its victimhood umbrella were unnecessarily suffering based on the color of their skin, on arbitrary policies bent to divide rather than uplift.

So Lin started looking. Little did she know, the stories she was looking to uncover were right in her state. In Hartford, Connecticut, one of the toughest educational climates in America. There, Lin met a parent, Gwen Samuel.

Gwen, a single Black parent and veteran, did not have the most encouraging schooling as a child. She often felt excluded because of her academic interests. "I didn't get along much with the African Americans [at my school]," Gwen said. Her peers would say she "was acting like a white girl . . . you got criticized by your own African American peers for acting like a white person because you liked school." In other words, Gwen Samuel did not fit the narrative that had been conferred to her, often by her own peers, as a Black woman. And she paid for it.

Then, her mother did something for her that changed her life: She enrolled Gwen at a private Catholic school, despite having barely any money to pay for it. Gwen's mom worked three jobs so Gwen could get an acceptable education and go to college. Gwen did. She went to a military school, in fact, and joined the military soon after graduating. Leaving the military and having kids, she eventually found herself in Hartford with her children, who needed an adequate education.

Gwen, who had worked her way up to middle-class standing, did not want her child to suffer the same educational fate as she did. Lin, an Asian American who lived in wealthier New Haven, was moved by Gwen's testimony. Their mutual desires were the same: Both wanted their children to get the world-class education they deserved. Both sought every opportunity for her children to get the education she felt they needed, but Gwen was looking in one of the most difficult school districts in America.

Hartford, Connecticut, a low-income city with over 81 percent of its population being Black and Hispanic, is hardly a model of public education excellence. The 2018 graduation rate at Hartford Public Schools was 68.8 percent, below the national average of 81.1 percent. But it had one thing that motivated Gwen to see an educational future for her kids.

In the early 2000s, Connecticut started to build gleaming new magnet schools in the middle of the city in an effort to at least stymie the city's terrible trends. Gwen saw one of these schools, Capitol Prep Magnet School—sturdy, with high ceilings and fresh, clean windows—and knew it was the kind of school to which she wanted to send her child.

But there was a catch. Ostensibly, the way to get her child into one of these schools was straightforward—enter him in a lottery for a random selection. The lottery, which randomized the names, was supposed to fairly pick kids to attend these high-demand magnet schools. Her kids stood just as much of a chance as everyone else's to get in. Supposedly.

That is, until a state court decision mandated "diverse" schooling in all Connecticut magnet schools. In the eyes of school administrators, it meant that schools could not be more than 75 percent "one race." The claim was that there needed to be at least 25 percent white students in the school so that Black students could be considered "reduced-isolation;" that is, around enough white people to reap the benefits of a sufficiently "diverse" student body. There was only one problem: Hartford was more than 80 percent Black, and the applications to the magnet school were overwhelmingly from Black students. In fact, more than 87 percent of Hartford's mostly Black population applies to these magnet schools.[36] (Although the magnet schools were completely beyond the quality of the local public schools around them, wealthier white parents in the suburbs were still not interested in paying for busing into the city.)

Yet despite not attracting any white demand, the diversity mandate persisted. If they continued to admit Black kids—which was the overwhelming demand for these schools—over white kids, they would upset the status quo and possibly increase the ratio of Black and Hispanic kids versus white and Asian kids higher than 75 percent. So what did the school do? They left "empty seats," Gwen said. Empty seats her child should have taken.

So important was this arbitrary 75–25 ratio to the Connecticut State Court that Superior Court Judge Marshal K. Berger saw the clear discrimination against Black and Latino students, and did nothing about it:

> "The placement of all students who seek a seat in a magnet school is a laudable goal, but it does not justify a change in the standard . . . Equity cannot favor more segregation, especially in light of the 1996 Supreme Court decision which directs a reduction in racial and ethnic isolation."[37]

How did we arrive at a place where something as grotesque as this exclusionary 75–25 ratio could be called "diversity?" Where fundamental rights to an education and a fair shot at admissions are completely trampled in the name of a number?

It was so important that a certain percentage of white kids populate this school that a judge *prevented Black and Hispanic kids* from enrolling so that it could maintain this diversity ratio—because there were too many Black students.

Trying and failing to get her kids into Capitol Prep Magnet School, one of the diversity-enforced magnet schools, led Gwen Samuel to contemplate how her lawmakers' seemingly good intentions were being used against parents like her. Ensuring a diverse student body "doesn't trump the Constitution," she said. "In Connecticut we're treated like such victims," she said. "They'll tell us all the terrible things that happened during the civil rights era, your era. But there were people that despite the oppression, despite the challenges—they overcame. But those stories aren't told here, and we're treated as victims. Like you really need to be saved."

And it is from this victim mentality, Gwen asserted, that educators advance their diversity agenda onto you. "They're sending a message that you have to be in a classroom with a white and Asian child to learn, like there's some osmosis. We're starting to internalize that."

The unequal treatment devastated Gwen. She felt the only thing that mattered to the state was her skin color. Any other part of her life did not matter one iota to them. Not that she was a military mom, that her mom trained her to value academics, and that she had tried to raise her kids the same way. To the state, she was just another single Black parent, probably destined to raise an ill-tempered Black kid who would drag down school performance metrics unless there were enough white kids at his school to keep the numbers afloat.

She found Lin, and the two of them formed a powerful bond. Together, they enlisted the help of Pacific Legal Foundation, an individual liberty-based legal firm, and sued the Hartford City School System for discriminating against Black parents. A lawsuit wouldn't be easy. The NAACP quickly rushed to defend the school system, giving the city the moral self-righteousness to fight back. But Gwen and Lin found allies in unusual places. They recruited a former Dr. King ally, Terrence Roberts. Lin arranged for him to speak at a Chinese restaurant in Hartford in front of a group of educational allies; an intimate crowd composed of families of all races appeared for his talk. A small pack of dissidents trying to make a difference.

Terrence Roberts, a former professor and now consultant, started life in the roughest of waters—as a member of the famous "Little Rock Nine," the Black kids who had to be ushered by National Guards into the school they were desegregating, Little Rock Central High School in Little Rock, Arkansas. He became an intellectual and civil rights advocate, a moral force in the community. So when Lin invited him to give a speech in front of the Pacific Legal Foundation, near the courthouse where Gwen's case was being argued, Roberts held nothing back in his scathing indictment of what the civil rights system he fought for had devolved into. He even lamented the most consequential Supreme Court decision of the twentieth century: *Brown versus Board of Education.* Although he agreed with the initial outcome, Roberts felt that *Brown*'s reasoning would bite this country in the back, later on—as it does now.

"I think what happened with the *Brown* decision was actually somewhat problematic, because there was a great deal of emphasis put on the need for Black people to feel better about themselves by being in classrooms with white kids . . . The real issue has always been resources, materials, opportunities," he said. And who could blame him? The racial ratios attached to these Connecticut magnet schools created a veneer that Black kids couldn't help themselves, that they needed a critical mass of white kids to "educate" them.

And it raises this question: How much of this whole diversity and inclusion logic is in fact about elite white liberals thinking that their culture—elite white culture—is the necessary salvation to what ails Black people? How much of this is a subconscious white savior complex, saying, "You know what you really need, bucko? A dose of *me* and people *like me*," to signal to Black people, "You cannot succeed without turning to people like me." The elite liberals who frequent red-carpet charity galas may think the solution to failing schools and widening success gaps is to import more white people into those schools and get rid of achievement markers. Ha! No achievement marker, no achievement gap, no problem. Anyone actually concerned with whether Black children are learning anything would be pushed to the wayside.

But Gwen *is* concerned. She is hungry for opportunities for her children. Unlike the NAACP, she does not believe demographics determine destiny. "Everything is not Black and white. I went to private school, you know. Life and its challenges and its choices play a part."

And there are so many moms, like Gwen and Lin, who just want a *fair shot* for their kids. The setting may be different. But the principles are the same.

As of December 2020, litigation is ongoing in Gwen's city. The courts might strike her, Lin, and Terrence Roberts down. "Diversity, equity, and inclusion" might win out in the end, but these fights must be had. Asian Americans are being harmed, and they're not the only ones. Everyone who is the wrong color, whose story does not match the stereotype, loses out in this broken meritocracy.

Lin reflected on the experience. "My heart has turned towards the Black community," she said. "They're suffering the same way we're suffering."

AMERICAN DREAM

Part of the reason why Marx and Mao were wrong about the perpetual envious clash between the classes is because they did not take into account the power of leadership. The power of great leadership to turn people towards something good, something better than what is expected of them.

A great leader not only changes minds, he defines a generation.

Does anyone seriously doubt that the individual influence of Dr. Martin Luther King Jr., saved this country from a descent into racial discord and moral chaos? Without his leadership, there would be no March on Washington, no Civil Rights Act. No Voting Rights Act. Without his leadership, it is guaranteed that there would have been even more social discord, disharmony, rioting, and fuming white resentment against Black people that would have made their struggle for civil rights much more difficult—and perhaps would have spiraled this nation out of control and into another Civil War.

Even when King organized rallies for more controversial positions, like his opposition to war and poverty created by unbridled capitalism, he planned them strictly—with a kind of moral discipline that allowed his protesters to stand unimpeachable for their cause. He did so because he stood for more than simply the gain of his group over the gain of another group. He said in his Letter from Birmingham Jail: "Before I was a civil rights leader, I was a preacher of the Gospel. This was my first calling and it still remains my greatest commitment. You know, actually all that I do in civil rights I do because I consider it a part of my ministry. I have no other ambitions in life but to achieve excellence in the Christian ministry."

I pointed to Malcolm X's response to King and the ideology that eventually became critical race theory, equity, and antiracism. But I haven't yet elaborated on how King responded to Malcolm X's scathing critique. Malcolm X believed that there was no room within the white system for Black flourishing. With slavery and a Jim Crow legacy lasting hundreds of years, it is tempting to believe that. But King believed America was capable of more, that the stain of racial animus could in some way be neutralized.

One of King's greatest confidants was Reverend Wyatt Tee Walker, installed by King as the director of his Southern Christian Leadership Conference during the high noon of the civil rights battle. Reverend Walker believed that the Black race could advance in America *without* resorting to taking from white people. He believed so stridently that there was room in America for both races that in 1999, he set up Harlem, New York's first charter school, the Sisulu-Walker Charter School of Harlem, which sought to provide an alternative to the difficult educational experience of so many young Black children in New York City.

Today, because of the precedent Walker set, students who attend city charter schools from kindergarten to eighth grade can close about 86 percent of the "Scarsdale-Harlem" gap—the difference in scores between Black students in Harlem and those in the affluent, white, New York suburb—in math and about 66 percent of the gap in English.[38] Walker's charter school reflected his vision that Black children prosper through a combination of classic best practices and classroom rigor; that a Black child was just as well-prepared to achieve as a white one if he was subjected to the right pressures and organization. They didn't excuse white people, but neither did they castigate them. They didn't need to look through the lens where one man prospers only if the other falls.

In 2015, Walker cowrote an article where he came out against the critical race theory starting to blossom in mainstream popularity. He wrote presciently:

> "Today, too many 'remedies'—such as Critical Race Theory, the increasingly fashionable post-Marxist/postmodernist approach that analyzes society as institutional group power structures rather than on a spiritual or one-to-one human level—are taking

us in the wrong direction: separating even elementary school children into explicit racial groups, and emphasizing differences instead of similarities.

"The answer is to go deeper than race, deeper than wealth, deeper than ethnic identity, deeper than gender. To teach ourselves to comprehend each person, not as a symbol of a group, but as a unique and special individual within a common context of shared humanity. To go to that fundamental place where we are all simply mortal creatures, seeking to create order, beauty, family, and connection in a world that—on its own—seems to bend too often toward randomness and entropy."[39]

In a world where a certain skin color by birth seems to define you, it is true that in some circles, both on the Left and the Right, you are marked. But what Reverend Walker understood is that *your race should not define you* in an America that truly lives up to its ideals.

The whole idea of the American Dream—the same dream Reverend Walker wishes for Black Americans to fully experience one day—is that you can come from any background and make a *life* in this country. But in order to unlock that potential, people of all races must, in some sense, trust the other. Racial divides will have to fade away slowly, like a cloud that has given hail and thunder and lightning, but eventually drifts to the horizon and leaves well alone. There will be mistakes made, Walker knew. The key is to never let another group's past slights define the present. The present must be made up of laws to which race is of minimal importance. The only thing that matters is what you contribute to the world.

Perhaps that sheds new light on King's words that fateful, sweltering day in August: "I still have a dream. It is a dream deeply rooted in the American dream." King's vision was of a country where the *rules of the game* are not based in the color of your skin but the content of your character.

What racial separatists do, however, is lock in race. Ironically, in trying to retribute the sins and slights of others, they define people according to factors they cannot control and create a reality in which background matters more than anything else. They work against the American Dream. They take this country from a land of opportunity into the same sort of land that today's immigrants to America have departed.

Worst of all, they create an industry out of it. It is an industry of equity money and antiracism that doesn't help low-income Black and Hispanic Americans, of racial preferences that give advantages to the elite and leave the rest behind. It turns people against each other. It fragments American solidarity.

But there's hope. There are brave fighters out there, people like Lin Yang and Gwen Samuel and Wenyuan Wu and Ward Connerly and Yukong Zhao and Yiatin Chu and Eva Guo. People carrying out a greater purpose than one just themselves. Fighting against something: Identity politics. The diversity industry. The cultivated arrogance of liberal elites.

And fighting for something. For the right to be judged based on your character, not the color of your skin. The right to carry out the fundamental proposition of the American Dream: that whatever your background may be, it does not have to define you, and that your hard work, your character—*that's* what ultimately matters.

Afterword
Model Minority

S ome may wonder about the lack of my own anecdotes through *An Inconvenient Minority*. I would rather my case be made through the testimonies of others rather than myself, as I find personal narrative is often clouded by hasty judgements, exaggerations, and selective editing.

But that doesn't mean I don't have anything to say about myself.

My journey to understanding my racial identity began in fourth grade. I had transferred into the county's gifted and talented program, where I met the boy who changed my life. Henry was a Chinese American like me, except much more perfect than I could ever hope to be. He was short, cute, acquiesced to everything his teachers told him, and got A pluses on every test. I was chubby, nerdy, and merely got As. At our fifth grade graduation ceremony, my teachers went on stage to present Henry with a star student award, unveiling a bike. Henry was "very special," the teachers said in unison, and he was bound to do great things.

We were friends for a while before I began to resent him as we followed each other to the county's top middle school, an accelerated International Baccalaureate program. I compared myself to him, partially because other people kept comparing me to him. He was, after all, the perfect Chinese boy—better grades, better "personality," more popular than I could ever be. I was the brooding rebel who sat in the back of the bus, plotting how I could prove I was better than him at something.

That something was writing. Henry had the popularity, the squeaky-clean obedience, the apparent bashfulness it seemed only I could tell was inverted self-aggrandizement. But I had the pen. I wrote for days on end, got lost in science fiction and released book after book, writing three novels before I reached high school.

Yet my consciousness wouldn't shake Henry. I was so tired of being compared to him, of people sizing up me and all the other Asians in my school who inevitably came up short, that I began to see my own Asianness as a harmful aspect of my life. I wouldn't be subordinated to a kid like Henry, I thought, if I were *white.* But I was reared in a Chinese family, and the burden of achievement was on me to be better than my overachieving Asian peers, of whom Henry was the pinnacle.

My feelings of inferiority dogged me for a long time. Constantly needing to prove myself, in a year I wrote a 144,000-word science fiction sports novel called *Trisk* and sold hundreds of copies to my friends. I dated several white girls; I relished the fact that they were white. I joined the cross-country team and made varsity. Things were going well. Suddenly, I was accumulating some status in high school.

But there was one whale I hadn't yet caught. The whale every Asian American at my school was dreading. The one that would take your pleasant voyage across the sea and wreck your boat. The Ivy League admittance.

Some had been preparing for Harvard's admissions since elementary school. I had mostly focused on doing what I was passionate about—writing—but Harvard's glare put a different light on what I was doing. It became about whether I had sufficiently distinguished myself from all my Asian competitors in a way that was attractive to the Ivy League. Whispers went around my (very Asian) high school: "He played *squash,* colleges like that." Asians accumulated clubs like trophies to show how holistically gifted they were. I selected Princeton as the university for my early action application. Was my writing good enough for Princeton's admissions officers?

I remember my essay and my alumni interview. I had bet everything on my book *Trisk.* Asked to meet with an alumnus in an office on Princeton's famous Nassau Street, I came with my book. I told the alumnus about my process for writing it, how I'd love to be an author, and why I was sufficiently distinguished for the admissions spot. The alumnus smiled. He went into his wallet and pulled out a twenty-dollar bill. "I want to buy it," he said.

"No, I don't want to make you do that," I said.

The alumnus laughed. "No," he said, shaking his head and smiling. "You sold me."

I left thinking: Wow, maybe I have a chance after all.

Henry and I applied the same class year, he to Yale, I to Princeton. Henry got into Yale. I didn't get into Princeton. There was only enough room in the Ivy Leagues for one of us—the perfect student, or the brooding author. The Ivy League made its decision, and I was once again consigned to the wilderness of inferiority to Henry, as rated by the powers that be.

I accepted a scholarship to Davidson College, where I began to build my reputation as a politically outspoken person. Things were going well. I was sporting a stellar GPA, a declared Math major, and the kind of notoriety that made me a name on campus.

And then the consulting firms came around. I didn't particularly care for consulting, but I became convinced—like so many other high achieving Asians—that an elite consulting job at a place like Bain was the preferred path of the excellent. I didn't make the McKinsey interview rounds (I wasn't *summa cum laude*, for crying out loud), but I was a semi-finalist for the Deloitte internship role. I prepared for two weeks straight to master the interview. Day and night, I practiced. The day came. I made my case. The recruiter told me they would have their finalist round at 1 p.m., and they would let me know beforehand if I got in. I waited. One o'clock passed and I heard nothing. My heart sank; they weren't even going to tell me they rejected me. I sat on my bed, heartbroken.

Then, at 1:20 p.m., they asked me to come in for the finalist round in thirty minutes. No apology for calling late.

I hiked to the Career Development Office, where I met the other three competitors. I was the only man there. The other three were attractive women who I knew only vaguely (Davidson was a small campus, about 2,000 people, so students generally had reads on each other). Briefly, the thought crossed my mind—were they looking for a certain "type" from

Davidson?—but I quickly dismissed it and focused on preparing myself for the finalist round.

I performed admirably, scything through every behavioral query and answering every consulting question with easy, practiced grace. At the group round, where all four of us were clumped in a room and asked to make a case for a certain business strategy, I took the lead, explaining rationally what we were trying to do and how a preferred strategy would fall into place. The girls seemed to agree. Things were going well.

I waited for the phone call—acceptance or rejection—into this prestigious club. That Wednesday, driving with friends to Five Guys, I received a call from a random Atlanta number. It was the Deloitte guy. I answered and my Bluetooth picked up the phone, so that everyone in the car—my friends—heard: "Kenny, I thought I might tell you personally," he said, "because I wanted to tell you about how you could improve."

My hands could barely hold onto the steering wheel.

"You did great on all of the consulting interview questions," he said. "We all knew you were smart."

Okay, I thought to myself. *So I was being judged on something else.*

"As for your performance on the group interview, we thought you were being a little too dominant."

I was not accepted to the consulting internship. And the deciding factor was that I was perceived as a dominant personality, somebody who couldn't "work well" with the team. Never mind that our team solved the problem. Never mind that I didn't get an inkling, even from my competitors, that the way I had approached the group interview was off-putting or hostile. Something about the way I was acting didn't fit the interviewers' vision for who should get the only internship from Davidson College.

"Okay," I croaked, "thank you."

"Wish you the best of luck, Kenny," the Deloitte guy said. And he hung up.

I finished the drive and let the boys out. "I'm sorry," my friends told me. "That's okay," I said weakly. "Give me a moment."

I sat in the car alone for ten minutes, looking at the night sky and the steering wheel. It seemed that everything I was trying for, that I seemed to really want, I was shut out of for one reason or another. I tried so hard and I always fell just short, seemingly in the final rounds. My feelings of rejection would have eaten me up if my friends had not come back to the car. "Come out, Kenny," they said. "We'll get you Five Guys."

I told my parents that night what had happened. "It's okay," Mom said. "We love you," said Dad. Swallow your pride. There are so many opportunities out there.

I was never particularly concerned about money, or managing other people's finances. So why did this Deloitte rejection sting so hard? Maybe because people like me know, preternaturally, that just being around other high-achieving Asians means we will be judged against them. I had somehow lost a life race for which Asian Americans could come out on top. And I was twenty-one years old.

We went along with our lives, and I continued to locate where God wanted me to be. One day, my dad and I were sharing a bit of wine and we started talking about the whole Deloitte saga. "You gave it all you got," he said. "Sometimes, no matter how hard you try, they just want someone else."

■   ■   ■

I wrote this book for three audiences: my parents, my Asian American community, and the world. I wanted to warn about what happens when elite discrimination is legitimized and abetted by the world's most powerful institutions. I wanted to write to my Asian American community to help them stand up for themselves and show that they are part of a larger story about America. And I wanted to write to my parents.

My father came to America from China in 1991 and worked as a business professional in the United States for nearly thirty years. He knew a thing or two about climbing. After reaching a gap of rungs in the corporate ladder, where he specialized in banking and finance, he started his own business. For a while our family was thriving. Dad could afford to take us to Europe for extended vacations. Then the Great Recession hit in 2008; his business lost steam, and he had to wade his way back into the world of corporate politics. There, he found more missing rungs, unrelated to his personal talent or merit, preventing his advancement.

Even as a Senior Vice President of a big bank, my father couldn't find his footing in a corporate environment littered with internal strife. It became more about making alliances and kissing up to the next guy than actually doing his job. Eventually, my father left that job, too, sick and tired of the politics, and formed a second business he could retire on.

My mother came over to America with Dad. She passed her Certified Public Accounting Exams on the first try and became a CPA. But since our immigrant family had little to no extended family in the US, when the kids came, Mom devoted her full-time role to motherhood, sacrificing much of her career to raise me and my sisters. Many years later, after my youngest sister went to school full time, my mother wanted to go back to work. An accounting firm hired her. But merely two months later, she left the firm; the work had become too technologically advanced, the hours too long and taxing for a woman now in her fifties.

My parents' stories informed me that life is hardly the straight-ahead meritocracy I wished for in my younger life. What would have happened if I got into Princeton? Into Deloitte? Would this book have been written? Would I have been able to interrogate myself in the harsh, biting ways that eventually led me to sympathize with my fellow aspirational Asian Americans and push that energy into *An Inconvenient Minority*? Or would an acceptance have propelled me into an even more ruthlessly competitive environment that would stoke more jealousy of other Asians, rather than sympathy?

These are some of the questions that threaten to uproot one's entire self as an Asian American, knowing people hold you up to a higher standard for reasons you cannot control. But in a country like America, there are multiple paths to succeeding in your field.

In the end, we have to be comfortable in our own talents and gifts. That is what I've realized about human nature. The reason why some make it artificially harder for people of other skins is because they aren't comfortable in their own skin. Why does Harvard feel the need to racially balance its class? Because the elite administration is guilt-ridden over their privilege, their compliance, but enjoys the benefits too much to bear their responsibility to help those less fortunate. Racial preferences are the salve. Its unseen victims are Asian Americans like me, who question the order of the world around them and their place in it.

I bore that self-questioning and self-loathing for a long time. Occasionally I think back to Henry. My friends inform me he's going to be a doctor. I don't press. I don't really need to know.

Because I wouldn't trade my life for his. Some people play the elite game, and that gives them life. But I could never see myself doing that. I have too much to say, too much to love, to be comfortable with being another model minority, chasing a model dream that isn't mine.

I have my own dreams to chase.

A Note on Anti-Asian Violence

While on travels, I have been asked about the wave of recent news coverage of anti-Asian crimes in the United States and whether attacks on Asian American excellence are related. The answer is that they are. Harvard's race ideology is a product of the same kind of resentment of success that often undergirds anti-Asian hate crimes. This resentment of success has come in the form of political exclusion: Labor leader Denis Kearney, the lead organizer of Chinese Exclusion in the late 1800s, attacked Chinese Americans for being "curs" and mongrels. This resentment has come more recently in the form of targeted violence. In New York City, Oakland, and Los Angeles, thugs beat up Asian American bystanders for seemingly no reason other than their color and perceived vulnerability. One assailant, after shoving a sixty-eight-year-old Sri Lankan immigrant to the ground, allegedly said, "You motherf–king Asian!" as he punched the elderly man multiple times in the head.[1] There are latent reasons for this animus. Sometimes, suspicion and hostility against Asian shopkeepers in inner cities—and suspicion of fellow customers who are Black—boils over. Before a group of rioters and gangsters stormed Koreatown in the 1992 Los Angeles Riots, the rapper Ice Cube preached: "So pay respect to the black fist. Or we'll burn your store right down to a crisp. And then we'll see ya. 'Cause can't turn the ghetto into Black Korea."[2] Asian Americans are not aloof to these kinds of narratives, either: During those riots, one Korean magazine asked those same Koreans to "engage in self-reflection" as "a subject of envy from Americans of different minority races."[3]

Sometimes, especially in elite circles (as explored in *An Inconvenient Minority*), this resentment is more subtle—but just as invidious. In fact, these more raw and visceral incidents of anti-Asian violence help us to clarify exactly what is meant when Asian Americans are accused of "privilege" or "white adjacency." What is meant, in this elite Leftist-speak, is that Asian Americans are taking things away from other races in an apparent zero-sum game to the top. A narrative is advanced: that Asians are taking all the business opportunities, just as Asians are taking all the best school spots.

This doesn't have to be the portrait of who we are as a nation. We should not harbor grudges like this forever; we are a rapidly diversifying country, in many ways. But we cannot stand to allow policies that continue to divide our nation on the basis of race and allow for discrimination to occur. We must target the media, government, and education systems that attempt to divide our country to infighting racial blocs. Only then can we stand up—not just for Asian Americans, but against envy, bitterness, and resentment of anyone on the basis of their skin color.

Kenny Xu
April 8, 2021

Acknowledgments

This book has been a special journey, and many people deserve thanks for making it possible. To my supporters—thank you! Without your support and encouragement, *An Inconvenient Minority* would have never existed, and these critical perspectives on education, meritocracy, and racial identity would have never made it into mainstream culture. Special thanks go out to the Asian American Coalition for Education, the Gale Foundation Trust, the Silicon Valley Chinese Association, Edward, Ward, Lin, Eva, Barbara and Jack, Larry, Ning, Zhen, Edward, Emma, Amelia, James, and to many others for believing in the vision for this book. Thanks also to my agent, Andrew Stuart, and the publishing team at Diversion. Thanks to many others who were willing to give candid interviews and important perspectives to share with the world. The greatest thanks to God and Jesus Christ for providing me with the gift of a voice, to be used to serve Him. Romans 12:3–8.

Bibliography

Chua, Amy. *Battle Hymn of the Tiger Mother*. Penguin, 2011.

Chua, Amy and Jed Rubenfeld. *The Triple Package*. Penguin, 2014.

Fincher, David. *The Social Network*. Columbia, 2010.

Gladwell, Malcolm. *Outliers*. Little, Brown and Company, 2008.

Golden, Daniel. *The Price of Admission*. Crown, 2009.

Gonzalez, Michael. *The Plot to Change America*. Encounter, 2020.

Kendi, Ibram X. *How to Be an Antiracist*. One World, 2019.

Mac Donald, Heather. *The Diversity Delusion*. St. Martins, 2018.

McKay, Adam. *The Big Short*. Paramount, 2015.

Mulligan, Thomas. *Justice and the Meritocratic State*. Routledge, 2019.

Markovits, Daniel. *The Meritocracy Trap*. Penguin, 2020.

Taylor, Stuart and Richard Sander. *Mismatch: How Affirmative Action Hurts Students It's Intended to Help, and Why Universities Won't Admit It*. Basic Books, 2012.

Tough, Paul. *The Years that Matter Most*. Houghton Mifflin Harcourt, 2019.

Yang, Wesley. *The Souls of Yellow Folk*. Norton, 2019.

Notes

FOREWORD
Within Our Many, an Inconvenient One

1. Delgado, Richard, and Jean Stefancic. *Critical Race Theory: An Introduction* (NYU Press, 2017). 3.

PREFACE FOR NEW EDITION

1. https://www.washingtonpost.com/news/worldviews/wp/2013/05/15/a -fascinating-map-of-the-worlds-most-and-least-racially-tolerant-countries/
2. https://www.pewresearch.org/social-trends/2017/05/18/1-trends-and -patterns-in-intermarriage/
3. https://samv91khoyt2i553a2t1s05i-wpengine.netdna-ssl.com/wp-content /uploads/2018/06/Doc-415-1-Arcidiacono-Expert-Report.pdf

A BROKEN MERITOCRACY

1. Vikram Achuthan, "(Un)Equal Opportunity: Breaking down Demographics at Jefferson," *TjTODAY* (June 2020), www.tjtoday .org/29044/showcase/unequal-opportunity-breaking-down -demographics-at-jefferson/.
2. Sonia Kanchan, "Dwindling Diversity," *TjTODAY* (Nov. 2018), www .tjtoday.org/24808/showcase/dwindling-diversity.
3. Hilde Kahn et al., "A Stubborn Excellence Gap," *Education Next* (Mar. 2020), www.educationnext.org/stubborn-excellence-gap-despite-efforts -diversity-stalls-elite-public-high-school/.
4. Ibram X. Kendi, *How to Be an Antiracist* (New York: One World, 2019), 19.
5. "Fairfax County schools defending $20K presentation from anti-racism scholar," *Fox 5 DC* (Sept 2020), https://www.fox5dc.com/news/fairfax -county-schools-defending-20k-presentation-from-anti-racism-scholar.
6. Rashida Green, *Twitter* (Aug 2020), https://twitter.com/RashidaJGreen /status/1291359988808589317.
7. Kendi, *Antiracist*, 101.

8. https://thehighlandernews.com/24236/news/fcps-proposes-merit
    -lottery-for-tj-admission/.

9. https://patch.com/virginia/oakton/supt-presents-recommendations
    -improve-diversity-thomas-jefferson-high-school.

10. Tyler Currie, "The Quest," *The Washington Post* (Aug 2005), https://www
    .washingtonpost.com/archive/lifestyle/magazine/2005/08/07/the-quest
    /e459494c-2cb3-4db2-8313-0ae6846bd8ba/.

11. Asra Nomani, "Merit on the Ropes," City Journal, *Manhattan Institute*
    (Sep 2020), https://www.city-journal.org/lefts-campaign-against
    -educational-excellence-suburbs?utm_source=Twitter&utm_medium
    =Organic_Social.

12. Frank L. Samson, "Altering Public University Admission Standards to
    Preserve White Group Position in the United States: Results from a
    Laboratory Experiment," *Comparative Education Review* 57, no. 3 (2013):
    369–396, *JSTOR*, www.jstor.org/stable/10.1086/670664.

13. Kanchan, "Dwindling Diversity."

14. "Virginia Education Secretary Compares Test Prep to Using Illegal
    Performance Enhancing Drugs," *YouTube*, uploaded by Asra Nomani
    (September 2020).

15. Thomas Mulligan, *Justice and the Meritocratic State* (New York: Routledge,
    Taylor & Francis Group, 2018).

16. Tomás R. Jiménez and Adam L. Horowitz, "When White Is Just Alright:
    How Immigrants Redefine Achievement and Reconfigure the Ethnoracial
    Hierarchy," *SAGE Journals* (June 2014), journals.sagepub.com/doi
    /full/10.1177/0003122413497012.; Chang, Bettina. "The Problem With a
    Culture of Excellence." *Pacific Standard.* 18 June 2014. psmag.com
    /education/tiger-mom-asian-americans-achievement-education-the
    -problem-with-a-culture-of-excellence-83744.

17. Scott Jaschik, "Harvard Faces Scrutiny for the Black Applicants It Rejects,"
    Inside Higher Ed. (Nov. 2019), www.insidehighered.com/admissions
    /article/2019/11/25/harvard-faces-scrutiny-black-applicants-it-rejects.

18. Charles Burress, "Asian Students Study Twice As Much, Says Study
    Sparked by 'Tiger Mom' Book," *El Cerrito, CA Patch* (May 2011), patch
    .com/california/elcerrito/asian-students-study-twice-as-much-says-study
    -sparked12ddc45a73.

19. Kathy Seal, "Asian-American Parenting and Academic Success," *Pacific
    Standard* (Dec. 2010), psmag.com/education/asian-american-parenting
    -and-academic-success-26053.

20. Amy Chua, *Battle Hymn of the Tiger Mother* (New York: Penguin Group,
    2011).

21.   *America Without Entrepreneurs: The Consequences of Dwindling Startup Activity*, The Committee on Small Business and Entrepreneurship United States Senate Cong. 2016, Testimony of John W Lettieri; Co-Founder & Senior Director for Policy and Strategy Economic Innovation Group.

22.   Joe Heim, "On the World Stage, U.S. Students Fall Behind," *The Washington Post* (Dec. 2016), www.washingtonpost.com/local/education/on-the-world-stage-us-students-fall-behind/2016/12/05/610e1e10-b740-11e6-a677-b608fbb3aaf6_story.html.

23.   David Willman, "Contamination at CDC Lab Delayed Rollout of Coronavirus Tests," *The Washington Post* (Apr. 2020), www.washingtonpost.com/investigations/contamination-at-cdc-lab-delayed-rollout-of-coronavirus-tests/2020/04/18/fd7d3824-7139-11ea-aa80-c2470c6b2034_story.html.

24.   Adam Andrzejewski, "10,600 CDC Employees Earn $1.1 Billion Annually," *Forbes* (Feb. 2020), www.forbes.com/sites/adamandrzejewski/2020/02/29/10600-cdc-employees-earn-11-billion-annually/?sh=2627dcdf24da.

25.   Andrzejewski, "10,600 CDC Employees."

26.   "Public Trust in Government: 1958-2019," *Pew Research Center—U.S. Politics & Policy*, (Pew Research Center, Apr. 2019), www.pewresearch.org/politics/2019/04/11/public-trust-in-government-1958-2019/.

27.   Jeffrey M. Jones, "Confidence in Higher Education Down Since 2015," *Gallup* (Oct. 2018), news.gallup.com/opinion/gallup/242441/confidence-higher-education-down-2015.aspx\.

28.   Daniel A. Bell et al., "Is the China Model Better Than Democracy?" *Foreign Policy* (Oct. 2015), foreignpolicy.com/2015/10/19/china-democracy-theory-communist-party-politics-model/.

29.   Bell, "China Model."

30.   Craig Chapple, "TikTok Crosses 2 Billion Downloads After Best Quarter For Any App Ever," *SensorTower* (Apr. 2020), https://sensortower.com/blog/tiktok-downloads-2-billion.

31.   Nathaniel Hilger, "Upward Mobility and Discrimination: The Case of Asian Americans," *NBER Working Paper Series*, Working Paper no. 22748 (2016).

32.   William J. Collins and Marianne H. Wanamaker, "Up from Slavery? African American Intergenerational Economic Mobility Since 1880," *NBER Working Paper Series*, Working Paper no. 23395.

33.   "Chapter 6: Political and Civic Life," *Pew Research Center's Social & Demographic Trends Project* (June 2012), www.pewsocialtrends.org/2012/06/19/chapter-6-political-and-civic-life/.

34.   Gonzalez-Barrera, Ana, and Jens Manuel Krogstad, "US Naturalization Rates Increase Most for Those from India, Ecuador," Pew Research Center

(Jan. 2018), www.pewresearch.org/fact-tank/2018/01/18/naturalization
-rate-among-u-s-immigrants-up-since-2005-with-india-among-the
-biggest-gainers/.

35.   "Vietnamese: Data on Asian Americans," *Pew Research Center's Social &
Demographic Trends Project* (Sept. 2017), www.pewsocialtrends.org/fact
-sheet/asian-americans-vietnamese-in-the-u-s-fact-sheet/.

36.   Markovits, *The Meritocracy Trap: How America's Foundational Myth Feeds
Inequality, Dismantles the Middle Class, and Devours the Elite* (New York,
NY: Penguin Press, 2019), 27.

37.   Michael Martin and Algernon Austin, "Asian-Americans: Smart, High-
Incomes And . . . Poor?" *NPR* (2020), www.nhpr.org/post/asian-americans
-smart-high-incomes-and-poor#stream/0.

38.   Rakesh Kochhar and Anthony Cilluffo, "Income Inequality in the U.S. Is
Rising Most Rapidly Among Asians," *Pew Research Center's Social &
Demographic Trends Project* (July 2018), www.pewsocialtrends.org/2018
/07/12/income-inequality-in-the-u-s-is-rising-most-rapidly-among-asians/.

39.   Victoria Tran, "Asian Americans Are Falling through the Cracks in Data
Representation and Social Services," *Urban Institute* (June 2018), www
.urban.org/urban-wire/asian-americans-are-falling-through-cracks-data
-representation-and-social-services.

40.   John Creamer, "Poverty Rates for Blacks and Hispanics Reached Historic
Lows in 2019," *The United States Census Bureau* (Sept. 2020), www.census
.gov/library/stories/2020/09/poverty-rates-for-blacks-and-hispanics
-reached-historic-lows-in-2019.html.

41.   U.S. Department of Justice and Office of Juvenile Justice and Delinquency
Prevention, "Estimated Number of Arrest by Offense and Race, 2019,"
Ojjdp.gov (2018), www.ojjdp.gov/ojstatbb/crime/ucr.asp?table_in=2.

42.   Gretchen Livingston, "Facts On Unmarried Parents in the U.S.," *Pew
Research Center's Social & Demographic Trends Project* (Apr. 2018), www
.pewsocialtrends.org/2018/04/25/the-changing-profile-of-unmarried
-parents/.

43.   Michael Martin, "Asian-Americans: Smart, High-Incomes And . . . Poor?"

44.   Irene Jay Liu, "Chinese Immigrants Chase Opportunity in America," *NPR*,
NPR (Nov. 2007), www.npr.org/templates/story/story.php?storyId
=16356755.

45.   Hoyt Bleakley and Aimee Chin, "Language Skills and Earnings: Evidence
from Childhood Immigrants*," *Review of Economics and Statistics* 86,
no. 2 (2003).

46.   Kimmy Yam, "Asian Americans voted for Biden 63% to 31%, but the reality
is more complex," *NBC News* (Nov. 2020), https://www.nbcnews.com

/news/asian-america/asian-americans-voted-biden-63-31-reality-more
-complex-n1247171.

47. Will Bredderman, "Councilwoman Raises Concerns About 'Blocs' of
Asians Moving Into NYCHA," *Observer* (Mar. 2015), observer.com
/2015/03/councilwoman-raises-concerns-about-blocs-of-asians-moving
-into-nycha/?fbclid=IwAR34nTxqvT5YeI4jmWfHf1uHkZyrMYJxEAIXV
anjj_cavaEwZYuMNZq0UdY.

48. Gotham Gazette, "New York City District 35 Central Brooklyn Searchlight
2002," *Searchlight on Campaign 2001* (Aug. 2001), www.gothamgazette
.com/searchlight2001/dist35.html.

49. Carla Marinucci, "#MeToo Movement Lawmaker Made Anti-Asian
Comments," *POLITICO* (Apr. 2018), www.politico.com/story/2018/04/22
/metoo-asian-garcia-california-544974.

50. Iris Kuo, "The Whitening of Asian-Americans," *The Atlantic* (Aug 2018),
https://www.theatlantic.com/education/archive/2018/08/the-whitening
-of-asian-americans/563336/.

51. Viet Thanh Nguyen, "Asian Americans Are Still Caught in the Trap of
the 'Model Minority' Stereotype. And It Creates Inequality for All," *Time*
(June 2020), time.com/5859206/anti-asian-racism-america/.

52. John Rawls, *A Theory of Justice* (Oxford: Oxford UP, 1999), 274.

53. Claire Jean Kim, "The Racial Triangulation of Asian Americans," *Politics
& Society* 27, no. 1 (1999): 105–138.

54. "Estimated Cost of Attendance," *San Joaquin Delta College*
(Jan. 2020), www.deltacollege.edu/student-services/
financial-aid-scholarships-veterans-services/estimated-cost-attendance.

55. Kriston McIntosh, Emily Moss, Ryan Nunn, and Jay Shambaugh,
"Examining the Black-White Wealth Gap," *Brookings* (Feb. 2020), www
.brookings.edu/blog/up-front/2020/02/27/examining-the-black-white
-wealth-gap/.

HARVARD IS ROTTING

1. This finding alone does not prove discrimination; Harvard returned a
model suggesting that Asian Americans' lower personality scores are
not the result of Harvard's discrimination, but other factors external to
Harvard.

2. Anemona Hartocollis and Ted Siefer, "On Eve of Harvard Bias Trial,
Dueling Rallies Show Rifts Among Asian-Americans," *The New York
Times* (Oct. 2018), www.nytimes.com/2018/10/14/us/harvard-protest
-affirmative-action.html.

3. More on this later.

4. Peter Arcidiacono et al., "Asian American Discrimination in Harvard Admissions," *IZA Institute of Labor Economics Discussion Paper Series*, no. DP No. 13172 (Apr. 2020), doi:10.3386/w27068.

5. Ron Unz, "The Myth of American Meritocracy," *The Unz Review* (Nov. 2012), www.unz.com/runz/the-myth-of-american-meritocracy/.

6. Delano R. Franklin and Samuel W. Zwickel, "Internal Harvard Review Showed Disadvantage for Asian Applicants," *The Harvard Crimson* (June 2018), www.thecrimson.com/article/2018/6/15/admissions-internal-report/.

7. Kanchan, "Dwindling Diversity."

8. "Our Efforts to Fight against Ivy Leagues Discrimination," *Asian American Coalition for Education* (Aug. 2015), asianamericanforeducation.org/en/our-efforts-to-fight-against-ivy-leagues-discrimination/comment-page-217/.

9. Anemona Hartocollis, "Harvard Victory Pushes Admissions Case Toward a More Conservative Supreme Court," *The New York Times* (Nov. 2020), www.nytimes.com/2020/11/12/us/harvard-affirmative-action.html.

10. United States District Court for the District of Massachusetts, *Students for Fair Admissions, Inc., v. President and Fellows of Harvard College (Harvard Corporation)*, Civil Action No. 1:14-cv-14176 (Dec. 2017), Filed Jun. 15, 2018.

11. Kenny Xu, "Parents Sue Schools for Discriminating Against High-Achieving Asian Kids," *The Daily Signal* (Sept. 2020), www.dailysignal.com/2020/09/02/parents-sue-school-system-for-discriminating-against-high-achieving-asian-kids/.

12. United States District Court for the District of Massachusetts Boston Division, *Students for Fair Admissions Inc., v. President and Fellows of Harvard College (Harvard Corporation) United States' Statement of Interest in Opposition to Defendant's Motion for Summary Judgment*, Court Case No. 1:14-cv-14176-ADB, Filed Aug. 2018, cdn.cnn.com/cnn/2018/images/08/30/harvard_statement_of_interest_filed_0.pdf.

13. Anemona Hartocolis, "Presiding Over the Harvard Admissions Trial: A Judge Who Was Rejected From Harvard," *The New York Times* (Oct. 2018), https://www.nytimes.com/2018/10/22/us/harvard-admissions-trial-judge-burroughs.html.

14. Camille G. Caldera, Delano R. Franklin, and Samuel W. Zwickel, "Federal Judge Rules Harvard's Admissions Policies Do Not Discriminate Against Asian American Applicants," *The Harvard Crimson* (Oct. 2019), www.thecrimson.com/article/2019/10/2/admissions-suit-decision/?from=groupmessage.

15. Max Fisher, "A fascinating map of the world's most and least racially tolerant countries," *The Washington Post* (May 2013), https://www .washingtonpost.com/news/worldviews/wp/2013/05/15/a-fascinating -map-of-the-worlds-most-and-least-racially-tolerant-countries/.

16. Scott Jaschik, "Inside Higher Ed," *Appeals Court Backs Harvard on Affirmative Action* (Nov. 2020), www.insidehighered.com/admissions /article/2020/11/16/appeals-court-backs-harvard-affirmative-action.

17. Ronald Turner, "Justice Kennedy's Surprising Vote and Opinion in Fisher v. University of Texas at Austin," *Wake Forest Law Review* (Oct. 2016), wakeforestlawreview.com/2016/10/justice-kennedys-surprising-vote -and-opinion-in-fisher-v-university-of-texas-at-austin/.

18. Max Larkin, "Harvard Has Become More Racially Diverse, But Most Of Its Students Are Still Really Rich," *WBUR: Edify* (Oct. 2018), www.wbur .org/edify/2018/10/24/harvard-diverse-wealth.

19. Peter Arcidiacono et al., "Legacy and Athlete Preferences at Harvard," *National Bureau of Economic Research* (2019), https://www.nber.org /papers/w26316.

20. "Anti-Semitism in the U.S.: Harvard's Jewish Problem," *Jewish Virtual Library* (2012), www.jewishvirtuallibrary.org/harvard-s-jewish-problem.

21. Courtney Rozen, "What To Know About Affirmative Action As The Harvard Trial Begins," *NPR* (Oct. 2018), www.npr.org/2018/10/16 /657499646/what-to-know-about-affirmative-action-as-the-harvard- trial-begins.

22. Burger Court, *Regents of University of California v. Bakke*, No. 7811, Argued 12 Oct. 1977, Decided Jun. 28, 1978, Citation: 438 US 265. *Regents of University of California v. Bakke*, Docket No. 76-811, 12 Oct. 1978, "Regents of Univ. of California v. Bakke, 438 U.S. 265 (1978)," Justia Law, supreme.justia.com/cases/federal/us/438/265/.

23. Andrzejewski, "10,600 CDC Employees."

24. *Regents of University of California v. Bakke*. Docket No. 76-811, Argued 12 Oct. 1978 Decided Jun. 26, 1978 "Regents of Univ. of California v. Bakke, 438 U.S. 265 (1978)," Justia Law, supreme.justia.com/cases/federal /us/438/265/.

25. Amy J Binder, "Why Are Harvard Grads Still Flocking to Wall Street?" *Washington Monthly* (2014), washingtonmonthly.com/magazine/septoct -2014/why-are-harvard-grads-still-flocking-to-wall-street/.

26. Nancy Walecki, "McKinsey and the Fig Tree," *Yale Daily News* (Nov. 2019), yaledailynews.com/blog/2019/11/01/mckinsey-and-the-fig-tree/.

27. Walecki, "McKinsey."

28.   Saffron Huang, "Harvard Creates Managers Instead of Elites," *Palladium* (July 2020), https://palladiummag.com/2020/07/27/harvard-creates -managers-instead-of-elites/.

29.   Christopher Eisgruber, "Letter from President Eisgruber on the University's efforts to combat systemic racism," *Princeton University* (Sep 2020), https://www.princeton.edu/news/2020/09/02/letter-president -eisgruber-universitys-efforts-combat-systemic-racism.

30.   Hannah Wang, "Unclear Whether U. Complied with DOE Deadlines, as Growing Chorus Calls for Investigation's End," *The Princetonian* (Oct. 2020), www.dailyprincetonian.com/article/2020/10/princeton-department -of-education-racism-discrimination-comply-investigation.

31.   Eileen Huang, "A Letter from a Yale student to the Chinese American Community," *Chinese American* (May 2020), https://chineseamerican .org/p/31571.

32.   Gemma Yoo, "GOOD TROUBLE: Eileen Huang," *Yale Daily News* (Oct. 2020), yaledailynews.com/blog/2020/10/29/good-trouble-eileen-huang/.

33.   Sergiu Klainerman, "How to Fight the Enemies of Academic Freedom," *Quillette* (Aug. 2020), quillette.com/2020/08/10/how-to-fight-the-enemies -of-academic-freedom/.

34.   Richard H. Sander, "A Systemic Analysis of Affirmative Action in American Law Schools," *Brown.edu* 57:367, https://www.brown .edu/Departments/Economics/Faculty/Glenn_Loury/louryhomepage /teaching/Ec%20137/Richard%20Sander%20on%20Affirmative%20 Action%20in%20Law%20Schools.pdf.

35.   Richard D. Kahlenberg, "Harvard Overuses Racial Preferences in Admissions. Here's How It Should Approach Diversity Instead," *Slate Magazine* (June 2018) slate.com/news-and-politics/2018/06/harvard -should-use-socio-economic-not-racial-preferences-in-admissions.html.

36.   "Most Black Students at Harvard Are from High-Income Families," *The Journal of Blacks in Higher Education* (2006), www.jbhe.com/news_views /52_harvard-blackstudents.html.

37.   W.E.B. Du Bois, "'The Talented Tenth' [Excerpts]," *The Gilder Lehrman Center for the Study of Slavery, Resistance, and Abolition*, glc.yale.edu /talented-tenth-excerpts.

38.   Emily DeRuy and National Journal, "Black HBCU Grads 'Thriving' More Than Non-HBCU Peers," *The Atlantic* (Oct. 2015), www.theatlantic.com /politics/archive/2015/10/ black-hbcu-grads-thriving-more-than-non-hbcu-peers/433236/.

39.   Peter Wood, "Caltech Competes," *NAS* (Apr. 2009), www.nas.org/blogs /article/CaltechCaltech_competes.

40.   "University Ranking - Citations per Faculty," *Most Cited Universities Citations per Faculty | Ranking | Colleges*, www.unipage.net/en/ranking _citations.

41.   Laura Bridgestock, "Top Tech Schools: MIT or Caltech?" *Top Universities* (June 2019), www.topuniversities.com/student-info/choosing-university /mit-or-Caltech.

42.   The university's annual budget for 2019–20, divided by the number of students attending in 2019–20.

43.   Princeton University, "Princeton Registrar Common Data Set" (Sept. 2019–2020).

44.   Nicole Chavez, "Lori Loughlin and Felicity Huffman Are Two Contrasting Faces in the College Admissions Scam," *CNN* (Oct. 2019), www.cnn.com /2019/10/22/us/lori-loughlin-felicity-huffman-fallout/index.html.

45.   Kim Parker, "Views of Higher Education Divided by Party," *Pew Research Center's Social & Demographic Trends Project* (Aug. 2019), www .pewsocialtrends.org/essay/the-growing-partisan-divide-in-views -of-higher-education/.

THE TRUTH ABOUT ASIAN STEREOTYPES

1.   Pew Research Center Social & Demographic Trends, *The Rise of Asian Americans* (June 2012), www.pewsocialtrends.org/2012/06/19 /the-rise-of-asian-americans/.

2.   Ariana Eunjung Cha, "A Martin Luther King Jr. Statue 'Made in China'?" *The Seattle Times* (Aug. 2007), www.seattletimes.com/nation-world /a-martin-luther-king-jr-statue-made-in-china/.

3.   Gonzalez also writes of Latino Americans: "That many Mexican Americans saw themselves as white was a problem for activists and elites. Indeed, the federal government counted them as white on the decennial US census and for legal purposes. When the census of 1930, in an exception to general practice, classified Mexican Americans as a race of their own, Mexican American leaders protested bitterly, and officials reverted back to the white classification in the 1940 census . . . The process of making all Mexican Americans into victimized 'people of color' (POC) came at a price. As Cristina Mora observes in her study Making Hispanics, it required that Mexican Americans '[accept] a disadvantaged minority status,' with no possibility of ever escaping minority status."

4.   Mike Gonzalez, *The Plot to Change America* (New York City: Encounter, 2020), 63.

5.   Jens Krogstad, "A majority of Americans say immigrants mostly fill jobs U.S. citizens do not want," Pew Research Center (June 2020), https://www

.pewresearch.org/fact-tank/2020/06/10/a-majority-of-americans-say
-immigrants-mostly-fill-jobs-u-s-citizens-do-not-want/.

6. Amy J. Cuddy, Susan T. Fiske, and Peter Glick, "The BIAS Map: Behaviors
from Intergroup Affect and Stereotypes," *Journal of Personality and Social
Psychology* 92, no. 631–684 (2007), doi:10.1037/0022-3514.92.4.631.

7. LC means low competence, HC means high competence, LW means low
warmth, HW means high warmth.

8. TED: The Economics Daily, "Asian Women and Men Earned More than
Their White, Black, and Hispanic Counterparts in 2017," *U.S. Bureau
of Labor Statistics* (Aug. 2018), www.bls.gov/opub/ted/2018/asian-women
-and-men-earned-more-than-their-white-black-and-hispanic-counterparts
-in-2017.htm.

9. Alexis Kleinman, "Black People And Asian Men Have A Much Harder
Time Dating On OKCupid," *HuffPost* (Sept. 2014), www.huffpost.com
/entry/okcupid-race_n_5811840.

10. Damona Hoffman, "Perspective | Date Lab: Daters Say They Don't
Tolerate Racial Bias. Their Actions Say They Do Have Racial Preferences,"
The Washington Post (June 2020), www.washingtonpost.com/lifestyle
/magazine/date-labdaters-say-they-dont-tolerate-racial-bias-their-actions
-say-they-do-have-racial-preferences/2020/06/18/0d1eace4-a039-11ea
-9590-1858a893bd59_story.html.

11. Wesley Yang, *The Souls of Yellow Folk* (W.W. Norton & Company, 2018), 48.

12. Hoffman, "Date Lab."

13. Yang, *Souls*, 48.

14. Paul Farhi, "Familiar Ad Trope: Pairing White Men and Asian American
Women," *The Washington Post* (Sept. 2012), www.washingtonpost.com
/lifestyle/style/familiar-ad-trope-pairing-white-men-and-asian-american
-women/2012/09/27/a959bc84-feb1-11e1-a31e-804fccb658f9_story.html.

15. Mary Kent, "Most Americans Marry Within Their Race," *Prb.org* (Aug.
2010), www.prb.org/usintermarriage/.

16. Amy Chua, *Battle Hymn of the Tiger Mother* (New York: Penguin Group,
2011).

17. *The Social Network*, Directed by David Fincher, performance by Andrew
Garfield, Sony Picture Entertainment, (2010).

18. Weike Wang, "Omakase," *The New Yorker* (June 2018), www.newyorker
.com/magazine/2018/06/18/omakase.

19. Eddie Huang, "Network TV Ate My Life: Eddie Huang on Watching His
Memoir Become a Sitcom," *Vulture* (Jan. 2015), www.vulture.com/2015
/01/eddie-huang-fresh-off-the-boat-abc.html.

20. Alison MacAdam, "Long Duk Dong: Last of the Hollywood Stereotypes?" *NPR* (Mar. 2008), www.npr.org/templates/story/story.php ?storyId=88591800.

21. Daniel Chin, "Three Portraits of Bruce Lee," *The Ringer* (July 2020), www .theringer.com/movies/2020/7/23/21334815/three-portraits-of-bruce-lee.

22. Kevin Smokler, "Gedde Watanabe Discusses 30 Years of Sixteen Candles and Long Duk Dong," *Vulture* (May 2014), www.vulture.com/2014/05 /gedde-watanabe-long-duk-dong-sixteen-candles-interview.html.

23. Thessaly La Force, "Why Do Asian-Americans Remain Largely Unseen in Film and Television?" *The New York Times* (Nov. 2018), www.nytimes .com/2018/11/06/t-magazine/asian-american-actors-representation.html.

24. Walter Benjamin, "The Work of Art in the Age of Mechanical Reproduction," *Marxists.org*, Translated by Harry Zohn, Transcribed by Andy Blunder (1998), (2005), www.marxists.org/reference/subject /philosophy/works/ge/benjamin.htm.

25. Liz Dwyer, "Connie Chung's Enduring Legacy," *Shondaland* (June 2018), www.shondaland.com/inspire/a20982396/connie-chung-legacy/.

26. Cameron Laux, "Is Japanese Anime Going Mainstream?" *BBC Future* (Dec. 2019), www.bbc.com/future/article/20191127-the-spirited-world -of-japanese-anime.

27. Andrew Yang, "Opinion | Andrew Yang: We Asian Americans Are Not the Virus, but We Can Be Part of the Cure," *The Washington Post* (Apr. 2020), www.washingtonpost.com/opinions/2020/04/01/andrew-yang-coronavirus -discrimination/.

28. Canwen Xu, "Opinion | Andrew Yang Was Wrong. Showing Our 'Americanness' Is Not How Asian-Americans Stop Racism," *The Washington Post* (Apr. 2020), www.washingtonpost.com/opinions/2020 /04/03/andrew-yang-was-wrong-showing-our-american-ness-is-not -how-asian-americans-stop-racism/.

DIVERSITY AND EXCLUSION

1. https://www.mercurynews.com/2012/11/29/asian-workers-now -dominate-silicon-valley-tech-jobs/.

2. "2020 Report – Diversity," *Facebook* (2020), https://diversity.fb.com /read-report/.

3. Mody, Seema. "Diversity officers are in demand across corporate America but are often underpaid." *CNBC* (Jul. 2019). https://www.cnbc .com/2020/07/29/diversity-officers-are-in-demand-at-us-companies-but -often-underpaid.html

4.   Melonie Parker, *Google Diversity Annual Report 2020*, https://diversity
        .google/annual-report/.

5.   Ruth Umoh, "Google Diversity Report Shows Little Progress for Women
        and People of Color," *Forbes* (May 2020), www.forbes.com/sites/ruthumoh
        /2020/05/05/google-diversity-report-shows-little-progress-for-women
        -and-people-of-color/?sh=7ac34632207f.

6.   Gee, Buck, and Wes Hom, (2009), cdn.ymaws.com/www.ascendleadership
        .org/resource/resmgr/research/failureof_asian_success.pdf.

7.   Heather Mac Donald, *The Diversity Delusion* (New York City: St. Martin's
        Press, 2018), 174.

8.   Kelly, Erin, and Frank Dobbin, "How Affirmative Action Became
        Diversity Management: Employer Response to Antidiscrimination
        Law, 1961 to 1996," *American Behavioral Scientist* 41, no. 7 (Apr. 1998):
        960–984, doi:10.1177/0002764298041007008.

9.   Kelly, "Affirmative Action," 960–984.

10.   Sundiatu Dixon-Fyle, Kevin Dolan, Vivian Hunt, and Sarah Prince,
        "Diversity Wins: How Inclusion Matters." *McKinsey & Company* (May
        2020), www.mckinsey.com/featured-insights/diversity-and-inclusion
        /diversity-wins-how-inclusion-matters.

11.   McKinsey cites a sample size of 186 in its evaluation of the United States
        and Canada's record of diversity.

12.   Jena McGregor, "Urged to Back up Pledges for Racial Justice, 34 Major
        Firms Commit to Disclose Government Workforce Data," *Washington
        Post* (Sept. 2020), www.washingtonpost.com/business/2020/09/29
        /corporate-diversity-data-pledge/.

13.   "Labor force characteristics by race and ethnicity, 2018," *The Bureau of
        Labor Statistics*, US Government (Oct. 2019), https://www.bls.gov/opub
        /reports/race-and-ethnicity/2018/home.htm.

14.   "Meet Google's first 19 Employees," *Gadgetsnow* (Jan 2017), https://www
        .gadgetsnow.com/slideshows/meet-googles-first-19-employees/larry
        -page/photolist/56425721.cms.

15.   Jack Nicas, Conor Dougherty, and Daisuke Wakabayashi, "How Google's
        Founders Slowly Stepped Away From Their Company," *The New York
        Times* (Dec. 2019), www.nytimes.com/2019/12/04/technology/google
        -larry-page-sergey-br.html.

16.   David Gelles, "Sundar Pichai of Google: 'Technology Doesn't Solve
        Humanity's Problems,'" *The New York Times* (Nov. 2018), www.nytimes
        .com/2018/11/08/business/sundar-pichai-google-corner-office.html
        ?action=click.

17.   Andy Smarick, "Toward Real Decentralization," *National Affairs* (2019), nationalaffairs.com/publications/detail/toward-real-decentralization.

SHUT UP ABOUT THE TEST

1.   Chris Fuchs, "Plan to Diversify New York's Top High Schools Divides Asian-American Groups," *NBC News* (June 2018), www.nbcnews.com/news/asian-america/plan-diversify-new-york-s-top-high-schools-divides-asian-n884316.

2.   Reema Amin and Sam Park, "Where Do NYC's Top-Scoring Middle Schoolers Go to High School? Hint – It's Not Just the Specialized High Schools," *Chalkbeat New York* (June 2019), ny.chalkbeat.org/2019/6/4/21108536/where-do-nyc-s-top-scoring-middle-schoolers-go-to-high-school-hint-it-s-not-just-the-specialized-hig.

3.   Heather Mac Donald, "How NYC's Gotham Elite High Schools Escaped the Leveller's Axe," City-Journal, *Manhattan Institute* (Spring 1999), https://www.city-journal.org/html/how-gotham%E2%80%99s-elite-high-schools-escaped-leveller%E2%80%99s-ax-12276.html.

4.   Dennis Saffran, "The Plot Against Merit," *City Journal* (June 2018), www.city-journal.org/html/plot-against-merit-13667.html.

5.   MetroFocus, "NYC School Segregation: Rethinking the SHSAT," *MetroFocus* (May 2019) www.thirteen.org/metrofocus/2019/08/separate-but-still-not-equal/.

6.   SHSAT, "SHSAT Practice Test - Free Pop Quiz," *Kaplan Test Prep* (2020), www.kaptest.com/shsat/free/shsat-pop-quiz.

7.   Eliza Shapiro, "How New York's Elite Public Schools Lost their Black and Hispanic Students," *The New York Times* (June 2019), https://www.nytimes.com/interactive/2019/06/03/nyregion/nyc-public-schools-black-hispanic-students.html.

8.   Elizabeth Stone, "Gifted Children's Programs: A Matter of Class," *The New York Times* (May 1990), https://www.nytimes.com/1990/05/06/magazine/gifted-children-s-programs-a-matter-of-class.html.

9.   Susan Edelman, "The racially diverse, high-achieving schools of NYC's past have vanished," *The New York Post* (Mar 2019), https://nypost.com/2019/03/23/the-racially-diverse-high-achieving-schools-of-nycs-past-have-vanished/

10.   Andrew Wolf, "Gifted Students Under Fire," *The New York Sun* (Nov. 2004, www.nysun.com/opinion/gifted-students-under-fire/5541/.

11.   Christina Veiga, "By the Numbers: New York City's Specialized High School Offers," *Chalkbeat New York* (Mar. 2019), ny.chalkbeat.org

/2019/3/19/21107139/by-the-numbers-new-york-city-s-specialized
-high-school-offers.

12.   Larry Cary, "The SHSAT Isn't Racist: A Careful Look at the Hecht-
Calandra Law Shows It Was Not Motivated by Bigotry, nor Did It Initially
Harm Blacks and Hispanics," *New York Daily News* (Sept. 2019), www
.nydailynews.com/opinion/ny-oped-the-shsat-isnt-racist-20190903
-ihtrstrombhd7lveugv2xr6shy-story.html.

13.   Kendi, *Antiracist*, 101.

14.   Reema Amin, "NYC Spends a Record $28K per Student, but the State Is
Footing a Smaller Portion of That Bill," *Chalkbeat New York* (Jan. 2020),
ny.chalkbeat.org/2020/1/27/21121084/nyc-spends-a-record-28k-per
-student-but-the-state-is-footing-a-smaller-portion-of-that-bill.

15.   NYS Education Department, "State Education Department Releases
Spring 2019 Grades 3-8 ELA & Math Assessment Results," *New York State
Education Department* (Aug. 2019), www.nysed.gov/news/2019/state
-education-department-releases-spring-2019-grades-3-8-ela-math
-assessment-results.

16.   "New York City Charter School Center on the Executive Budget Proposal
Fiscal Year 2020-2021" (2019).

17.   Selim Algar, "Over 140 NYC Schools Have Grades with 90 Percent State Exam
Failure Rate," *New York Post* (Dec. 2019), nypost.com/2019/12/17/over-140
-nyc-schools-have-grades-with-90-percent-state-exam-failure-rate/.

18.   Susan Edelman, "Critics Cry 'Grade Inflation' at NYC Schools as Students
Pass without Meeting Standards," *New York Post* (June 2019), nypost.com
/2019/06/29/critics-cry-grade-inflation-at-nyc-schools-as-students-pass
-without-meeting-standards/.

19.   Nicole Tortoriello, "Dismantling Disparities: An Analysis of Potential
Solutions to Racial Disparities in New York City's Specialized High
Schools Admissions Process," *Columbia Journal of Law and Social
Problems* (2016), jlsp.law.columbia.edu/wp-content/uploads/sites/8/2017
/03/49-Tortoriello.pdf.

20.   Seht Barron, "Diversity, Not Merit," *City Journal* (June 2018), www.city
-journal.org/html/diversity-not-merit-15948.html.

21.   Rachel M. Cohen, "This Is the Wrong Way to Fight Inequality," *The New
Republic* (Aug. 2017), newrepublic.com/article/144182/wrong-way-fight
-inequality.

22.   Savannah Jacobson, "Where Top Officials Stand on the SHSAT and
Specialized High School Admissions," *Gotham Gazette* (Mar. 2019), www
.gothamgazette.com/city/8406-where-top-city-officials-stand-on-the
-shsat-and-specialized-high-school-admissions.

23. Boaz Weinstein, "No Ethnic Group Owns Stuyvesant. All New Yorkers Do," *The New York Times* (June 2018), https://www.nytimes.com/2018 /06/13/opinion/de-blasio-stuyvesant-school.html.

24. Spectrum News Staff, "'Our Plan Didn't Work' *De Blasio Indicates Openness to Keeping the SHSAT*" (Sept. 2019), www.ny1.com/nyc/all -boroughs/politics/2019/09/26/shsat-bill-de-blasio-says-plan-to-scrap -specialized-high-school-exam-did-not-work.

25. D.C. Briggs, "The Effect of Admissions Test Preparation: Evidence from NELS;88," *Draft for Chance Magazine* (2007), https://nepc.colorado.edu /sites/default/files/Briggs_Theeffectofadmissionstestpreparation.pdf.

26. Kristie K. Waltman and David A. Frisbie (1994), Parents' Understanding of Their Children's Report Card Grades, Applied Measurement in Education, 7:3, 223–240, DOI: 10.1207/s15324818ame0703_5.

27. College Board, "Total Group Profile Report," *College Board* (2013), secure -media.collegeboard.org/digitalServices/pdf/research/2013/TotalGroup -2013.pdf.

28. The Upshot, "Some Colleges Have More Students From the Top 1 Percent Than the Bottom 60. Find Yours," *The New York Times* (Jan 2017),https:// www.nytimes.com/interactive/2017/01/18/upshot/some-colleges-have -more-students-from-the-top-1-percent-than-the-bottom-60.html?mtrref =www.google.com&assetType=REGIWALL.

29. Elizabeth Stone, "Gifted Children's Programs: A Matter of Class," *The New York Times* (May 1990), www.nytimes.com/1990/05/06/magazine/gifted -children-s-programs-a-matter-of-class.html.

30. Peter Arcidiacono et al., "Legacy and Athlete Preferences at Harvard," National Bureau of Economic Research (2019), https://www.nber.org /papers/w26316.

31. Dr. Susan Berry, "Asian-Americans: Mayor Bill De Blasio 'Pitting Minority Against Minority,'" *Breitbart* (June 2018), www.breitbart.com/politics /2018/06/06/asian-americans-mayor-bill-de-blasio-pitting-minority -against-minority/.

32. Andres O'Hara, "Asian-American Groups Protest Plan To Diversify Specialized High Schools," *Gothamist* (June 2018), gothamist.com/news /asian-american-groups-protest-plan-to-diversify-specialized-high -schools.

33. Christina Veiga, "What's Happened in the Year since Mayor Bill De Blasio Called for Overhauling NYC's Specialized High School Admissions," *Chalkbeat New York* (June 2019), ny.chalkbeat.org/2019/6/1/21108237 /what-s-happened-in-the-year-since-mayor-bill-de-blasio-called-for -overhauling-nyc-s-specialized-high.

34. William J. Collins, "Up from Slavery?"

35. Adam Andrzejewski, "10,600 CDC Employees."

36. Paula Katinas and Meaghan McGoldrick, "As Mayor Pulls Back from SHSAT Plan, Brooklyn Pols Call for Gifted Program Expansion," *Brooklyn Eagle* (Sept. 2019), brooklyneagle.com/articles/2019/09/26/as-mayor -pulls-back-from-shsat-plan-brooklyn-pols-call-for-gifted-program -expansion/.

THE RULES ARE CHANGING

1. Digital History, *Black Nationalism and Black Power* (2019), www .digitalhistory.uh.edu/disp_textbook.cfm?smtID=2.

2. Malcolm X, "Malcolm X, 'Racial Separation' (1963)," Contributed by BlackPast (Jan. 2013), www.blackpast.org/african-american-history /1963-malcolm-x-racial-separation/.

3. Kanchan, "Dwindling Diversity."

4. Tommy Curry, "Critical Race Theory," *Encyclopædia Britannica* (May 2020), www.britannica.com/topic/critical-race-theory.

5. Kendi, *Antiracist*, 19.

6. Pacific Legal Foundation, "AFEF v. Montgomery County Public Schools" (2020), pacificlegal.org/case/afef-v-montgomery-county-public-schools /?fbclid=IwAR29ymW9Rkw0QtaSk-9ApQsZTVMgL8OroErF02B-Qq -jLXduF_NMIv_7g8U.

7. "Montgomery County Public Schools," *Superintendent of Schools— Montgomery County Public Schools, Rockville, MD* (2020), www .montgomeryschoolsmd.org/superintendent/bio.aspx.

8. Pacific Legal Foundation, "AFEF v. Montgomery County Public Schools" (2020), pacificlegal.org/case/afef-v-montgomery-county-public-schools /?fbclid=IwAR29ymW9Rkw0QtaSk-9ApQsZTVMgL8OroErF02B-Qq -jLXduF_NMIv_7g8U.

9. Stanford, "The Educational Opportunity Project at Stanford," *Opportunity* (2019), edopportunity.org/explorer/.

10. Jack R. Smith, "The Growing Achievement Gap in Montgomery County Schools Must Be Addressed," *The Washington Post* (May 2019), www. washingtonpost.com/opinions/local-opinions/the-growing-achievement -gap-in-montgomery-county-schools-must-be-addressed/2019/05/02 /9cdf89ac-5bc5-11e9-842d-7d3ed7eb3957_story.html.

11. Lauren Lumpkin, "Report: Montgomery County's Attempt to Narrow Student Performance Gap Is 'Largely Ineffective,'" *The Washington Post* (Dec. 2019), www.washingtonpost.com/local/education/report -montgomery-countys-attempt-to-narrow-student-performance-gap-is

-largely-ineffective/2019/12/30/eec8729e-227e-11ea-bed5-880264cc91a9
_story.html.

12. Montgomery County Public School, "Montgomery County Public
     Schools," *Equity Initiatives Unit—Montgomery County Public Schools,
     Rockville, MD* (2020), www.montgomeryschoolsmd.org/departments
     /clusteradmin/equity/.

13. MCPSTV, "NAACP Parents' Council 2019 Kickoff Meeting Keynote
     Address," *YouTube*, uploaded 25 Nov. 2019, www.youtube.com/watch
     ?v=DhZqtR4xijk.

14. Montgomery County Public Schools, "Our Investment in Students:
     Excellence and Equity Operating Budget," *Montgomery Schools* (2018),
     www.montgomeryschoolsmd.org/uploadedFiles/departments/budget
     /fy2021/Budget-Inv-in-Equity.pdf.

15. Elaine Bonner-Tompkins, (2019), *Montgomery County MD*, www
     .montgomerycountymd.gov/OLO/Resources/Files/2019%20Reports
     /OLOReport2019-14.pdf.

16. Mulligan, *Justice and the Meritocratic State*.

17. HCPSS, "Bridge to Excellence," *Howard County Public School System
     Bridge to Excellence Comments*, www.hcpss.org/about-us/bridge-to
     -excellence/.

18. Jack R. Smith, *Montgomery County Public Schools FY 2021 Operating
     Budget* (2020).

19. Caitlynn Peetz, "MCPS Might Spend $450K on 'Anti-Racist System
     Audit,'" *Bethesda Magazine* (Nov. 2020), bethesdamagazine.com/bethesda
     -beat/schools/mcps-might-spend-450k-on-anti-racist-system-audit/.

20. Justin Wm. Moyer and Doona St. George, "Can You Skip 47 Days of
     English Class and Still Graduate from High School?" *The Washington Post*
     (May 2019), www.washingtonpost.com/local/education/can-you-skip-47
     -days-of-english-class-and-still-graduate-from-high-school/2019/05/25
     /be3318ca-1b84-11e9-88fe-f9f77a3bcb6c_story.html.

21. Kanchan, "Dwindling Diversity."

22. The Maryland-National Capital Park and Planning Commission, (2019),
     Montgomery Planning, montgomeryplanning.org/wp-content/uploads
     /2019/01/MP_TrendsReport_final.pdf.

23. Kanchan, "Dwindling Diversity."

24. Tunku Varadarajan, "The Duo That Defeated the 'Diversity Industry,'" *The
     Wall Street Journal* (Nov. 2020), www.wsj.com/articles/the-duo-that
     -defeated-the-diversity-industry-11605904415.

25. AssemblyAssets, "Assemblymember Dr. Weber Introduces Legislation to Restore Equity & Opportunity for All," *YouTube* (June 2020), www.youtube.com/watch?v=SygDublArvc.

26. California State Assembly, "Media on Demand," *California State Assembly Seal* (2020), www.assembly.ca.gov/media/assembly-public-employment-retirement-committee-20200505/video.

27. "Proposition 16 - ACA 5 (Resolution Chapter 23), Weber. Government preferences," California Secretary of State, *CA State government* (2020), https://www.sos.ca.gov/campaign-lobbying/cal-access-resources/measure-contributions/2020-ballot-measure-contribution-totals/proposition-16-aca-5-resolution-chapter-23-weber-government-preferences.

28. Justin Marion, "How Costly Is Affirmative Action? Government Contracting and California's Proposition 209," *The Review of Economics and Statistics* 91(3) (2009): 503–522.

29. Juliana Menasce Horowitz, "Americans See Advantages and Challenges in Country's Growing Racial and Ethnic Diversity," *Pew Research Center's Social & Demographic Trends Project* (May 2020), www.pewsocialtrends.org/2019/05/08/americans-see-advantages-and-challenges-in-countrys-growing-racial-and-ethnic-diversity/.

30. Jason Xu, "Racial Equality in Professional Sports (15% rule)," *Change.org* (2020), https://www.change.org/p/professional-sports-racial-equality-in-professional-sports?utm_source=share_petition&utm_medium=custom_url&recruited_by_id=e7cb7330-19d8-11e7-8e47-29ce442ff6cb.

31. California for Equal Rights, "#CFERTV Mr. Ward Connerly on Tucker Carlson to Discuss Prop. 16 | No on Prop 16," *YouTube* (Aug. 2020), www.youtube.com/watch?v=VTbUp2kYJnI.

32. Hi, that's me.

33. Tunku Varadarajan, "The Duo That Defeated the 'Diversity Industry,'" *The Wall Street Journal* (Nov. 2020), www.wsj.com/articles/the-duo-that-defeated-the-diversity-industry-11605904415.

34. Kamala Harris, "There's a Big Difference between Equality and Equity. Pic.twitter.com/n3XfQyjLNe," *Twitter*, Twitter (Nov. 2020), twitter.com/KamalaHarris/status/1322963321994289154?s=20.

35. Netflix is a Joke and Hasan Minhaj, "Affirmative Action | Patriot Act with Hasan Minhaj | Netflix," *YouTube* (Oct. 2018), www.youtube.com/watch?v=zm5QVcTI2I8.

36. Kenny Xu, "Parents Sue Connecticut, Saying Racial Quotas Are Hurting Black Students," *Washington Examiner* (Mar. 2019), www.washingtonexaminer.com/red-alert-politics/parents-sue-connecticut-saying-racial-quotas-are-hurting-black-students.

37. Vanessa De La Torre, "As Sheff V. O'Neill Case Persists, Frustrations Grow Over Minority Students Left Out Of Magnet Schools," *The Hartford Courant* (Sep 2017), https://www.courant.com/community/hartford/hc-hartford -sheff-case-discrimination-claim-20170912-story.html.

38. Tee Walker, Wyatt, and Steve Klinsky, "A Light Shines in Harlem," *RealClearPolitics* (2015), www.realclearpolitics.com/articles/2015/09/24/a _light_shines_in_a_harlem_charter_school_128189.html.

39. Kochhar and Cilluffo, "Income Inequality."

A NOTE ON ANTI-ASIAN VIOLENCE

1. Priscilla DeGregory, "Prosecutors probing subway attack on Asian man as possible hate crime," *NYPost* (2021), https://nypost.com/2021/03/22 /prosecutors-probing-attack-on-asian-man-as-possible-hate-crime/.

2. Ice Cube, "Black Korea," *Death Certificate* (1991).

3. Joong Ang Daily, "The Press: The Whole World Watches—and Reacts—to L.A. Riots," *LA Times* (1992), https://www.latimes.com/archives/la-xpm -1992-05-05-wr-1498-story.html.

Index

About the Author

Kenny Xu is the president of the nonprofit organization Color Us United, and the lead insider on the *Students for Fair Admission v. President and Fellows of Harvard College* case and a commentary writer for the *Federalist*, the *Washington Examiner*, the *Daily Signal*, *Quillette*, and *City Journal*. Xu has spoken on the consequences of the Harvard case and its identity politics ideology in front of groups as diverse as the nationally renowned Pacific Legal Foundation to the Boston Rally for Education Rights to the all-Black Connecticut Parents Union. His commentary has propelled him to interviews with NPR and features in the *New York Times Magazine*. He lives in Washington, DC.